# ROLF HARRIS

## THE DEFENCE TEAM'S SPECIAL INVESTIGATOR
## REVEALS THE TRUTH BEHIND THE TRIALS

# WILLIAM B. MERRITT

First published in Great Britain as a softback original in 2022

Copyright © William Merritt

Cover design by Finola Stack: finolastack.co.uk

Typesetting by UK Book Publishing: ukbookpublishing.com

ISBN: 978-1-915338-18-1

# INTRODUCTION

## JUNE 2015

I had recently completed a large and demanding investigation into the historic sexual assault trials of the ex-BBC Radio 1 disc jockey Dave Lee Travis, and I was looking forward to a well-deserved rest. I had been with DLT – as he is known – throughout his ordeal at Southwark Crown Court. This depressing building, along with the attention of the paparazzi, was something I was pleased to see the back of. The paparazzi had followed DLT like a pack of hungry wolves and, whilst he was used to this, I had never experienced anything like it.

From a professional point of view my investigations uncovered evidence that supported DLT's not guilty plea and assisted his barrister, Stephen Vullo QC, in presenting a sound defence, which enabled the jury to find him not guilty on all of the 14 charges that had originally been brought against him. We had found the evidence that the Metropolitan Police either could not find or did not want anyone else to find.

DLT was not a vile paedophile, to use tabloid-speak. Undoubtedly this must have caused some disappointment to certain newspapers in that they were unable to brand him as such. It was the conclusion of the court that he was neither a paedophile nor a sexual predator.

DLT was found guilty on a minor charge of touching a woman's breasts over her clothing 20 years previously. This was not one of the original charges. It was brought in by the police after he had been found not guilty on 12 of the 14 charges and a second trial on the two undecideds was imminent. The police knew the evidence on the remaining two charges was looking too weak to survive a retrial, so they brought in another. This time they got their conviction, and DLT received a suspended sentence. It was an eye opener for all of us – that if the Establishment want to get you, they will find a way.

From a personal point of view, it was a job, almost well done, and it was time for a break. Then the telephone rang and a female voice with an Australian accent said, "Hello, my name is Jenny Harris." Even though I had never met any of the Harris family, I knew instantly who Jenny was and if I thought I was going to get a rest, there was a shock in store for me, because what happened as a result of this one phone call completely enveloped every waking moment of my life for the next two years.

I had not followed the Rolf Harris trial because of my deep involvement with DLT but I knew that 12 months previously Rolf had been convicted on numerous counts of historic sexual assault and he was languishing in jail. The press had vilified him and labelled him a paedophile and sexual predator.

I came to the UK from New Zealand in 2000. I had never heard of Jimmy Savile or DLT until the media broke the news about the alleged historic sexual assaults that numerous people had come forward and complained about. However, the name Rolf Harris was well known to me. I was brought up with Rolf Harris and his various shows when I was a youngster living in New Zealand. Like many others I felt disappointed that he had been found guilty of the charges that had been brought against him, but I had believed the press reports and I was a strong believer in the justice system. Having been a member of the New Zealand police, I was also a strong supporter of the police. However, as I looked into Rolf's trial further, I suspected that he had been caught up, as was DLT and a number of other celebrities, in the Jimmy Savile debacle.

I met Jenny Harris in London a couple of weeks after the telephone call and learned from her that she was the Managing Director of Rolf Harris Enterprises, having taken over the running of the company after the retirement of her father, Bruce Harris, Rolf's older brother. Sadly, I never got to meet Bruce as he was living in Australia, and he has since passed away.

I spent about an hour and a half with Jenny. During that time I learnt a bit about how the court case had been conducted and just how weak the evidence was that was used to convict Rolf on all 12 counts.

The family wanted me to investigate the areas where they believed the police investigation had fallen short and to see if there was sufficient evidence to launch an appeal. They were particularly annoyed about the constant references by the media to the seven- or eight-year-old girl who the jury had found Rolf guilty of sexually assaulting in 1969.

After that meeting I had heard enough to agree that the police investigation fell short of what one would expect of experienced Scotland Yard detectives, and I was later to be proven correct.

In fact, I can say now, without fear of contradiction, that the standard of detective work fell well short of what the public would expect of this service. The same detectives who were involved in the DLT case were also involved in Rolf's case, so I recognised what I considered to be a similar pattern of both poor and lazy detective work.

I agreed to accept instructions and recommended Stephen Vullo QC as the ideal man to handle the appeal. The Harris family contacted and instructed him, along with a firm of solicitors. I was very happy with this as I had worked closely with Stephen during the DLT investigations. We had built up a good relationship and I trusted his judgement implicitly, as he had grown to trust mine.

In the following chapters I will outline in some detail the deficiencies in the police investigation and leave it for the reader to decide whether this was poor police work, lazy police work, or perhaps something even more sinister.

I should explain that lawyers are restricted in what they are permitted to present to a jury at trial. Often, for tactical reasons, evidence that overwhelmingly shows the complainant in a poor light is not communicated to the jury. This will become clearer later, but if a complainant or witness is not telling the truth, and an experienced barrister can see this, it is often better not to rub salt into the wound because this could backfire, and the jury may feel sorry for the complainant or witness and turn against the defence counsel.

In this book I will reveal evidence that has never been heard before by either the courts or the media. Only a few of us – those who were involved in the investigation into the complaints made against Rolf Harris – know the truth behind the allegations.

The police prosecution was based on selective evidence; anything that contradicted what they wanted the jury to hear was either ignored or overlooked. The media followed the police and reported what they wanted the public to hear. The police embarked on a worldwide fishing expedition and publicly declared to anyone who came forward with a complaint of historic sexual abuse, 'You will be believed'. This ill-conceived and misguided mantra is an embarrassing legacy.

'No win no fee' solicitors Slater and Gordon appeared on prime-time morning television urging women to come forward, advising them of the large amounts of money that they could be entitled to, and repeating what the police had said: 'You will be believed'.

Amid this media and police feeding frenzy, entertainers such as Rolf Harris had no chance. Rolf was an entertainer; he was a kind, artistic man who had spent most of his life relying on others to manage and organise his working life. He had no experience in the rough and tumble world that I come from, where most days are spent fighting for justice of some kind. His understandable naivety of how the justice system worked made him easy pickings for police detectives who had an almost unlimited budget and who were hell-bent on gaining a conviction against him, whatever the cost.

On 30th June 2014 Rolf Harris was found guilty by a jury at Southwark Crown Court on 12 counts of indecent assault on four girls under the age of 16 years. These offences were alleged to have taken place between 1969 and 1986. The complainants were four women who were aged between 43 and 52 when the trial started on 6th May 2014. Seven of the charges related to one woman, three to another and one each to the other two women.

Rolf was sentenced to five years and nine months in prison. At the time I was called in to carry out an investigation into the convictions he had already served over a year in prison.

Finally, I would like to point out that in cases involving sexual assault, the Sexual Offences (Amendment) Act 2000 grants a complainant a statutory lifelong right to anonymity, which is removed if the Court rules otherwise or if the complainant waives his or her right in writing.

# CHAPTER 1
# OPERATION YEWTREE

O peration Yewtree is the name that was given to the investigation carried out by the Metropolitan Police Service (MPS) into historic sexual abuse accusations made against the former disc jockey Jimmy Savile and others, many of whom were well-known men. The investigation, led by a specialist team, commenced in October 2012.

The MPS worked in partnership with the National Society for the Prevention of Cruelty to Children (NSPCC) and the National Association for People Abused in Childhood (NAPAC). The accusations predominantly involved children and related to assaults by Jimmy Savile that allegedly occurred between 1959 and the 1980s. Savile died at his home in Leeds in October 2011. The cause of death was pneumonia. He died two days before his 85th birthday.

Operation Yewtree initially involved 30 detectives who handled over 600 complaints, 450 of which related to Savile. However, by January 2013 the impetus had changed, and other celebrities were being investigated by Operation Yewtree officers. The cost of diverting police officers from their normal duties to the Operation Yewtree team was around £450,000 per year in 2012 but this soon increased to £2.2 million, with over 69 officers and civilian staff involved in investigating the allegations of historic indecency and sexual abuse. In addition, there was the cost of the court cases. Many millions of pounds of taxpayers' money was spent investigating, charging and prosecuting celebrities for these historic offences.

Other police forces set up similar squads to Operation Yewtree to investigate the huge number of allegations coming from all quarters of the country and involving a multitude of celebrities. Operation Yewtree still took the lead and assisted by providing information to the other police forces.

In response to media coverage encouraging anyone who claimed to have been abused or indecently or sexually assaulted to come forward and you will be believed, the National Police Chiefs' Council (NPCC) launched Operation Hydrant, which recorded the number of complaints that the media attention had generated. In May 2015, there were over 1,400 suspects from all walks of life: people of public prominence, people from TV, film and radio, people from institutions such as schools, children's homes, religious institutions and medical establishments.

Between 2012 and 2015, many other well-known music and show business personalities were investigated and charged. The rate of convictions was low but some, like Rolf Harris, were caught up in the media frenzy that followed their arrests. They were convicted, imprisoned and labelled paedophiles – a label that will probably stick with them for the rest of their lives.

I have no doubt that in years to come, when historians look back at these three years, they will be viewed as an embarrassment and remembered as a time when celebrities were subjected to trial by media. The hardy survived but those who trusted in the legal system were caught by surprise. It was not until they decided to fight back and employ their own detectives that they discovered the unfairness of the police investigation and how the evidence being leaked to the media, and presented to the court, was heavily biased and unbalanced.

During his first trial Rolf Harris did not have his own investigative team. His defence lawyers had to accept the evidence gathered by the Operation Yewtree officers – evidence that was later exposed as being inept and biased. Although it was too late for his first trial, it was not too late for his new defence team, of which I was a part, to thwart the second attempt by the police to add to his convictions.

The court cases that emanated from the three years of persecution of our celebrities continued to 2018. By this time the public had doubts about many of the cases that the police were bringing before the courts. Surrey Police launched Operation Ravine and charged the media mogul Jonathan King with 23 historic sex offences. I was employed by Jonathan King to investigate the evidence presented by Surrey Police, which I found wanting.

Jonathan King stood trial in June 2018. When the evidence presented by Surrey Police was challenged the trial collapsed, with Judge Deborah Taylor saying that Surrey Police had made 'numerous, repeated and compounded failings' in the disclosure process. She described the situation as a debacle. King received an apology.

In 2014 Operation Yewtree passed information about Cliff Richard on to South Yorkshire Police. The BBC subsequently, and controversially, filmed a police raid on Cliff Richard's home in Berkshire later that year, which led to Cliff Richard taking legal action against the BBC. He won. It took two years for the police to decide that no charges were going to be brought against Cliff. This was a bridge too far. The attack on the UK's favourite son had turned the tide on the police.

The final disaster, which in my opinion is on a par with what happened to Cliff Richard, was Operation Midland. This was launched in November 2014 by the Metropolitan Police. It involved accusations by a police informer known as Nick of sexual abuse and even murder against political figures. For 18 months the Metropolitan Police swore that the information their informer had provided was genuine. The 12 men who Nick accused of being part of an alleged VIP paedophile ring operating in London had their lives turned upside down and in some cases their reputations sullied. Amongst those accused were the retired Armed Forces Chief, Lord Bramall, and the former Home Secretary Lord Brittan.

Operation Midland ended in March 2016. It had been a complete failure. Nick, whose real name was revealed to be Carl Beech, was exposed as a fantasist and a liar. It was his conviction that finally spelled the end of the indecency and sexual abuse operations conducted by the Crown Prosecution Service and the police against well-known people. These operations were now being labelled as witch hunts.

The Metropolitan Police ran up a bill of several million pounds in operational fees, compensation, and the subsequent cost of the investigations against Carl Beech.

A 2016 inquiry into the conduct of the police task force condemned Operation Midland for its failings and left unanswered questions over the investigative conduct and accountability of officers. Carl Beech was arrested and charged over making the false allegations, and in 2019 he was jailed for eighteen years.

Amidst the aftermath of the various police operations headed by the Metropolitan Police there have been numerous inquiries and a lot of criticism over how the police conducted themselves.

I experienced this at first hand. Throughout this book I will record details of how, in order to gain a conviction, some police officers abused the trust and authority that the British public has bestowed upon them. My criticisms are not aimed at the police per se but more at individuals who allowed themselves to be coerced into gathering evidence that they were able to use to obtain a conviction, rather than gathering all of the evidence to enable a sound and fair decision to be made before a suspect was charged.

I am certainly not on my own here. There have been many who have openly criticised the Metropolitan Police's handling of complaints of historic sexual abuse and those in power who encouraged the complainants to come forward.

Some examples:

- In February 2016, the late Irish Supreme Court judge Adrian Hardiman criticised the methods used by Operation Yewtree. He was particularly critical of the treatment of Paul Gambaccini, the manner in which the investigation pertaining to Cliff Richard had been conducted and the Operation Midland cases of Leon Brittan and Edwin Bramall, for what he described as the radical undermining of the presumption of innocence.

- In the aftermath of the search of Cliff Richard's property in August 2014, human rights barrister Geoffrey Robertson wrote in The Independent that the long delays before announcing charges amounted to outrageous treatment. He said the delays had been the most intolerable features of other high-profile arrests for historic offences, namely the inability of police and prosecutors to deliver Magna Carta's truly historic promise that justice will not be delayed.

  Note: After many of those accused, including Cliff Richard, Jim Davidson and Paul Gambaccini, were left on bail for months, even years, before being told that they would not face charges, the then Home Secretary Theresa May proposed that bail time should be limited to 28 days. The 28-day limit came into effect in April 2017.

- Former Metropolitan Police Commander Peter Spindler admitted that the police had got some things wrong and that they had not had sufficient resources in place.

- English TV presenter, journalist and broadcaster Carole Malone claimed the case against Travis was a 'witch-hunt', adding, "If police spent more of their limited time and resources hunting dangerous sex criminals, and less time on celebrity gropers, the world would be a safer place."

I will add a little to what Carole Malone has voiced.

The one minor conviction against Dave Lee Travis (DLT) was the result of a witch hunt of the worst possible kind. It was fuelled by frustration but also by the need to get a conviction against him when all the original 14 charges against him had failed. The complainant in this case was a woman who had been working on the Mrs Merton television show in 1995, when DLT had appeared as a guest.

This complainant did not come forward of her own volition. After receiving information, the police contacted her and asked her to be a complainant. This was the kind of tactic used by the police and prosecution to get a conviction, any conviction, just so long as it was a conviction. DLT was set up, of that I have no doubt.

I am sure the judge did not agree with the verdict and, whilst he had to pass sentence on DLT, he gave him a suspended sentence. Sadly, this did not soften the blow and DLT has never worked again. The thought of having a conviction against his name, for something he maintained he never did, ruined him.

On the point made by Carole Malone, back in the early 1970s I was a police officer in Auckland, New Zealand. My girlfriend at the time was also a police officer. We were at a police party in Henderson, which is a suburb of Auckland. At some time during the evening her sergeant grabbed her breasts and said, "Boobs." My girlfriend took exception to this and left the party. I did not witness what happened, but I was told, and I went looking for her. When I returned, her sergeant apologised profusely and was clearly embarrassed.

The matter was resolved and that is where it was left. I understand that in later years her sergeant rose in rank within the New Zealand police and, if she had wanted to, she could have laid charges against him. Absolutely nothing would have been gained by this. We stayed in touch for many years, and I think it is fair to say that this brief incident did not ruin her life.

Whilst this happened in New Zealand, be sure the British police were not immune to indecent assaults on their female police officers. I recall watching a programme broadcast on Channel 4 in 2014 in which former policewomen talked about the unofficial initiation ceremony called 'the station stamp'. There was no hiding behind anonymity for the women who spoke out against this practice, which was often carried out by their senior officers, one of whom I recall held the rank of Inspector.

A policewoman would be grabbed, her knickers pulled down and her backside stamped with the station stamp. Some of the perverse activities described by these former policewomen were worse, yet despite this being brought to the attention of the British public, no-one did anything.

At the time when this was commonplace within the British police, if a policewoman wanted to keep her job then she had no choice but to accept this sexual abuse. To make it worse, the people who carried out these abuses were in positions of power.

What really infuriates me is the sheer hypocrisy of the police in abusing the authority that was bestowed on them by charging celebrities with offences far less serious than what their own colleagues had done during the same era. The perpetrators of these sexual assaults on female police officers in the 1960s and 1970s should be hunted down and brought to justice in the same manner in which they hounded celebrities between 2012 and 2015: dawn raids on their homes, confiscation of computers and laptops, and publicly naming and shaming them.

## MOTIVES

The reasons why complaints of historic indecent and sexual abuse are made are varied and can be very controversial. There have been calls for a statutory limit on bringing prosecutions, as there are in other countries. A period of 10 years has been suggested as sufficient time to lodge a complaint. There are arguments for and against.

A question I am asked regularly is, how many of the complaints of sexual abuse are genuine and why has the complainant waited up to 40 or 45 years to make a complaint? There is no simple answer to that because I know from experience that some complaints are genuine, and I also know that some complaints are not.

I will deal firstly with my experience of genuine complaints.

In my professional and personal experience, I believe the reason why many genuine cases of abuse are not reported is that the victim is of such a tender age when the abuse occurs that he or she does not know how to deal with it. The abuser normally has power over the victim and uses this position of authority in the most hideous and cowardly way in which any human being can behave. They are truly revolting individuals.

I have personal experience of this as when I was seven I was abused by my stepfather. Why people do nothing about it later in life could be, as in my case, that they move on and ensure that this does not rule their life. Others feel too embarrassed to talk about it and hide it from their family as they do not want anyone to know what had happened to them when they were a child.

I was recently involved in an investigation to assist a barrister/QC in preparing an appeal that involved a former scoutmaster to go before the Court of Appeal. The scoutmaster had been sentenced to a long term of imprisonment for offences against boys, but his supporters were convinced of his innocence. I was given several leads to follow but the witnesses I was locating and interviewing were not corroborating what the convicted former scoutmaster had told his supporters and what they were hoping to hear.

After finding a man who we believed would be a vital witness, I discovered the truth. He too had been abused by this man when he was a member of the scout troop. He had not come forward because he did not want his family to know. I then realised why there had been a wall of silence and reluctance by other potential witnesses, all of whom were male, to discuss the case with me. The offences committed by this man were far wider than we thought.

The appeal did not go forward, and my services were withdrawn. The wishes of those I had interviewed were taken into account and it was left to them to decide if they wanted to make complaints. They did not and they dealt with it in the same way as I had. They had made a good life for themselves and were all in good professions, so their way of dealing with the abuse was to rise above it and get on with their lives.

As a young detective constable in Auckland, I dealt with both genuine and false complaints of rape. The best result I had, and which I am truly proud of, involved a single mother who had a young son. They lived in an Auckland suburb. One night a man in his late teens broke into her house and raped her. She let him have sex with her because she was afraid that if she resisted he might harm her son.

Three detectives, who were far more experienced than I was at the time, had tried to obtain a confession from him but he was not admitting anything. We had found out that he had been in and out of boys' homes as a youngster and had previously been convicted of interfering with very young children. However, in recent years he had been charged with two other rapes, one being at knifepoint, but the charges against him had been dismissed owing to a lack of evidence.

After three long hours I obtained a confession and a signed statement. In those days we did not have video interviewing. The confession and statement were heavily challenged in court, but I had managed to obtain enough evidence from the scene examination to verify his confession. He was found guilty.

In New Zealand during the 1970s jurors did not go home at night whilst they were on jury duty and hearing a case. They were isolated from outside influences and stayed in hotels overnight, being watched over by a court official. I recall the jury sitting until quite late in the evening on the final day. After the guilty verdict had been handed down and the jury dismissed, the court registrar approached me and asked me to see the judge in his chambers.

The judge was Justice Peter Mahon QC, who years later became well known for heading the Royal Commission of Inquiry into the Erebus disaster. On 28th November 1979 an Air New Zealand DC10 on a 'flightseeing' trip had slammed into the side of Mount Erebus in the Antarctic, killing all 257 passengers and crew. It remains New Zealand's deadliest aviation disaster. I was quite nervous as I entered the judge's chambers as I was expecting some criticism.

However, I received just the opposite. Justice Mahon praised me for the work I had done on the case and said he had nothing but respect for the bravery of the victim for how she had handled the situation. He even confided in me that he would have to consider the length of sentence he would impart on the accused because of his age. He was still a teenager.

He said if he gave him too long a sentence then some do-gooder would appeal it and he would get out earlier, so he was probably going to sentence him to seven years. I really liked this judge; he was down to earth and realistic. I have always remembered this case and Justice Mahon.

At the other end of the spectrum was a case I dealt with concerning two young women who had been out on a date with a couple of young seamen. One claimed that she had been taken into a bedroom by one of these men and raped. Her friend backed up her story.

I spent weeks on this case only to receive a call from the mother of one of the girls, requesting a meeting. At the meeting I was told that the girls had made up the story because they were late home and had used this as a reason for arriving home in the early hours of the morning. One of the girls had had a sexual encounter but of her own free will.

I was devastated by this as they had been so convincing and I had believed them, even though the two men had pleaded their innocence.

So, I learned early on in my career that one can easily be swayed by a convincing story. The only way to be reasonably certain that someone is telling the truth is to complete a full investigation and to ensure that all the facts are known before making any decision. In my view this is something that the Scotland Yard team on Operation Yewtree did not do.

I will turn now to false complaints and why these are made. Historic complaints pose a particular problem in that it is very difficult to check out the validity of the complaint because a large amount of the evidence no longer exists.

There is no scene examination, DNA or scientific evidence to support the allegation. In the case of an accusation against a celebrity, the complainant often relies on photos or programmes, or documentation of some description, to confirm that he or she was in the same place as the celebrity at the time when the alleged abuse occurred. However, the ease with which such items can be bought online means that the complainant's possession of them has to be subjected to scrutiny. In some cases there is nothing at all to place the complainant in the same location as a celebrity at a particular time.

The police were neither prepared, nor adequately trained, to handle the number of historic sexual abuse cases they were asked to investigate between 2012 and 2015. Because of this they changed their normal procedure for gathering evidence. Instead of seeking evidence that could stand on its own, they embarked on a fishing expedition to see how many people – in most cases women – they could persuade to come forward to support allegations made against celebrities. The theory was, **they can't all be wrong**.

On 7th July 2017, just a week after Rolf Harris's first trial ended, the *Daily Star* ran the headline 'Rolf Harris victims to get £200k each'. With reporting such as this, the police referring to complainants as 'victims' and assuring them that '**you will be believed**' (with no regard for how lurid and unlikely the tale might be), and personal injury solicitors telling talk show hosts how much victims could expect to receive in compensation, it is no wonder that so many complaints were made. In fact, one of the complainants at Rolf Harris's second and third trials had come forward on the very day that the *Daily Star* article appeared.

For reasons of confidentiality, I am unable to comment on three of the four compensation settlements made after Rolf Harris's first trial (the fourth one is in the public domain), except to say that the *Daily Star*'s article was interesting to say the least.

On the point regarding **they can't all be wrong**, this insinuates that the UK is a country where everyone is honest, and no-one would chance coming forward with a false complaint in order to collect compensation. If a slightly dishonest individual, who has been tempted by the lure of money, was told by the police **you will be believed**, he or she might think they were not risking prosecution, so why not give it a go.

To put this in perspective, in 2016 the annual number of fraudsters prosecuted for benefit fraud in the UK was around 5,000, with a further 6,000 administrative penalties being issued. The cost to the UK taxpayer was £2.3 billion. In the same year insurers detected 125,000 dishonest insurance claims valued at £1.3 billion.

Why run the risk of committing benefit fraud or insurance fraud and being prosecuted when the police are advising you that if you come forward with a complaint of an indecent assault by a celebrity **you will be believed**? Carl Beech was believed. His macabre account of a paedophile ring and child murders linked to MPs and other prominent people was described by a Detective Superintendent, no less, as 'credible and true'. It netted him £22,000.

## COMPENSATION

Claiming compensation for sexual abuse can be done with or without a lawyer. However, most claimants prefer to use a 'no win, no fee', law firm that is experienced in handling compensation claims. These firms tout for business and are easy to find - that is, if they don't find you first.

A civil claim can be made against the perpetrator, or a claim can be made with the Criminal Injuries Compensation Authority (CICA) if the perpetrator is not able to pay compensation. At the time of writing the total fee recoverable for sexual assault is capped at £500,000, although to be awarded this amount is very rare. It is recorded that in 2016/2017 only 1.3% of applicants received £100,000 and over.

The usual amount awarded under the scheme ranges from £11,000 for minor sexual assault to £44,000 in more serious cases, such as rape. Additional amounts could be payable if the sexual assault caused physical injury.

Private civil claims are often made on behalf of a claimant by 'no win, no fee' solicitors. The *Daily Star* article referenced earlier identified law firm Slater and Gordon as having been contacted by up to a dozen people, whose cases were being carefully considered.

It was reported that a solicitor, Richard Walters, who is an expert in abuse claims, had said that victims who prove their cases in a criminal trial had very strong cases for compensation, which could be as much as £200,000 in the most serious of cases.

It is not necessary to obtain a criminal conviction against the perpetrator to claim compensation in a civil case. This applied in the case of one of the bad character witnesses called by the police in Rolf Harris's first trial. The alleged indecent assault occurred in Malta but owing to Malta being out of the jurisdiction of the UK courts the charge could not be heard in the UK. The Malta Police Force was not interested in pursuing this complaint.

Under the circumstances the complainant was called as a bad character witness. After the trial she instructed 'no win, no fee' solicitors Slater and Gordon to take out a private civil claim against Rolf Harris. Chapter 11 describes the interesting investigation that I carried out in relation to this Malta civil claim.

# WRONGFUL ALLEGATIONS

A disproportionate number of celebrities were investigated, and in some cases charged, over wrongful allegations of sexual abuse between 2012 and 2015.

Not all the complaints were made for the purpose of getting compensation. Some of the complainants had other reasons, although money was the key ingredient in most of the false allegations.

A few had a grudge and took the opportunity to exact revenge against the celebrity over a disagreement of many years' standing. One of the complainants in the DLT trials did just this. Fortunately, her plan failed, and her false complaint was exposed.

Many people will come forward of their own volition to report that they are victims of historic sexual assault. Their accounts may well be true, but in some instances a celebrity will become the embodiment of the person who assaulted them. As they try to make sense of their confusing life experiences, they genuinely believe that the celebrity was their abuser, especially if the real abuser is no longer alive and will never have to answer for what they have done. They tell a convincing story because they are relating what really did happen to them in terms of the assault itself.

False memories are far too common, much more so than I thought. As time goes by gaps appear in all our memories and we tend to fill these gaps with what we have heard from others.

This is why the constant media barrage and the speculation from tabloids are dangerous. By the time the complaint is reported to the police, the memory gaps have been filled and the account provided could differ significantly from what actually happened.

This is as far as I intend to take this because there are academics who have spent their lives studying why people make false allegations. This makes them much more knowledgeable than I am on this subject. They have presented their work in books and articles about false memories and wrongful allegations in relation to historic sexual abuse. One such book that I read recently is titled *Wrongful Allegations of Sexual and Child Abuse*. It is published by Oxford University Press and edited by Ros Burnett, DPhil. She is a Senior Research Associate, formerly Reader in Criminology at the Centre for Criminology, University of Oxford.

The book has twenty-two contributors from all around the world and focuses on why people make wrongful allegations of sexual and child abuse. There is a foreward by Professor Andrew Ashworth CBE, QC (Hon), LLB, MA, PhD, DCL, DJur (Hon), LLD (Hon), FBA – Emeritus Vinerian Professor of English Law, Oxford University.

Professor Ashworth writes about righting past wrongs in relation to victims of sexual abuse and why this should not be allowed to produce more wrongs.

For anyone who is genuinely interested in why people make wrongful allegations, this book is essential reading.

# CHAPTER 2
# 'TWO LITTLE BOYS'

O ne of Rolf Harris's convictions at the first trial resulted from an allegation made by complainant Wendy Rosher, who told the court that in 1969, around the time of her eighth birthday, she was indecently assaulted by Rolf Harris at the Leigh Park Community Centre in Havant, Hampshire. Rolf was convicted and sentenced to a term of nine months' imprisonment on this charge. This sentence was to run consecutively – that is, in addition to any other penalty imposed – rather than concurrently. Wendy Rosher, having waived her right to anonymity after the first trial but using a different name, appeared on television and in newspaper articles.

The charge was: *Indecent assault on a girl under the age of 16 years between the 1st day of January 1968 and the 1st day of January 1970.*

This charge related to an indecent assault that allegedly took place 45 years earlier. As such, it was truly historical. To add to Rolf's difficulty in having to account for his movements after so long, the charge covered a period of two years. In her evidence and during her police video interview, Wendy Rosher provided the following information in support of this charge.

In 1969 she went to a children's event at the Leigh Park Community Centre (which I will refer to henceforth as the LPCC) in Havant, Hampshire. She said that she had just had her eighth birthday, which was in October 1969. According to her evidence, Rolf Harris, who was then aged 39, was there and he was entertaining the children.

She also said that:

- Rolf Harris was promoting his new hit single 'Two Little Boys' by singing it and signing autographs.
- He had big hairy hands, big black glasses and curly black hair, and was quite a big man with a big smile and a very strong Australian accent.
- At the time she was living in Warsash Close, Leigh Park, where there were a lot of children. (Leigh Park is a suburb of Havant. Warsash Close is a cul-de-sac on the housing estate and is about five to ten minutes' walk from the LPCC.)
- She alleged that while she was on the stage at the LPCC getting Rolf Harris's autograph he put his hand between her legs and around her vaginal area, but his hand did not go under her clothing.

## SCOTLAND YARD DETECTIVES

The investigation into the claims against Rolf Harris was spearheaded by Detective Sergeant Gary Pankhurst. DS Pankhurst, who took early retirement at the conclusion of the inquiry, gave evidence in court that the police had searched local newspaper archives and had found no record of Rolf Harris ever having performed at, or otherwise visited, the LPCC. He added that the Metropolitan Police had arranged a mail drop to residents in the Leigh Park area regarding an investigation in which they were involved and asking for information. The letter read in part:

*The investigation relates to an incident alleged to have taken place during an event held at Leigh Park Community Centre. This would have been between the years 1968-1972 and many children from the local area would have attended. If you or anyone you know attended events at the Community Centre as a child or adult during these years, we would be grateful if you could call and speak to one of our investigators on the following number or email.*

Only one person came forward: an older man by the name of David James. I do not know how the name Rolf Harris came up because Rolf's name was not mentioned in the letter, but somehow – maybe as a result of having been interviewed – David James became aware that Rolf was the subject of the investigation. He told the court that he had attended the LPCC for many years, and that he recalled Rolf Harris being there around 1967.

The police did use another witness, Philip Wilbourn, whose family were living in Leigh Park in 1968/69. Mr Wilbourn, who was 12 at the time of the alleged incident and who no longer lives in the area, recalled reading in a local newspaper that Rolf Harris had visited the Havant area in the late 1960s. He did not see Rolf Harris when this supposed visit took place, and in evidence he conceded that he did not recall anyone at school mentioning a visit by Rolf Harris to Leigh Park. There was no reason for the prosecution to call Mr Wilbourn as a witness because he could not provide any evidence. I suspect that he was there as a 'filler' to boost the number of supporting witnesses from one to two.

What was notably missing from the police case were family members. According to Wendy Rosher's evidence, her brother, Paul, had dropped her off at the LPCC and left her there. She claimed that she was at the LPCC with someone else – either her sister or a friend (reports vary on this point). Astonishingly, neither her brother nor her sister were called as prosecution witnesses, and the friend was never identified.

Also missing as witnesses were her mother and father, whom one might think would have had some knowledge of where their eight-year-old daughter was, or who at least would have been able to inform the court if she had ever visited the LPCC without them around the time of her eighth birthday. They would also surely have remembered if Rolf Harris had visited the LPCC in 1969, or for that matter at any other time.

## THE DEFENCE

The defence solicitors did not contact any members of Wendy Rosher's family. During the trial Lorna Madden, a solicitor at law firm Kingsley Napley, which defended Rolf Harris at the first trial, gave evidence that she had carried out research at the Portsmouth Central Library and reviewed the local newspaper coverage of the years 1968 to 1970. *The Hampshire Telegraph* covered Havant and provided regular, specific news and updates from the LPCC.

Following a thorough and intensive review of the microfilm, Lorna Madden gave evidence that she had formed the view that had any individual, whether high profile or amateur, performed at the LPCC it would have been announced in the relevant section of this newspaper. She provided the dates and names of personalities, some known, others not well known, who had visited the area from 1968 to 1970. She also itemised news from the LPCC, which reported on cheese and wine evenings, the Saturday Cinema Club, Junior Jive Club, a local concert party and other events that one would expect to occur in a small-town community centre.

Lorna Madden reached the same conclusion as DS Gary Pankhurst, which was that there was no evidence that Rolf Harris had ever visited the LPCC. Therefore, the judge and jury had overwhelming evidence to support Rolf's assertion that he had never been there. That being the case, Rolf should never have been convicted of an indecent assault on

Wendy Rosher when he had not been there to commit the assault.

The defence team had the opportunity to challenge the evidence and ask the judge to dismiss the charge before it was presented to a jury, because the evidence against Rolf was so weak that a prima facie case against him could not be made. They decided not to challenge the charge as in their opinion it was so unbelievable that it could be used to show the jury how weak the evidence against Rolf was. It is hard to think of any other example of tactical thinking that backfired so spectacularly.

## THE CONVICTION

In 2014 the media frenzy over well-known people being linked to historic sexual offences was in full swing, underpinning a moral panic and leading many to believe that any complaint in this regard had to be genuine. There were warning signs that were ignored. Logic appeared to have completely disappeared from the English justice system, so much so that even evidence from the police was ignored. Proof beyond a reasonable doubt seemed to be overlooked. The celebrity was deemed to be guilty before the trial started and was expected to prove his innocence in court.

Aided by a huge media smear campaign against Rolf, the Crown Prosecutor, Sasha Wass, put on an Oscar-winning performance. She managed to convince the jury that Rolf had lied about assaulting the then eight-year-old Wendy Rosher. Once this had been planted in the minds of the jury it was able to be used to attack Rolf Harris's credibility in respect of the other charges.

In 1969, Rolf Harris was a world-renowned celebrity who was very much in demand. He often performed at high-capacity venues such as the Royal Albert Hall and Sydney Opera House. Despite the police and a solicitor for the defence testifying that they had found no evidence that Rolf Harris had ever been to the LPCC – a community centre on a local authority housing estate – the jury decided that Rolf Harris somehow covertly visited the LPCC and whilst there committed the indecent assault on Wendy Rosher. The jury preferred to believe Wendy Rosher over the mountain of evidence confirming that Rolf Harris had never been to Leigh Park. He was found guilty as charged.

## COMPENSATION

Following Rolf's conviction, 'no win, no fee' solicitors Slater and Gordon instigated a civil claim on behalf of Wendy Rosher for compensation to cover the psychological trauma she claimed to have suffered in the years since the indecent assault. However, in the civil claim the allegation was altered to read, "You indecently assaulted our client by touching her under her clothing and touching her genital area." This more serious allegation meant a far larger compensation payment if it was 'proven' to be correct.

The civil lawyers acting for Rolf successfully challenged the authenticity of the more serious allegation. As a result, Wendy Rosher received an out of court settlement of £22,000, which had been negotiated upwards from £12,500, rather than a higher figure that one might reasonably assume she had been expecting. Although the details of the amounts paid in compensation are confidential, Wendy Rosher chose to publicise how much she received. This was seized on by certain newspapers to ignite the ire of their readers. On 27th September 2015, the Mail Online reported that the sum equated to 76p per day for '40 years of nightmares.'

If Wendy Rosher was having nightmares, they could not be pinned on Rolf Harris. And whilst £22,000 might not sound a huge amount to some people, to someone undergoing bankruptcy proceedings, as Wendy Rosher was at the time of making her allegation, this would have been a large sum of money.

I should point out that paying £22,000 to Wendy Rosher was not an admission of guilt on Rolf's part. As he had been found guilty of indecently assaulting her, he had no choice but to pay the money. He had no defence other than to challenge, as his legal team did successfully, the more serious allegation made by Slater and Gordon.

It did not stop there. Wendy Rosher waived her right to anonymity so she could sell her story to various media outlets for undisclosed sums. Her brother, Paul, who was very vocal about her treatment at the hands of Rolf Harris, appeared in newspaper articles alongside her. To my knowledge, no journalist ever questioned either of them as to how Rolf could have indecently assaulted someone at a place that he had never set foot in.

## THE JURORS

On the face of it, the guilty verdict was based on the evidence of Wendy Rosher and one other person, namely David James, who despite his less-than-ideal credentials was called as a witness. But was it solely their evidence that convinced the jury that Rolf Harris had been at the LPCC in 1969 and that the alleged assault had taken place?

The calibre of a jury is always a concern, as to come to the right decision requires the ability to interpret evidence and apply some critical thinking. Whilst there will always be those who are convinced of the defendant's guilt before the trial has begun, those jurors who have fundamental deficits in understanding can easily be swayed by other jury members. There was a person on the jury at Rolf Harris's first trial who is of particular interest because of his occupation (about which I will write later), but it is worth mentioning here the Vicky Pryce speeding case.

Vicky Pryce is the ex-wife of a former Cabinet minister. In February 2013 she was on trial at Southwark Crown Court, having been accused of accepting demerit points for speeding ten years earlier when it was her then husband who had been driving. I do not intend going into this case in any depth as most of it won't be relevant to Rolf Harris.

The jury in the Vicky Pryce case was discharged after being unable to reach a verdict. This is not unusual, and indeed happened in Rolf Harris's second and third trials. But in the Vicky Pryce case it wasn't just any 'ordinary' deadlock. The judge, Justice Sweeney – the same judge who presided over Rolf's first trial – announced that the jury had 'absolutely fundamental deficits in understanding'. Putting it less politely, they had no idea what they were doing and were expected to make a decision that would affect someone's life.

## THE INVESTIGATION

I was provided with a summary of the evidence that convicted Rolf Harris when I first met Jenny Harris. After reading this, I was satisfied that Rolf had not received a fair trial and the conviction was unsafe. This first instinct of mine was later to be ratified by the Court of Appeal.

On my team I had two investigators named Douglas. Doug Quade was a retired Detective Superintendent of the Hampshire Police who had headed the Police Intelligence section. He was a very knowledgeable man who had come well recommended by another colleague. He quickly formed the same opinion as I had and struggled to understand how a jury could have reached a guilty verdict based on the evidence that was presented at trial.

The other Doug was Douglas Bainbridge, ex-marine, ex-Special Forces and an ex-police detective. Doug had served his country in the Falklands War and in Northern Ireland. He formed the same view as the rest of us and was very keen to do whatever was necessary to uncover the truth.

Doug Quade, who was in his mid-seventies, had an advantage in terms of the investigation as he had spent all his working life in Hampshire and was familiar with Leigh Park.

I had to cast my mind back to 1969 and remember what it was like back then. Although I was living in New Zealand in 1969, I still recall clearly how famous Rolf Harris was. My parents had moved back to the UK in 1968, so I had close contact with England. New Zealand in those days closely followed England, as it was very much reliant on the UK for trade at that time.

Even the police forces were very similar, with many English police leaving the UK to join the New Zealand police. From December 1976 to June 1977, I spent six months playing rugby in England. During this trip I lived on the south coast. That also assisted me in visualising how Leigh Park would have been in 1969.

The Leigh Park estate was built to accommodate the many local people who had lost their homes during the Second World War. Nearby areas on the South Coast, such as Portsmouth, which is about six miles from Leigh Park, were heavily bombed during the war, firstly because of the naval ships based there and secondly as it was the ideal place for German bombers to drop their excess bombs to reduce the weight of the plane before flying back over the English Channel.

I was told during my enquiries that at one time Leigh Park was the largest council estate in Europe. I am not sure of the accuracy of this but there is little doubt that it is a large estate. The LPCC was built in 1963 and was operated by a committee and executive committee elected by locals in the community. It was funded by grants from Havant Borough Council and Hampshire County Council plus any income derived from the cafeteria, bingo and social events. In 1969 the LPCC was desperately short of funds and operated on a shoestring budget.

The maximum number of people that could be seated in the centre was 200. Children's entertainment consisted of a Thursday evening disco from 4.30 pm to 6.45 pm. The council had supplied a projector and screen, so volunteers were able to run a Saturday morning and afternoon cinema show, which usually included a singalong of popular songs of the day. Entry was sixpence. Parents used the LPCC as a babysitting service whilst they went shopping or visited the Saturday market in the adjacent car park.

I spoke to most, if not all, of the officials who were still alive and who were involved in running the LPCC. They told me unanimously that no celebrity had ever appeared at the LPCC because the venue was too small, and there were no funds available to pay for such a person.

Although based in the UK, Rolf was an Australian icon and undoubtedly Australia's best-known export back in the 1960s and 1970s. He had a high profile on British television and his songs were played regularly on the radio. In late 1969 he released 'Two Little Boys', which topped the charts in the UK within the first three weeks of its release. Rolf's appearances were newsworthy. His performances would be advertised and reviewed in local papers and often they would receive national coverage.

I was aware of the enquiries made by the police and the defence solicitor. When we made our own enquiries, we came up with the same result: there was no record anywhere of Rolf Harris having visited Leigh Park at any time, let alone in 1969.

I sent researchers to the British Library in London, where newspapers that covered Leigh Park and the surrounding areas were reviewed. There were two in 1969: *The Hampshire Telegraph* and *The Southern Evening Echo*.

*The Hampshire Telegraph* was a weekly paper that included a section headed 'News from the Community Centres'. Leigh Park was included in this. There was no mention of Rolf Harris appearing at any of the community centres, including Leigh Park.

*The Southern Evening Echo* was a daily newspaper. We searched through every paper covering 1969, paying particular attention to the latter part of that year. There was no mention of Rolf Harris ever appearing at the LPCC. There was a page detailing forthcoming events on which there was an advertisement for Rolf Harris appearing with the Irish folk band The Pattersons at the Bournemouth Winter Gardens on 16th November 1969. This was part of his 16-day tour of one-nighters around England. In 1969, Bournemouth to Leigh Park by car was a four-hour return journey.

There was mention of singer and entertainer Anita Harris (who is no relation to Rolf) appearing in Southampton and of Tommy Steele aboard HMS Victory in Portsmouth, so one would certainly have expected there to be mention of Rolf Harris if he had appeared at Leigh Park.

Doug Bainbridge drew the short straw and had the job of foot slogging around Leigh Park to complete the local enquiries that the Metropolitan Police should have done, instead of arranging a mail drop that really produced nothing other than an eccentric elderly man who was known in the area as a fantasist. Doug did the real police work.

As part of our local enquiry planning, we drew a circle on a map of Leigh Park that was large enough to cover the streets where one would have expected the children who attended the Saturday morning film show to live. Certainly, they would be within walking distance of the LPCC.

My researchers then set about checking electoral rolls for Leigh Park in the late 1960s and early 1970s. They cross-referenced them with the current electoral roll and identified the people who were still living in the area. Then the door knocking started. Doug Bainbridge covered 32 streets. He also spoke to people at bus stops and in the shopping centre and anyone else along the way who looked to be of the age of those who would have been living in Leigh Park when this alleged incident occurred. Doug seemed to enjoy this part of the job, and he was ideally suited for it. Maybe it was all the years of foot slogging around parade grounds or in later years knocking on doors electioneering (he has served as a city councillor for many years).

Many days later, and after meeting some very interesting characters, Doug had not found anyone who knew of a visit to Leigh Park by Rolf Harris, at any time. The type of responses he received were:

*"If Rolf Harris had been to Leigh Park I would have known, as I was a big fan."*

*"Rolf Harris never came to Leigh Park because, if he did, I would have been first in line."*

*"We heard about the case and thought the police must have had some information that we didn't because no-one ever remembered Rolf Harris coming here."*

A couple of people knew of the prosecution witness David James, describing him as an old fantasist who sometimes hung around the shopping centre telling tall stories. They couldn't comprehend that the police had believed him and had called him to provide evidence against Rolf Harris.

There are two people in particular who spring to mind who were of great assistance to us when we were conducting our local enquiries.

After the trial it soon became apparent that those who were supportive of Rolf, or who queried the guilty verdict, were leaving themselves open to vicious verbal attacks on social media. For this reason, many supporters took to using pseudonyms. One such person was Debbie Wright, a former resident of Leigh Park

Doug Quade arranged a meeting with Debbie, at which she informed him that she had lived with her parents in West Leigh between 1961 and 1977 and had attended a local secondary school. As a young girl she would hang around the LPCC and regularly visited a little café nearby. In those days there was nowhere else for young people to go, so she was always around the LPCC. Had there been any news of a visit by Rolf

Harris she is adamant that she would have known.

Debbie provided a signed statement. In it she stated that she was totally confident that Rolf Harris had never been to Leigh Park.

A retired woman, who I will refer to as Winnie, told Doug Bainbridge that she had lived in Leigh Park all her adult life and still resided in the same house as she did in the 1960s. She remembered Wendy Rosher's family when they lived in Warsash Close in the late 1960s.

Winnie took it upon herself to keep an eye on the children who played in and around Warsash Close and look after them if need be. Winnie was originally from the East End of London, and she spoke with the same forthright and direct manner that East Enders are renowned for.

During the conversation Winnie had with Doug she spoke about Wendy, who she said regularly told lies to get the other kids in trouble.

Winnie recounted an incident that she said happened when Wendy was about seven. Wendy complained that two little boys (her words) who lived close by had been playing with her and had touched her private parts. We do not know the actual words used by Wendy as a seven-year-old to describe where they had touched her, but that is what she meant. Apparently, a local policewoman was called, and she spoke with both families, including the three children.

It seemed to me to be far too much of a coincidence that Wendy Rosher had dated the alleged indecent assault on her by Rolf Harris as being around the same time that she was complaining about having been interfered with – to use the parlance of the times – by the two young boys. Perhaps she recalled making this complaint when, 45 years later, she decided to make the same type of complaint against Rolf.

As it turned out, Winnie was unaware of the charges and convictions against Rolf Harris, let alone that he was lodging an appeal – which, of course, was the reason for Doug's enquiry. Also, she had no idea whatsoever that Wendy Rosher had made an accusation against Rolf.

Doug asked her if she could recall Rolf Harris visiting the LPCC. She said that she was absolutely certain that Rolf Harris had never been to Leigh Park and, more specifically, to the LPCC. If he had, she said, it would have been the highlight of her life.

A mail drop is a lazy way of making an enquiry. It epitomised the poor way this police investigation was handled. Most of the people Doug Bainbridge spoke to said they had never received the letter that the Metropolitan Police claimed they had distributed in Leigh Park, and those who did receive it either had no idea what it was about or had no interest in helping them.

The people who lived on the Leigh Park estate in the 1960s and 1970s tended to sort out their own problems. The police were not viewed as their friends. In fact, according to the retired police officers I encountered who had worked in Leigh Park in the 1960s and 1970s, there were several no-go areas.

It was naive to believe that the locals would respond to a police circular, let alone one from the Metropolitan Police. If the Operation Yewtree team had swallowed a bit of the attitude the Metropolitan Police often have towards a County Constabulary, and asked Hampshire police for their help, they would not have made so many mistakes and this matter may never have come before the court.

In 2011, a documentary funded by the Lottery Commission and commissioned by the BBC was produced for television. The documentary, which was directed by Lynne Dicks, was called 'On the Street Where We Live' and covered the history of Leigh Park. Local people were invited to bring along memorabilia and share their memories.

Doug Quade interviewed Lynne Dicks, who told him that during the making of the documentary there had been no mention by anyone of a visit to the LPCC by Rolf Harris.

Doug Quade also spoke with Philip Hammond, who was the author of the 2000 publication entitled *Leigh Park – The First Fifty Years*. He told Doug that he was interviewed by the police during their investigations, but he was not asked to make a written statement, nor was he called as a witness.

As part of his research, he trawled through local records and newspapers. He found no reference to Rolf Harris visiting the area and he never encountered anyone who mentioned such a visit. He was contacted again by the police in late 2013. To put his mind at rest and to be absolutely certain, he returned to the Portsmouth Library and searched through the newspaper records to make certain he had not missed anything. Once again, he found no record of any visit by Rolf Harris to Leigh Park.

What happened to the hundreds of children who, according to Wendy Rosher, were at the LPCC in late 1969, and all the autographs that she claimed Rolf had signed? Where were the photos of the event? The carefully preserved programmes and ticket stubs? How did Rolf Harris manage to indecently assault her when he was signing autographs on the stage in front of a crowd, with a pen in one hand and a steady stream of paper and autograph books in the other? Where were the LPCC staff who would have been keeping an eye on things? Above all, why did no-one on the estate apart from Wendy Rosher, her brother Paul and witness David James remember this event, which would have been one of the most exciting things ever to happen to Leigh Park?

During Rolf's trial, and ever since, fans and supporters have asked where the evidence was that he had been at Leigh Park. Each time they were shot down either by the news media or on social media. The interesting point is, for all the loudmouths out there, no-one has produced even the tiniest scrap of evidence to show that Rolf had been at Leigh Park, either when Wendy Rosher stated that he had indecently assaulted her or at any other time. Media interest was so intense that anyone with photos of Rolf Harris performing at the LPCC, or who had a programme, could have sold them to the highest bidder. No-one did.

The investigations my team made, and the investigations made by the police and defence lawyers, simply confirmed that Rolf was never

*Two photos of Rolf performing (not at Leigh Park) in the 1960s from his personal collection. There are no security guards or orderly lines on this occasion, and he would have had no chance to single anyone out whilst being mobbed by autograph hunters.*

there. So why were there uninformed people who still claimed that he had indecently assaulted this woman when she was a seven- or eight-year-old girl? This was the question that still hung over this investigation like a heavy 1950s London smog.

There appeared to be only one logical answer, but it seems that the jury had not used logic in reaching their decision, or perhaps I am being unfair. They could work only with the information that they had been provided with.

The public's perception of the police was that they must have known what they were doing, and there was no reason for the jury not to share this view. The selective police evidence, a brilliant theatrical performance from the prosecutor Sasha Wass (nicknamed 'The Wasp' during the trial), along with what was effectively the media's trial and conviction of Rolf, meant that the jurors were manoeuvred away from what they were there for, and that was to reach a verdict based on the evidence and legal arguments presented.

## THE POLICE STATION

Leigh Park is policed from Havant police station, which should have been the first port of call for any Scotland Yard police detective who is out of his area. Now, had DS Gary Pankhurst and his band of Scotland Yard's finest asked for help from the local police, they would have found out that in 1969 Hampshire Constabulary based their Leigh Park police station in a two-storey house sited on the corner of Dunsbury Way and Bishopstoke Road. The house is still there but is now privately owned. It is the closest house to the LPCC, being about a 50-metre walk away.

Along with uniformed staff, there was a CID section that comprised a Detective Inspector, Detective Sergeant and five Detective Constables. The 50-metre walk across the car park to the LPCC allowed a clear view from the CID offices of anyone using the car park or visiting the LPCC.

A two-storey brick extension, built on the car park site in 1980, was not there in 1969.

The Leigh Park police station closed around 1972. All the staff were transferred to Havant police station, which is about one and a half kilometres away. From then on, Leigh Park was policed from Havant police station.

It is unforgivable and an absolute embarrassment for so-called highly trained detectives from Scotland Yard to have completely missed the fact that in 1969 there was a police station only 50 metres away from the LPCC. It is not that they never went to the area; in fact, they spent a great deal of time and resources in and around the LPCC.

Doug Quade did not miss this. Once he discovered that at the time of the alleged visit by Rolf Harris the local police station was only about 50 metres away, he focused his investigations on identifying and locating any former police officers who would have worked at the police station during this time. Doug Quade found two. Both were retired and still living in Hampshire.

It did not take long for Doug to locate the two retired police detectives. They were both willing to assist and provided him with as much information as they could recall about the operation of the Leigh Park police station in 1969.

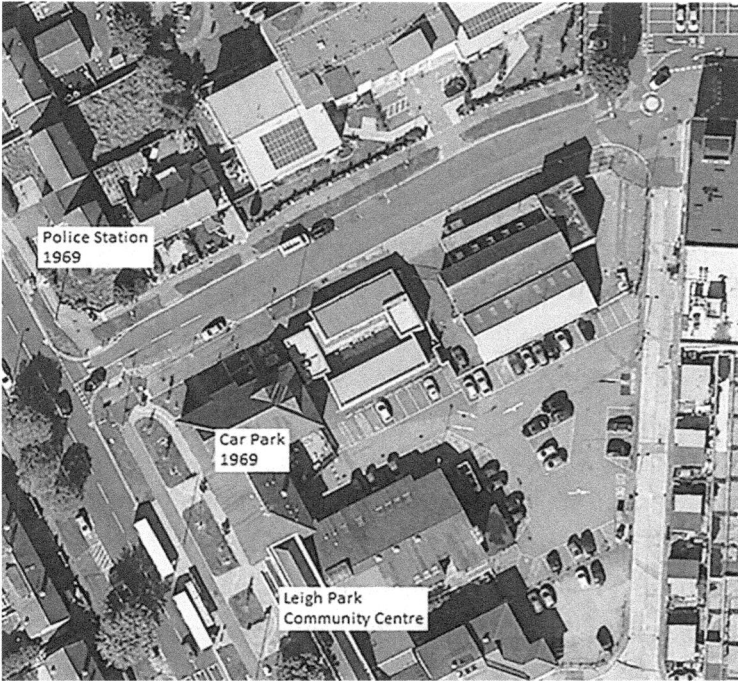

*An aerial view of the Leigh Park Community Centre today. The car park has been built on and the police station is now a private home.*

# LEIGH PARK POLICE IN 1969

### Peter Spencer

Peter, who is retired, was a Detective Constable based at the Leigh Park CID office from 1967 to 1972. He told us that the CID had their morning meeting inside the LPCC at 10.30 am each day. He was adamant that Rolf Harris had never visited the LPCC and he would have known if he had. He served with the Hampshire Constabulary from 1964 to 2003, retiring with the rank of Sergeant.

Peter Spencer was well known in the Hampshire police for his ability to cultivate informers and for his local knowledge. He knew everyone and everything that was happening in the area. He, above anyone else, would have known if Rolf Harris had ever been to Leigh Park.

### Raymond Piper

Raymond Piper, who is also retired, was a Detective Constable based at the Leigh Park CID office from 1968 to 1971. He worked out of this office for three years with Peter Spencer. He also said that the detectives based at this office had their daily meetings in the lounge of the Leigh Park Community Centre at 10.30 am each day.

Ray said that he was not aware of any celebrity appearing at the LPCC and this included Rolf Harris. He considered that he would have known if Rolf Harris had appeared because there would have been a buzz about the place, and he would have been interested in seeing him.

Ray further referred to a police order that would have been brought to their attention because of management of traffic, people and security. He pointed out that Leigh Park was a large council estate, and, in those days, there were some rough areas. Someone as famous as Rolf Harris would have attracted a lot of attention.

Raymond Piper served with the Hampshire Constabulary between 1959 and 1994, retiring with the rank of Detective Superintendent.

### Margaret Sinnott

Margaret was employed by Hampshire Constabulary as a Communications Operator between 1966 and 1985 and was based at Havant police station. She has been living at the same address since 1949, which is a five-minute walk from the LPCC. She went to school in

Leigh Park and of all the people we interviewed was probably the most senior in terms of age.

Margaret was involved with the LPCC for about 15 years from 1967. She was on the committee from 1968 onwards and served as the treasurer for a while. She attended functions and dances and assisted her mother, who ran the café on a voluntary basis. Her mother was once the president of the LPCC.

Margaret said she does not recall Rolf Harris appearing at the LPCC and, if he had, she is positive she would have a recollection of it. She was involved with the day-to-day operations of the LPCC during the relevant period and she would have had to know if Rolf Harris was appearing there.

Margaret did comment on the police witness David James. She spoke of her amazement and the amusement of some of her friends that he had been called to provide evidence about Rolf Harris visiting the LPCC. They had read about him in the paper and could not understand how anyone would believe this man.

David James had never been an official at the LPCC, and as far as she could remember, never a member, but he was known to have lived in the area. He was known as a fantasist and someone who made up stories that no-one ever believed. Margaret heard that he had been convicted for shoplifting, which was later confirmed in court, and friends had told her that he was in a care home.

### Gordon Burrows

Gordon, who is retired, has lived on the Leigh Park Estate since 1958. In 1965 he became a member of the Leigh Park Community Association. Gordon met and married his wife, Joyce, as a result of their meeting at the LPCC.

Gordon, an electrician, worked as a volunteer at the LPCC. His responsibility was the stage management and lighting, so any performance being held there would have required his input.

He described his involvement in the type of activities that were held at the Centre as running the children's Saturday Cinema Club and the Thursday afternoon Junior Jive. In 1968 he became involved as a DJ and worked at other events that were held at the LPCC.

Gordon served on the Executive Committee. In 1970 he was elected Vice Chairman, becoming Chairman in 1973. He was heavily involved with the LPCC on more than a weekly basis and is a hundred per cent certain that "There was no way Rolf Harris could have appeared within the Havant area, let alone the Leigh Park Community Centre, during the 1960s or 1970s without me knowing about it."

**Joyce Burrows**

Joyce Burrows is Gordon's wife. She has lived on the estate all her life and is now retired. Her brother, John Tabbner, gave evidence at the first trial and told the jury he had never heard anything about Rolf Harris coming to Leigh Park or to the LPCC.

Joyce's mother and father were actively involved with the LPCC as volunteers. Her father, Jim Tabbner, who is now deceased, was the Chairman in the 1960s and early 1970s. Her mother, May Tabbner, ran the Saturday Cinema Club.

Joyce described how she and her younger brother attended the Saturday Cinema Club with their mother every Saturday. She further advised that in 1969 she had started working at the Gateway supermarket, next to the Community Centre, but continued to visit her mother for lunch at the Centre on Saturdays. She is sure that Rolf Harris never appeared at the LPCC and said she would have known if he had.

# TIMELINE AND 'TWO LITTLE BOYS'

Whilst all these enquiries were being undertaken my research team put together a timeline that covered every Saturday of 1969. This was a very ambitious undertaking. As Rolf was an energetic and busy performer, it was expecting a lot to be able to obtain evidence of where he was on every Saturday 45 years ago.

We decided to have two timelines – the 1969 Saturday timeline and a 'Two Little Boys' timeline, so named as this was Rolf's hit single that Wendy Rosher referred to in her evidence.

We could use the 1969 timeline to show the type of venues that Rolf Harris was performing at in 1969 and the type of venues that his agents were using to promote his new single 'Two Little Boys'.

'Two Little Boys' had become an integral part of the investigation owing to Wendy Rosher having claimed that Rolf had sung this song at the LPCC on the day of the alleged incident. The two timelines displayed the programme that had been planned and executed for the release of 'Two Little Boys', the type of venues Rolf had been booked into, and his heavy work schedule.

By the time we had completed the two timelines we had accounted for every Saturday in the latter part of 1969.

## Bruna Zanelli

After all this hard work I struck gold, so to speak, and the gold medal went to Bruna Zanelli. Bruna, like most of those who assisted us with our enquiries, is now retired. She is a charismatic woman who doesn't mince her words.

In 1969, Bruna was the assistant to Phyllis Rounce of International Artistes Representation, which had its offices in London's West End. This was the management agency that was representing Rolf Harris in 1969. Phyllis passed away in 2001, so the police closed this line of enquiry. Perhaps it would have been too much to ask for them to have thought about who actually worked for International Artistes in 1969 and to find these people.

Bruna had not been contacted by anyone regarding Rolf's first trial, which I find surprising given that she had worked closely with Rolf during the time period in which Wendy Rosher claimed that he had indecently assaulted her.

Bruna was the person who arranged Rolf's personal appearances and kept his diaries. A big part of her duties in 1969 was the promotion of 'Two Little Boys', which meant spending a lot of time with Rolf.

Bruna told me that prior to hearing about the LPCC from news reports during the first trial in 2014 she had never heard of the place. There was one thing that she was absolutely positive about, which is that she had never booked Rolf to appear there. Bruna enlightened me as to the large entourage she would have needed to arrange to accompany Rolf to any venue in 1969.

She also made an important point, which was that the cost of a personal appearance by Rolf Harris in 1969 was between £500 and £1,000. That equates to between £8,000 and £17,000 in today's money. The children who attended the Saturday Cinema Club paid sixpence.

Moreover, as the venue could accommodate only 200 people, the LPCC would have needed to heavily subsidise the appearance of any celebrity, and on its shoestring budget this is money that the LPCC didn't have. The finances simply did not stack up.

The new defence team called Bruna as an important defence witness for the second trial, which started in January 2017. As part of their strategy in defending Rolf on the new charges, they sought to bring to the jury's attention the glaring omissions on the evidence front that my team had identified since the first trial.

The next person I located and spoke to was Barry Booth, who is a retired concert pianist, musical director, producer and composer. Barry still composes and produces as a hobby.

In 1970 Barry became Rolf's musical director. Whilst he was not Rolf's musical director at the time of the release of 'Two Little Boys', he took over this role very shortly afterwards and was involved in the arrangement of this song for many years. He knew it intimately.

Barry remains unconvinced that Rolf sang 'Two Little Boys' unaccompanied at the time of its release in late 1969, nor at any other time during the promotion of this recording. He provided some very good reasons for this, not least being Rolf's fastidious attention to detail in preparation for his stage performances.

Wendy Rosher had told the court that Rolf sang 'Two Little Boys' when he was at the LPCC. She said it was around the time of her eighth birthday, which was in the latter part of October 1969.

'Two Little Boys' was not released until 22nd November 1969 and as part of its promotion Rolf was contracted to attend large venues to promote it. His promoters and others involved in its production would not have allowed him to sing it without the orchestral musical accompaniment. As the years passed, and the song became well known, this lost its importance and Rolf would then have sung it without full musical accompaniment, but not in 1969.

Wendy Rosher also stated that on the day of the alleged incident there was a DJ at the LPCC who was playing records that were in the charts. One of the records she recalled was, 'One drop of rain on your windowpane, pitter, patter'.

She was referring to a song called 'Storm in a Teacup', which was sung by a group called The Fortunes and released in the UK in 1972. It could not have been playing at the LPCC in 1969.

**Rolf Harris was never at the Leigh Park Community Centre in 1969, nor at any other time. The evidence was so overwhelming that it was conclusive and could not be ignored.**

# FAMILY

By this time, it had become clear that the investigation by Scotland Yard detectives had been poor at best and, at worst, selective. I decided, along with Rolf's legal team, to extend our investigations to locating and interviewing family members of both Wendy Rosher and the witness David James.

I was in Gosport where, incidentally, I was born. I was with Doug Bainbridge, and we were visiting the home of Wendy Rosher's mother. We were interested in finding out why she was not called to give evidence in support of Wendy's accusation and why Wendy's siblings had not been called. We had heard that they had been interviewed by the police and that none of the three were prepared to confirm that Wendy was at the LPCC in 1969.

We knew that Wendy Rosher's mother, Margaret, was a Jehovah's Witness. Having known people when I was young who followed this religion, my impression was that they tend to be honest and live their lives strictly by the testimony in the Bible. We had also heard that Margaret was not well, so we had to tread carefully when speaking with her. I was prepared for her not to want to speak to us, but I sincerely believed that if she was well enough to talk to us, she would be truthful.

I located the council flat occupied by Margaret, which was on the second floor of a two-storey block, and knocked on the door. It was opened by a man who appeared to be in his late seventies. I introduced myself and asked if Margaret was at home. The man said that he was Margaret's carer, and she was asleep. I gave him my business card and advised him briefly of the purpose of my call. He then asked me if the police were supposed to take a statement when they interviewed someone. I replied yes, they should if the person being interviewed has anything relevant to say.

He thanked me and said he would pass my business card and message on to Margaret when she woke up. Just as I was leaving, I asked him if I could have his name for my file, and he replied that his name was Jeff. Something twigged. I then asked him if he was Jeff, Wendy Rosher's father, and he confirmed that he was. I told him that he was next on our list to visit as he lived only five minutes away. Jeff said that he could see us in about 15 minutes after he had checked on Margaret, so we drove to his lodgings and waited for his arrival.

Three hours later we left, and over the coming weeks I got to know Jeff quite well. He later proved to be another vital witness in Rolf's appeal.

Jeff was not Wendy Rosher's biological father. He had adopted her when she was two years old.

Jeff told me that he had met Margaret in the summer of 1963, shortly after she had moved to Leigh Park to live with her mother.

I found Jeff to be an honest man who, whilst hesitant about upsetting members of the family, was not about to avoid telling the truth. He provided me with a formal signed statement.

At the time Jeff met Margaret he was serving in the Royal Navy. They became a couple and later married. As Wendy was the youngest and not quite two years old when he met Margaret, she always knew him as her father. Jeff said he was closer to her than he was to Margaret's other children.

Around this time Jeff was based on shore for two years. He told me that the family enjoyed a happy home life. Unfortunately, Margaret became ill and spent several weeks in hospital. Jeff was able to be at home every night for the children.

In 1966 Jeff went back to sea. For the next 10 months he was on various patrols but returned every two months or so on shore leave. Whilst on such a break in 1967, and when he was due back at sea, it became obvious to him that Margaret was very ill. His GP contacted his captain and it was arranged that Jeff would stay on shore. This was the end of his naval career. The Admiralty agreed that he should be compassionately discharged. This took place in 1968, without pension, gratuity and final salary. Jeff left the Royal Navy with no job, no money, no assistance, three children and one on the way, a wife who was unwell and a mortgage.

Jeff had to earn money somehow because things were desperate, so after finding that there was a demand for a local delivery service, he started selling pre-packed potatoes and fresh eggs door to door during school hours. That way he could at least earn money on a daily basis and be at home for Margaret and the children.

Financially things got harder, which culminated in them having to sell their house and find other accommodation. Portsmouth Council was very good to them and found the family a house in Warsash Close, Leigh Park, to which they moved in September 1969.

This move worked well as Jeff had built up his potato and egg round over the previous 16 months. Most of it was around Leigh Park. On his round he came into contact with many locals on a daily basis and got to know Leigh Park intimately. He continued to prepack the potatoes late at night and to load up for the following day. This enabled him to see the children off to school in the morning and then get off on his round, taking their one-year-old son with him until later in the morning, when Margaret would be able to take care of him. Jeff would always be at home when the children arrived home from school.

Despite the hard financial times, the children were looked after. Warsash Close had lots of other children for them to play with. Wendy was a bright child and she seemed to be happy throughout the time they lived there. At no time did Jeff ever notice any change in her attitude.

Jeff told me that he was not involved in the first Rolf Harris trial (more about that later) but he did become aware of some of the accusations that Wendy had made against Rolf Harris. What particularly concerned him was that she claimed to have been at the LPCC when she was only seven or when she had just turned eight years of age. This did not ring true with Jeff because he and Margaret were quite strict with the children. In late 1969 they had only just moved to Warsash Close and were still getting to know their way around the estate.

One thing Jeff was certain about was that they would never have allowed Wendy to go to the community centre as a seven- or eight-year-old without either Margaret or himself being there. By 1971/72 Wendy was older and she would go to the LPCC on a fairly regular basis, with her elder sister, but not in 1969.

Jeff reiterated what Doug Bainbridge had been told previously by Winnie, that she looked out for the children in and around Warsash Close when they played out in front of the houses, and also about the incident involving Wendy and two young boys.

The police were informed, after which a policewoman came and spoke to the family. She also spoke with the boys and their parents. Later, the policewoman told them that the boys were very young and so was Wendy, so she was not going to take the matter any further.

At the time Jeff had found the incident very unpleasant, and he felt bad about what had been alleged. He described the boys' father as a nice guy who held a good position in the dockyard.

In early 1972 Jeff was offered a position with a property investment group at their office in Southampton, which he accepted. They moved into a large privately rented detached house in Bassett, which was a sought-after area of Southampton. The children went to schools with excellent reputations and Wendy progressed very well.

In the summer of 1973, the group Jeff worked for went out of business and the lease expired on the house he had rented. He was forced to change his employment and accept a job with Husband's Shipyard. The family moved to Osborne Road in Portswood, a less desirable area of Southampton, which was close to St Denys Station and the local pub. There was an underlying current of social problems, which came as something of a culture shock after living in Bassett. The children changed schools and went to Hampton Park, a failing school in Portswood that eventually closed.

By this time, it was 1974. Wendy was just becoming a teenager. She and her sister had made friends with local children. Margaret considered the children from one particular family to be such a bad influence that she stopped Wendy from associating with them. This caused a lot of resentment on the parents' part towards Margaret and Jeff, which eventually led to an assault on Margaret during which a clump of her hair was pulled out. The police became involved.

It was around this time that Wendy's personality began to change. Throughout the rest of 1974 her behaviour became more challenging, not only at home but at school as well.

In December 1974 PC Malcolm Craig was shot in the stomach by the IRA outside the house where Jeff and his family were living. His injuries were serious but not life threatening. According to a news report at the time, a hundred detectives were drafted in to conduct door-to-door enquiries.

The years during which the family lived in Osborne Road became increasingly stressful. Wendy's behaviour and conduct had become very worrying. Then, at some point in 1976, new owners took over the pub across the road. Jeff could not remember exactly when or how the girls became acquainted with the owners' sons – bearing in mind that he and Margaret were not pub-oriented, and the girls were still in their early teens – but he was concerned about it. Wendy and her sister, who over time had become more or less entrenched in the pub, struck up relationships with the pub owner's sons.

Margaret and Jeff spoke to the boys' parents about their concerns, but to no avail. The girls went out of control, and their family life disintegrated. Wendy became aggressive and rebellious at school, and at home she would pay no attention to Margaret. Her sister was completely under the influence of the eldest son.

Despite numerous visits to the Portswood police to raise concerns about their two daughters' underage drinking at the pub, Margaret and Jeff lost any influence they had over the girls. Wendy became pregnant at 15 and married the youngest son, Paul, soon after her sixteenth birthday. The marriage did not last long.

Jeff said that he had heard, while the court case against Rolf Harris was in progress, that Wendy had told the court that it was the assault by Rolf Harris in 1969 that had caused her to change. He said that was incorrect because Wendy had been a bright, happy girl until they moved to Portswood when she was 12 or 13. That is when all the problems started.

Jeff was not able to enlighten me as to why he thought Wendy would have made a complaint against Rolf Harris, although he was certainly of the belief that Wendy was more than capable of making a false accusation. He described Wendy as very manipulative. At times she would say some really vile and nasty things. She had been bound over by the court previously because of her behaviour.

Jeff said that Wendy was good at learning things. She familiarised herself with the computer very quickly and taught herself how to deal with legal matters. When a family member was arrested and sentenced to a term of imprisonment, she tried unsuccessfully to get the charges dropped. She then set about studying criminal law and researching the appeals procedure to assist the family member in deciding whether to lodge an appeal against his conviction.

## OPERATION YEWTREE INTERVIEWS

During the Operation Yewtree enquiry into Rolf Harris in 2013, two officers interviewed Margaret and Wendy's older sister at Margaret's home and took statements from them. Jeff was there as he was caring for Margaret, but he was not involved in the interviews. He waited in the kitchen while they were being interviewed separately in the lounge.

A couple of weeks after the interviews a message was left on Margaret's answering machine from one of the Operation Yewtree officers, who requested a meeting with Jeff. An arrangement was made for them to come and see Jeff. They told him that they wanted to clarify some dates because they had been told by Margaret that he was good with dates. I can vouch for this as I found Jeff to have a very good memory. Jeff's interview by the Operation Yewtree officers occurred a week or two later.

There were two Operation Yewtree officers involved in the interviews. One was an older man who said he was a retired police officer and had been employed as a civilian investigator by the police for the Operation Yewtree enquiries, and the other was a younger man who Jeff thinks was still a serving police officer. The older man seemed to be in charge and did most of the talking.

During our investigations we discovered that there was a pattern to the method of interviewing that had been adopted by the Operation Yewtree officers. The retired men engaged to work on this case had held a far higher rank when they retired from the police than the younger men who were the actual serving police officers. They tended to have a strong influence over the Operation Yewtree enquiries, which in my opinion was dangerous because as former police officers they were not subjected to the same disciplinary procedures as serving officers.

The interview was conducted by the older retired man. Jeff told me of his concerns regarding the negative way in which this investigator had handled the interview. Jeff had been asked to clarify dates such as when they had moved to Leigh Park, and he was asked about various other events that had occurred. He had no problem in recalling this information but when he had started telling this investigator that he found it hard to accept that Rolf Harris had been in Leigh Park at this time, this was countered by the reply, "Other people have stated he was."

Jeff also thought it strange that the Operation Yewtree investigators did not want to take a statement from him, as Wendy's father. He told them that most of the people he knew from Leigh Park had young children in 1969 who would have been very excited at seeing Rolf Harris, and that he knew so many people there because of his delivery rounds on the estate. Despite his best efforts the interviewers were just not interested in what he had to say about Rolf Harris not having visited Leigh Park.

The older investigator told Jeff that they did not want to take a written statement from him, but Jeff had observed that they were making notes. He was not given the notes to check, and he was not asked to sign them as being correct.

During the court case leading up to the appeal, the young police officer who was with the older man tried to deny that Jeff had provided them with this information. He was unconvincing. Jeff finally gave the evidence that he should have been called to give at the first trial, when Rolf was convicted of assaulting Wendy Rosher.

Interestingly, none of these three members of Wendy Rosher's family were called to give evidence at the first trial. If they had been called, then I am sure the jury would have viewed Wendy's fanciful story as being false and Rolf would never have been convicted on this charge.

## SUPPORTING WITNESSES

This was an exhausting investigation, made even more difficult by the fact that by the time I came on board Rolf had already been convicted of indecently assaulting Wendy Rosher. The guilty verdict that the jury returned did not reflect the fact that there was a lack of evidence that Rolf had ever been to Leigh Park, let alone to the LPCC. However, it would be fair to say that at the time he was convicted this might not have been quite so apparent. Most of the evidence on this front was garnered by my team in preparation for lodging the appeal.

There was a widespread belief, bolstered by the media, that the guilty verdict meant that Rolf Harris must have been lying about not having visited Leigh Park. This made it very difficult a year or two later to find people who were prepared to discuss this case publicly for fear of reprisals from the media.

Some newspapers seemed incapable of reporting objectively. Instead, they fell over themselves to vilify Rolf at every opportunity and to be critical of anyone who questioned the safety of this conviction. My team and I had to use every ounce of skill we had acquired over many years of carrying out investigations whilst at the same time keeping within the rules set down by the court. Any deviation from this could well have put Rolf's appeal in jeopardy.

I decided to turn my attention to the only two witnesses for the Crown who had given corroborating evidence that Rolf had been to the LPCC.

### David James

David James was called by the prosecution and testified that he recalled Rolf Harris opening a shop near the LPCC. He said that afterwards they all went back to the Centre and that this was sometime around 1967. He also remembered other celebrities coming to the area, including Norman Wisdom and Diana Dors. He did not say that they visited the LPCC.

At the time of giving evidence David James was residing in a care home and walked with the aid of a Zimmer frame. He was quite vocal when challenged and remained adamant throughout the court case that he had got it right about Rolf visiting the LPCC. He added that in 1967 he had just returned from a long tour of duty in Korea, so he was able to be fairly accurate with the date.

He said that he remembered Rolf coming back to the LPCC and having a cup of tea with them, and that Rolf gave him his autograph, which he later gave to his children for their autograph books.

Although 1967 was two years earlier than the date when Wendy Rosher alleged that she had been indecently assaulted by Rolf Harris, David James's witness evidence was able to place Rolf at Leigh Park. For reasons known only to members of the jury, they accepted the evidence of this rather eccentric old man.

Media reports described David James's testimony as 'rambling'. It was suggested to him by the defence counsel that he was making up stories, to which he replied in an outraged voice that he was not a man who 'is stupid or otherwise'. He told the defence counsel that she should go and check council archives for a record of Rolf Harris's visit to the area.

The council archives were checked. Nothing whatsoever surfaced regarding a visit by Rolf Harris to Leigh Park.

As far as I was concerned the investigation was not complete until I learned the truth about why this man had come forward and was being used as a witness. Surely the police had checked his credibility before calling him as a witness in such a high-profile case. Or were they that desperate to find anyone who was prepared to testify, under oath, that Rolf Harris had visited the LPCC?

So, it was back to the drawing board and further in-depth historic investigations.

We identified a celebrity who had visited Leigh Park to open the Greywell Shopping Centre in September 1966. This shopping centre is next to the LPCC. The local newspaper reported that it was a low-key affair as the shops had been open for a number of months. After the opening, officials and local authority representatives were entertained to a buffet at a Chinese restaurant at one end of the main precinct. The celebrity to which the article referred was Sid James.

I need to mention here that Sid James was in no way connected to the complaint against Rolf Harris. His visit in 1966 was for the purpose of opening a shopping centre. David James was close, but he recalled the date of Sid James's visit as 1967, whereas Wendy Rosher claimed that the indecent assault by Rolf Harris took place in 1969. Not only was David James two or three years out with his date for when a celebrity visited Leigh Park, he got the name of the celebrity wrong.

A further clue that one would have expected police detectives to pick up on was David James testifying that he had only just returned from a long tour of duty in Korea. He claimed to have been a member of the armed forces, but it was never made clear in his evidence which of the forces he claimed to have served in.

The Korean War began on 25th June 1950 and ended, albeit unofficially, on 27th July 1953. British and Commonwealth forces fought beside USA and South Korean forces. The last country to withdraw its forces from Korea was the USA, in August 1954.

Background checks were carried out on David James. These checks entailed putting together a full family history. We obtained his marriage certificate and the birth certificates of his children with a view to establishing any former addresses and how his occupation had been described. On all of them his address was given as Leigh Park and his occupation was stated as lorry driver. There was no mention of him having been a member of the armed forces.

Based on the documentary evidence I had collated, David James was never in the armed forces. He could not have 'returned recently from a long tour of duty in Korea in 1967' as the Korean War had been over for 14 years. The evidence that David James had not been telling the truth was mounting. There was one more enquiry to make, which, as it turned out, was what finally convinced the court that David James had lied.

**Daphne James**
We identified David James's former wife as Daphne James, who had not been located or spoken to by the police. Our enquiries established that she still resided in Havant. The problem we encountered was that she lived in a high-rise block of flats that could not be entered without the security access code.

Doug Quade made a number of attempts to raise someone at Daphne's flat but even though he tried at different times of the day, he was unsuccessful. This left him with no option but to wait in the main car park at night until the lights in the flat were turned on, which hopefully would mean that someone was in there.

Had the Scotland Yard detectives who worked on Operation Yewtree shown the same initiative and diligence towards their work that Doug did, I would not be writing this today, as Rolf Harris would never have been convicted. At the time, Doug was in his mid-seventies and a retired Detective Superintendent, yet he was prepared to sit outside a high-rise block of flats for hours, night after night, waiting for Daphne's flat to show signs of occupancy. To add to his problems, it was in the middle of winter and freezing.

Finally, all of Doug's hard work paid off and he established Daphne's movements. It turned out that she was an active woman who had plenty to keep her occupied, so she did not spend a lot of time at home in her flat. I teamed up with Doug and, using the information he had obtained, we turned up at the high-rise block and managed to bluff our way through security and get to Daphne's flat. No-one was home, so I dropped my business card with a note through the door. Shortly after we left, I received a phone call from Daphne. At her invitation Doug and I returned to the flat, where we had the chance to interview her.

Daphne's account of her previous life with David James, who by then was her very ex-husband, completely rebutted the evidence he had given during the trial. To help me I had the documentary evidence relating to his address and occupation through the 1960s that my researchers had located. This enabled me to verify the information that Daphne provided to us. Incidentally, there was no malice or hard feelings involved on Daphne's part towards her former husband, as the marriage had ended a long time ago.

Daphne, who had lived in Leigh Park for most of her life, had met David James there in 1959. About a year after meeting they decided to live together and moved into a council house on the Leigh Park estate with Daphne's two children from her previous marriage. They had children of their own before eventually getting married in 1970. Daphne separated from David James in 2004.

In the late 1960s they would go to the LPCC to play bingo, normally on a Wednesday. None of their children went there. Daphne told me that she had no recollection of Rolf Harris ever coming to Leigh Park, and if

Rolf Harris had attended the LPCC she would definitely have known.

David James had told the court that he had obtained Rolf Harris's autograph at the LPCC for his children. Daphne's response to this was, "That is a lie. He did not do that. I would have known for certain had he done so." She added that none of her children collected autographs and David did not get any autographs for them.

Daphne told me that David James did not do National Service, but he was a member of the Territorial Army before and during their relationship. He was never a regular in the armed forces and did not go to Korea. He would go away with the Territorial Army for short periods for camps in the UK, but never abroad. He was one of their drivers.

David James had worked as a driver throughout the time Daphne knew him. Two of the firms that had employed him as a delivery man were Clements Coal Merchants and Hartley's Stores in Bedhampton.

Daphne told me that when she left David James in 2004 he had suffered a breakdown, following which he was living in a care home. Daphne was adamant that if David James had told the court that he had obtained Rolf Harris's autograph at Leigh Park he was definitely lying. She went everywhere with him in the 1960s and 1970s and it didn't happen.

## Philip Wilbourn

Philip Wilbourn was the other witness called by the prosecution to provide evidence that Rolf Harris had been to Leigh Park. He gave evidence that he had lived in Leigh Park from 1957 and attended the local schools. He recalled Sid James opening the Greywell Shopping Centre in Park Parade.

At the time of giving evidence, Philip Wilbourn was residing in the north of England. He told the court that he had become an avid reader of the *Daily Mirror* and *Portsmouth Evening News* from 1969 onwards following the reports of the moon landings. He said that he did not recall any discussions or chatter regarding Rolf Harris within the school he attended at the time, through his parents or from any other source, but he lists Rolf Harris as one of the celebrities who had visited the area. The others were Sid James, Roy Castle and Frankie Vaughan.

Local newspapers covering the relevant time period and the years either side were researched thoroughly by the police, legal firm Kingsley Napley, who formed part of Rolf's defence team, and our researchers. There is a report in Portsmouth-based *The News* for Monday, 14th August 1978 of a visit by Rolf Harris and Frankie Vaughan to Southsea, Portsmouth.

In short, Philip Wilbourn used the words 'visited the area', which of course would cover Portsmouth. Havant, of which Leigh Park is a suburb, is around six miles from Portsmouth. News reports at the time often referred to the alleged assault on Wendy Rosher as having taken place in Portsmouth rather than in Havant, presumably as the former is much larger in terms of area and population and is also very well-known. Portsmouth's claims to fame are the Naval Dockyard, Lord Nelson's flagship HMS Victory, of Battle of Trafalgar fame, Henry VIII's flagship Mary Rose and the Spinnaker Tower. In contrast, Havant's only landmark of note is The Spring Arts & Heritage Centre.

Philip Wilbourn did not provide any dates. It now appears that he had read about Rolf Harris visiting Portsmouth in August 1978, which was nine years after the alleged Leigh Park incident. By this time 16-year-old Wendy Rosher was married with a baby and had been living in Southampton for six years. Philip Wilbourn provided no worthwhile evidence and should never have been called as a prosecution witness.

## THE LEIGH PARK COMMUNITY CENTRE'S NON-EVENT

Even those of a cynical disposition must by now be prepared to accept that the event described by Wendy Rosher never took place. Rolf Harris did not visit the LPCC and neither did Wendy Rosher attend an event there without a parent around the time of her eighth birthday. Moreover, the family had only just moved to Warsash Close and were still finding their feet in their new home.

Had the police completed a full and unbiased investigation they would have discovered this. However, even with the limited investigation that was carried out, the warning signs were there, as they failed to uncover any evidence to confirm that Rolf Harris had visited Leigh Park.

Wendy Rosher's family, who had tried to make it clear to police interviewers that they had no recollection of the events described by Wendy, had not been required to give evidence. Also, the police failed to advise the defence that they had interviewed her father, who had given them more than enough information to throw strong doubts on the authenticity of her claim. Why, then, did the Crown Prosecution Service accept such a weak and unsubstantiated complaint?

As an investigator it is not for me to speculate so I will leave this for others to reach their own conclusions. All I know is that an innocent man was convicted of a crime that he did not commit and was sentenced to nine months' imprisonment on this charge.

## THE APPEAL

The evidence gathered by my team was so overwhelming that the Court of Appeal agreed to allow Rolf Harris leave to appeal against his conviction for indecently assaulting Wendy Rosher, even though he was well outside the time limit.

When an appeal is heard there is no jury, as there is in a Crown Court. The appeal is heard by three judges. In November 2017, after considering the evidence, the judges agreed unanimously that Rolf Harris's conviction for indecently assaulting Wendy Rosher was unsafe. His conviction was quashed.

The tabloids and some regional newspapers, which had labelled Rolf Harris a paedophile based on his conviction for indecently assaulting an eight-year-old girl, were somewhat restrained in their reporting of the overturning of this conviction. For many months following the decision of the Court of Appeal, newspapers still referred to Rolf's 'youngest victim' as being eight years of age whenever a story was written about him. Gradually the wording changed from 'victim' to 'complainant' and only recently have the tabloids managed to tone down their content to reflect the true situation when referring to this case.

Rolf Harris was never compensated for the nine months' imprisonment to which he was sentenced on this charge. Wendy Rosher did not have to repay the £22,000. Unlike Carl Beech – a fantasist who accused MPs and other high profile public figures of murder and crimes of a sexual nature, and who coincidentally also received £22,000 – she never faced charges. It was far easier to sweep Operation Yewtree's embarrassment under the carpet than to charge her with perjury. Why, one asks. Well, once again it is not for me to speculate but when those making enquiries into alleged historic sex offences publicly encourage people to 'Come forward and you will be believed', it makes it difficult to charge those who did come forward, even when they did not tell the truth.

## NO APOLOGY

Following Rolf's convictions at the first trial he was lambasted in the media, with journalists demanding that he 'apologise to his victims'. I was present during the media scrums outside Southwark Crown Court when the second and third trials were taking place, when reporters would yell out to Rolf, "When are you going to apologise to the victims, Rolf?" Such was the pushing and shoving that I felt an alarming sense of being swept along in a tidal wave of microphones and cameras. I was just not used to the tactics of reporters and photographers who were all keen to be first in line.

When Rolf was found not guilty of the nine new charges – those heard at the second and third trials collectively – and when the conviction for indecently assaulting Wendy Rosher was quashed by the Court of Appeal, there was not one apology from the Crown Prosecution Service, the police or the media. Rolf had endured three trials and a wrongful conviction. An application to overturn the remaining convictions, which were all from the first trial, was rejected by the Court of Appeal on the grounds that he was out of time and that no further evidence had emerged at the time of the application to cast doubt on the safety of the convictions.

As Wendy Rosher had been the first complainant to give evidence at the first trial – on the basis that the prosecution had determined the order in which the counts would be heard, with the oldest first – there exists, in my view, the probability that the jury was sufficiently dismayed by what she alleged to the extent that it swayed their thinking in relation to the remaining counts. It is also likely that, as she was a child at the time of the alleged offence, this charge had the greatest impact on the jury.

## THE LETTER

Wendy Rosher's brother, Paul, who is three years her senior, was 11 at the time of the alleged incident. He did not come forward to support his sister when the allegation was first made, and when spoken to by the police he said that he could not recall Rolf Harris appearing at the LPCC.

Paul was in court during the first trial, and after the verdict had been returned, he became quite vocal in support of his sister.

Just over a year after the conclusion of the trial, Paul, who appeared to style himself as an actor and reporter, arranged with a journalist the publication of a letter that he had written to Rolf Harris. In it he called for Rolf to offer an apology to his younger sister and enclosed with the letter a photo of Wendy taken around the time of the alleged incident. It might not have occurred to him, in his possibly lucrative quest for publicity, that to send a photo of a young child – and not just any young child, but the child that the intended recipient had been found guilty of indecently assaulting – was a very odd thing to do.

The letter appeared on the *Mirror*'s website on 26th September 2015, accompanied by a photo of Paul in what I can only describe as his English gentleman finery.

Paul's letter was in essence a covering letter for the photo of Wendy Rosher as a child that he intended – or claimed that he intended – to send to Rolf Harris, who at that point was in Stafford Prison. The photo itself was in very poor condition. It was creased and damaged to the point where part of her face had been obliterated.

I should point out that Rolf Harris had already seen this photo, as it had been included with the documents prepared for his defence. Paul even referred to this in his letter – 'You had this picture of Wendy as a little girl in your files'. The question arises as to whether he thought Rolf might be willing to view it again – a scenario that I would consider extremely unlikely – or whether this crumpled image might be useful in generating an opportunity for publicity, which would be very useful for an actor, along with any associated fees that might be paid.

In the letter Paul stated that he had been sitting behind Rolf Harris in court 'when the judge heard [Rolf Harris] had £11 million in [his] bank account'. One wonders what impact the mention of £11 million might have had, because Paul went on to dismiss the £22,000 that Rolf had paid in compensation, which he had been obliged to pay on the basis that he had been found guilty, as 'paltry'. He then went on to say that Rolf's failure to apologise to his sister – for something that had never happened, I might add – was 'worst of all'.

It seems that the main thrust of Paul's intention in sending a photo of his sister to Rolf Harris was to make him 'reflect on his actions' and then to apologise to her. It has to be said that such a move could have been made privately and not through the medium of a national newspaper. I do not know how much, if anything, Paul and Wendy were paid for this article, though it would seem more likely than not that a payment was made to one or both of them. My view is that it would probably have been a lucrative move given the high but negative profile that Rolf Harris had at that time.

Paul went on to remind Rolf Harris that he had 'rubbished' his sister's claims that his hands were 'black and hairy' by holding up his hands and turning them over to show them to the jury. His recollection here seems a tad inaccurate, as in her evidence Wendy Rosher had claimed that Rolf Harris had 'big hairy hands, big black glasses and curly black hair' – not 'black hairy hands'. Regardless, the reason that Rolf held up his hands was to prove to the jury that his hands were not 'big and hairy' and therefore did not fit the description given by Wendy Rosher in her evidence.

Paul concluded his letter by asking whether Rolf Harris was 'man enough' to write to him with an apology for his sister. In the same paragraph he referred again to the compensation payment as 'paltry'. This does suggest to me that perhaps they had expected the settlement to be somewhat higher than it was.

It is a hard-hitting letter with no substance, written in such a way as to tug on the heartstrings of the gullible. Paul must have suspected that his sister Wendy was not telling the truth. When Rolf was convicted on the charge of indecent assault against Wendy, it seems that Paul seized the opportunity to take on the support role of a big brother and arrange for media interviews. I have no idea how much they raked in from courting the media in this way, but Paul's use of the word 'paltry' in his letter – not once but twice – did start to take on a new significance.

I do not know if Rolf ever received Paul's letter. What I do know is that there was never an apology, as Rolf maintained all along that he had been wrongly convicted. His stance was justified nearly three-and-a-half years later when three Court of Appeal judges unanimously quashed the conviction, having deemed it to be unsafe. To my knowledge there has never been any published comment from Paul regarding the overturning of Rolf's conviction.

So, where is Paul now? Surely he owes Rolf Harris an apology for the letter that he wrote to a man in prison who was serving a sentence for something he hadn't done?

## THE 'IGNARAMOUSE' POSTS

On the 25th June 2015, Wendy Rosher unexpectedly posted some rambling comments on the social media site 'Support Justice for Rolf Harris'. These were posted from one of her known accounts. It is my view that these posts are genuine, and that Wendy Rosher had become rattled about the existence of 'Support Justice for Rolf Harris' – probably because Lizzie Cornish, who runs it, and others posting on it were asking too many sensible questions.

Wendy Rosher had waived her right to anonymity as early as August 2014, just a few weeks after the end of the first trial, and had since made herself available when the media felt that a comment was required on something that Rolf Harris had reportedly said or done. However, she was referred to in newspaper articles and on television by a different name.

One of Wendy Rosher's posts on 'Support Justice for Rolf Harris' contained groundless allegations and an implied threat – that someone would come for the site administrator, Lizzie Cornish, to whom she referred as 'Lizzard', 'so, so soon'.

> Wendy Rosher Blow it up ya ASS you ignaramouse , Any one can link you Lizzard to the child/ satin/ child abuse site you and yours crawled out of their Lizzard, you carry on talking shit to ya self their Honest, no one will notice its you , Or yourself and I.../ ..Honest " Their, their some one will come for you SO, so... Soooooooon ! Promise ! x

In the event that any reader should require a translation, to the best of my knowledge it reads:

*Blow it up your ass, you ignoramus. Anyone can link you, Lizzard, to the child/Satan/child abuse site you and yours crawled out of. There, Lizzard, you carry on talking shit to yourself there. Honest, no-one will notice it's you, or yourself and I, honest. There, there. Someone will come for you so, so soon! Promise! x*

Another post accused Lizzie Cornish of having multiple personalities. Wendy Rosher was in essence querying whether those who posted on the site in support of Rolf Harris were actually Lizzie using a multitude of pseudonyms. The truth is that Lizzie didn't have to. There was an abundance of support for Rolf, which clearly was not what Wendy Rosher wanted to see. And if those on the site weren't Lizzie, they must all be – as she put it – 'thick as f..k' or 'retards'.

> Wendy Rosher Because he is guilty.........A convicted pedophile num nut... WERE YOU IN COURT ?? NA........ You twats .........You lot are the same person Multipal personalitys aye Lizzie....! ARE YOU ALL THICK AS F..K or Lizzie ?? Please tell me their are not this many retards walking the earth !

This is not quite the eloquent language that was used in her Victim Impact Statement. One does, of course, acknowledge that these statements are put together by solicitors in consultation with the client, but nevertheless the differences between the language in her Victim Impact Statement and the semi-literate missives reproduced here are quite startling. Part of her Victim Impact Statement read:

*All these questions left me angry and confused. I became an angry child unable to express myself and unable to trust men. I took this with me into my teens and did not like to be touched. It made having normal relationships difficult.*

Aside from the differences in language, how someone who 'did not like to be touched' became pregnant at 15, married at 16, and then had four further children, is a bit of a mystery. But I digress.

## AN ORCHESTRATED LITANY OF LIES

Being a New Zealander, I remember only too well the tragic crash of Air New Zealand flight TE 901 in Antarctica in 1979. This was mentioned in the previous chapter, where I also made mention of Judge Peter Mahon QC. He was appointed to head the Royal Commission of Inquiry in the wake of the disaster.

There was an attempt by Air New Zealand officials to blame the crash on pilot error, but the inquiry found that the cause was down to a correction having been made to the computerised flight path coordinates on the morning of the disaster and the failure to inform the flight crew of this change. When presenting his findings, Judge Peter Mahon QC referred to the evidence of the Air New Zealand officials as 'an orchestrated litany of lies'. This phrase has ever since been embedded in New Zealand's collective psyche. It is a phrase that sits just below the surface of one's conscious thought, and which occasionally rises up in response to something that has dishonesty written all over it.

Paul's letter was written on the basis that Rolf Harris had been convicted of indecent assault. However, it is important to acknowledge that the letter would never have been written had it not been for the deeply flawed testimony of his sister, which in my view fits the description of 'an orchestrated litany of lies.'

## POSTSCRIPT

Since the appeal, and the resultant quashing of the conviction, Wendy Rosher and witness David James have passed away. Wendy Rosher died of natural causes in 2019, less than two years after Rolf Harris's conviction for indecently assaulting her was overturned.

It was disappointing – and really quite outrageous – to see some newspapers reporting in such a way as to suggest that Rolf Harris must shoulder some of the blame for her death at the age of 57.

It was astonishing to see newspapers that should have known better referring to 'the eight-year-old who had been abused by Rolf Harris'. To be fair, some online news outlets, such as the *Mirror* and *Birmingham Live*, pulled their coverage, obviously having been made aware that Rolf's conviction for indecently assaulting Wendy Rosher had been quashed in 2017. Others updated their reports to state that she had 'claimed to have been assaulted', which at least was a more accurate description, or they sprinkled inverted commas everywhere and carried on with their usual Rolf-bashing regardless.

However, in terms of inaccurate reporting nothing could quite match the coverage afforded by the *Manchester Evening News* of 17th June 2019. It completely ignored the fact that Rolf Harris's conviction on this charge had been overturned on appeal in 2017 and quoted Paul as saying that Rolf Harris 'should be aware of the grim legacy he left her to cope with'. It is really quite staggering that the *Manchester Evening News* was able to get away with this. Over two years later, the article still had not been updated or removed. Interestingly, it quoted the *Mirror* as the source of the information contained in the article, yet the *Mirror* had removed the original article from its website soon after publication.

The following extract is taken from the aforementioned article:

*The youngest victim of Rolf Harris has died – she was seven [sic] when he groped her at a children's disco. [She] had asked for the*

*Aussie entertainer's autograph before he attacked her. She had said the event haunted her for the rest of her life. Wendy has died at the age of 57 – and her brother Paul said Harris had never shown any remorse, the Mirror reports.*

I will make this quite clear once and for all, so there can be no further misunderstanding. Rolf Harris had never met Wendy Rosher. He had never visited the Leigh Park Community Centre.

**He did not indecently assault her.**

# CHAPTER 3
# BOLD AS BRASS

I n 1971 the Lyceum Theatre had a huge ballroom. It was one of the largest standing venues available in London, although there was seating on the balcony overlooking the dance floor. Until 1968 it was used for the Miss World contest. It was also used for big bands, as a pop concert venue and for television broadcasts. The Lyceum formed the backdrop to Count 1 at the second trial.

In July 2014, shortly after Rolf Harris had been found guilty on historic indecent assault charges at the first trial, the boyfriend of a woman now in her late fifties contacted the National Society for the Prevention of Cruelty to Children (NSPCC) helpline to tell them that in 1971, when his girlfriend was 14 years of age, she had been sexually assaulted by Rolf Harris.

At the time of the alleged assault the complainant was a member of a youth brass band in the north of England and an attendee at the 1971 Music for Youth event, which was held over two days – a Saturday and Sunday – at the Lyceum Theatre. Rolf, as the guest of honour, presented certificates and trophies to the winners, as well as signing autographs for the many children and young people who were there. The complainant, and the other members of the youth band she played in, attended only on the Saturday. They travelled to London and back to their hometown by coach on the same day.

## ANONYMITY

The complainant has anonymity. For this reason, I have changed her name along with the names of those closely connected to her.

For ease of reading, I will refer to the complainant as Victoria Pringle.

### The Charge

*Count 1 – Indecent assault on a girl under the age of 14 years between 10.07.1971 and 11.07.1971 at the Lyceum Theatre, London.*

The Australian news media had followed the first trial closely. Rolf was an Australian icon and an informal ambassador for all things Australian. There was huge public interest in the trial and in subsequent developments. Hence when the second trial was under way, the Australian reporters were on board.

The following extracts, which relate to the alleged incident at the Lyceum, are from Australian news outlets. I am including these as they are quite succinct in describing Victoria Pringle's version of what happened.

*It was alleged that during the event, Harris picked her up by the waist and put her on his lap. Whilst on his lap Harris placed his hand up her skirt and touched her vaginal area over her knickers. She immediately moved away.*

- News Corp Australia Network's news.com.au, 18th March 2016

*... he allegedly spotted a 14-year-old at Lyceum Theatre in central London where she was attending with a youth band. He was smirking at her before he put a hand on her waist, pulled her onto his knee, then his lap, and put his hand up her mini dress onto her vaginal area.*

– The Weekend Australian, 18th March 2016

Victoria Pringle made her complaint on 3rd July 2014, at a time when an unprecedented number of celebrities were facing police investigations, prosecution, and court trials over allegations of historic sexual abuse. The adverse publicity that had accompanied Rolf's first trial was in full swing. He had just been convicted on 12 counts of indecent assault and was due to be sentenced the following day, 4th July 2014.

The news that Rolf Harris had been found guilty at the first trial led to a number of other people – one assumes all or mainly women – coming forward. The following are some examples of the type of reporting immediately post-trial.

## 30th June 2014

Several publications quote the NSPCC. *The NSPCC said it has received 28 calls relating to Harris to date, involving 13 people who claim they fell prey to the performer.*

## 1st July 2014

The *Daily Telegraph* reports: *Richard Scorer, abuse lawyer for Slater & Gordon, who represents 176 victims of Jimmy Savile, said they had been contacted by 'up to a dozen people' with allegations about Harris and were considering them carefully.*

**1st July 2014**

Several publications report that *'NSPCC chief executive Peter Wanless said they had received 'an explosion of calls' in the last 24 hours from people concerned about sexual abuse, not directly related to Harris himself.*

**2nd July 2014**

Liz Dux, abuse lawyer for Slater and Gordon, appeared on ITV's *Good Morning Britain* shortly after the conclusion of the first trial. A partial transcript of this programme includes the following:

> *Victims should contact the police. We'll assess the evidence and decide whether or not to bring a civil claim against Mr Harris. In a civil court they still have to prove their cases on the balance of probabilities. We don't think these people are jumping on a compensation bandwagon – the onus is on them to prove their case.*

**7th July 2014**

The *Daily Star* runs a story, *Rolf Harris victims to get £200k each.*

Anyone who came forward to claim that they had been indecently assaulted by Rolf Harris had nothing to lose. It wasn't going to cost them anything, their name wouldn't be made public unless they chose to waive their anonymity, and – if the *Daily Star* were to be believed – they could end up with £200,000. It is little wonder that so many people came forward, not just in relation to Rolf Harris but other celebrities as well.

## THE VENUE

Larry Westland CBE was the founder and Executive Director of Music for Youth, a national charity dedicated to providing young people with free access to live music-making opportunities for all styles of music and at all levels of accomplishment. He chose the Lyceum as the venue for the 1971 Music for Youth event, which was held over a weekend and attended by approximately 1,000 children and young people aged between four and nineteen from schools and youth organisations all over the country. They were accompanied by family and friends. The venue was awash with musical instruments, instrument cases and performance clothes.

Mr Westland said that he had arrived at the Lyceum at about 9.00 am on the Saturday. The event finished late in the afternoon on both days.

## THE COMPLAINT

In February 2016, the Crown Prosecution Service announced that Rolf Harris, who was by then almost 86 and already serving a term of imprisonment in HMP Stafford after having been found guilty on all counts at the first trial, would face further indecent assault charges. One of these new charges related to Victoria Pringle. On 17th March 2016, the BBC reported that Rolf Harris had pleaded not guilty via video link at Westminster Magistrates' Court to indecently assaulting seven girls and women. The alleged assault on Victoria Pringle was subsequently listed as Count 1 at the second trial.

In February 2016 Rolf was charged with indecently assaulting Victoria Pringle and six others. He then had to endure two further trials.

The NSPCC, on being contacted by Victoria's then boyfriend, had referred the matter to the police. Victoria told the police, and later the court, that in 1971 she was a member of a youth brass band and was attending the Lyceum Theatre with the band to participate in a youth music festival. Although the festival was being held over a weekend, she and her companions were there only on the Saturday, which is when she met Rolf.

It was Victoria's version of events that was presented to the court. She said that she felt Rolf Harris had singled her out during the day.

According to her account, he kept following her around. At one stage she had her photograph taken with him. Later in the day he was seated behind a table signing autographs. She said that she was standing near him when he pulled her from behind onto his lap, whereupon he placed his hand up her skirt and touched her vaginal area over her tights and knickers.

She moved away immediately and went to find her father, who was with her mother, aunt and uncle. They were all at the event. Her parents had travelled down with her, and her aunt and uncle, who lived in London, had met them there. What she omitted to tell the police was that her older brother had travelled down with the family and was also with them at the Lyceum. He is two years older than Victoria, which made him 16 years of age at the time.

Victoria claimed that when she found her father, she did not tell him where Rolf Harris had touched her, only that he had touched her. She said her father was shocked and confronted Rolf Harris about what had happened. She did not hear what was said but recalled that Rolf Harris left shortly afterwards.

Victoria handed over to the police a scrapbook containing a programme of the event and two photographs. One of the photos was of her with Rolf and the other showed her in her band uniform at the event.

## WITNESSES

Victoria's friend, who I will refer to as Patricia, was also in the band and was with her at the Lyceum. Patricia gave evidence that she remembered being with Victoria when Rolf Harris pulled her onto his lap, but she did not see anything untoward happen and she was not aware that anything had happened.

A man I will refer to as Geoffrey came forward as a witness. Geoffrey claimed that he was a member of the band and had attended the event at the Lyceum with his parents. He said they had caught the train down to London, whereas the other band members stated that they had travelled to and from the venue by coach. He recalled Victoria and Patricia going off to see Rolf Harris and sometime later seeing Victoria with her parents, looking upset. He said that his mother had told him later that Victoria had gone off to see Rolf Harris and that when she sat on his lap, he put his hand up her skirt, and that Victoria's father had gone to see Rolf Harris about this.

## THE INVESTIGATION

At first glance it appeared that there were witnesses who could testify as to the accuracy of Victoria's account. However, there was a dearth of witnesses put forward by the Crown Prosecution Service. My first task was to establish why there were so few witnesses available.

My second task was to seek out former members of the youth band and interview them as to their knowledge and memories of the event. My third task was to check the credibility of the witnesses who had come forward in support of Victoria's allegations.

## FAMILY

As is often the case with historic allegations, people associated with a complainant or a particular event will either be deceased or unable to be interviewed owing to medical conditions such as dementia. This can sometimes give a less-than-honest complainant an advantage in that there is no-one around to refute their allegations, or it can work to the disadvantage of a genuine complainant in that there is no-one to corroborate what they are saying.

In Victoria's case, her father was deceased, and her mother was not interviewed. When the NSPCC was contacted by her then boyfriend in July 2014, her mother was in her late eighties.

As a result of the call to the NSPCC, Victoria was contacted by the police in August 2014. She told officers that her mother was still alive, and she would remember her telling her father about what Rolf Harris had done to her.

The police contacted Victoria again in January 2015, around six months after she had made her complaint, with the intention of interviewing her mother. Victoria told them that her mother had dementia and that her memory had declined rapidly, so she was not going to remember anything. As a result, Victoria's mother was not interviewed by the police. As she was classed as a vulnerable person, I could not interview her either.

Victoria's uncle, who had been at the event with her parents and aunt, had died some years earlier. Her aunt was alive, and in a care home. According to Victoria, her aunt had lost her memory owing to the onset of dementia. She could not remember anything, and I understand the police did not attempt to interview her. I was not permitted to approach her because she was also classed as a vulnerable person.

I decided to look further into this. A researcher traced one of Victoria's aunt's sons (Victoria's cousin) to where he was living overseas. I arranged for a local investigator to speak with him. The investigator reported that he had been co-operative and what he had been told.

*"I am unaware of any allegation made by [Victoria] in relation to Rolf Harris. No-one has spoken to me about this, and I find it strange that I never heard that my parents attended the Youth Festival in London in 1971. In 1971 I would have been living at home with my parents in South London. I never heard of anything to do with this allegation from my parents and I believe I would probably have heard about it at some time, if not at the time, then*

*likely in later years. As I said previously, I never heard anything."*

*I find it strange that [Victoria]'s father would have given up a day at the farm to attend a festival as he would not have wanted to pay someone else to run the farm, even for one day.*

*If there had been an indecent assault on [Victoria] by Rolf Harris, her father would have confronted Rolf about it and others would have heard, as he would not have been quiet about it. I would have expected him to have either hit Rolf or reported it to the police.*

*My mum is in a rest home and has dementia so she may be unreliable regarding this allegation, although she does sometimes have very vivid memories of things that happened a long time ago, so it could be worth talking to her.*

*I understand that my aunt, [Victoria]'s mother, also has dementia and I do not know where she is living.*

*You know a lot of this stuff is just people jumping on the bandwagon. I'm not saying that this is true in [Victoria]'s case, but I can't rule that out either."*

Victoria's brother, who I will call Peter Pringle, still lives in the area where he and Victoria were raised on the farm that had been the family home for generations. He also played in the youth band.

Peter is something of an enigma because Victoria failed to mention him in the first two statements that she gave to the police – the first on 15th August 2014 and the second, a year later, on 2nd August 2015. She gave a third statement on 12th October 2016 when she identified him in a band photo but even then she did not tell the police that he was at the Lyceum as a band member in 1971, or that he was on the coach with the rest of the band and her family.

Peter was not called by the prosecution to give evidence in support of his sister in either of the two trials in which she was involved.

One of my researchers located an address for him. Following several unsuccessful attempts to contact him, my investigator Mike Kelly called at his home one Saturday afternoon in September 2016 when his wife happened to be in. She said that her husband was due home from work shortly, so Mike waited outside in his car.

When Peter drove into the lane alongside the house it was evident that he was aware that Mike was waiting for him, as he nodded to him as he drove by. He parked his car away from the house, near a local cricket ground, and walked towards Mike holding a large cardboard box with both hands. Names were not exchanged. As he walked near to Mike his first words were, "I am not speaking to anyone."

Peter then asked Mike if he was with the police. When Mike informed him that he was acting for the defence, he stopped and said, "I will tell you what I told the police. I was in a band that travelled to London to perform in a competition where Rolf Harris was present to give out awards." He added that the police then told him that because of his answer they would need to speak to his aunt, who his sister had said was present at the Lyceum. Peter then said that he had told the police that he had been unaware that his aunt had been at the Lyceum.

Peter told Mike that he had no knowledge or memory of any allegations made by his sister against Rolf Harris. He also told Mike of his concern for his elderly mother, who was very ill. He did not want her to get involved in any of this.

Mike asked Peter if his father had spoken to him about the allegation his sister had made while at the Lyceum in 1971. Peter answered, "My father was a farmer. Why would he be there anyway? I can't remember." He declined to say anything more and walked towards the house.

As Mike was sitting in his car writing up his notes of this conversation, Peter knocked on the front passenger window. He asked

Mike if he was the same person who had been making enquiries of his neighbours, asking about him. He was told yes, but the neighbours were being asked only if he lived at the address and if he was away.

He was satisfied with this. Then he asked Mike if he was Australian. When Mike said yes, he shook his head and walked back towards his house.

## THE BANDMASTER

We then focused our attention on the young people who had played in the band and the adults associated with it. We established that the band had been set up by two men who were both ex-army. The bandmaster had been a sergeant in the Signals Regiment, following which he had pursued a career in education. According to the former band members we spoke to, he had a quick temper when roused. Had any misconduct of the type alleged by Victoria Pringle been brought to his attention, he would have raised the roof.

Sadly, both men had died before this allegation was made. We did manage to locate the bandmaster's wife and daughter, and we spoke with both of them. Neither had heard of the allegation. His wife told us that she had no recollection of ever having been informed of an assault on any of 'our girls' who played in any of the bands that she and her husband had been associated with.

## THE BAND MEMBERS

Between 30 and 35 band members had taken part in the trip to London. Forty-five years had passed, and as might have been expected many were no longer living in the local area. Some of the girls had married more than once, so tracking them down was no easy task. However, many were spoken to, and a sample of the answers provided by them follows.

**Tuba Player** – He remembered Rolf Harris being there and said, "Whilst there I managed to get an autograph from him. I remember he drew a picture of his face on the autograph. He was busy signing autographs and had a lot of people queueing to see him. I never saw him being on his own with anyone. I am not aware of anything untoward taking place that day and never anyone saying that anything happened. One of the reasons I remember Rolf being there that day was that I am a big music fan, and he had a Number One hit with 'Two Little Boys' only a year before and this was the closest I had got to someone who was then a big star."

**Bass Player** – He said he could not really remember anything about the day. He did not remember anything untoward happening that day and did not remember seeing any celebrities at the Lyceum.

**Euphonium Player** – He confirmed that Rolf Harris was present at the event and said, "I think there were photo calls. It was a long day, but I recall photographs going around of the girls with Harris. There were some pretty girls in the band, certainly [Victoria] was one and she would have been one you would have picked out. She was stunning. I have been asked if I knew of anything inappropriate or of concern. I can say I knew or heard of nothing on the day and since."

**Conductor's Daughter** – She was the 13-year-old daughter of one of the conductors. He had not been conducting the band at the event but had come along to support them and had brought her with him. She did not remember anything untoward or out of the ordinary happening at the event.

**Cornet Player 1** – He remembered Rolf Harris being there as he was a star on television at the time. When asked if he had heard of, or knew of, anything inappropriate having taken place, or if he had had any concerns at the time, he replied, "The answer is no, not then or since."

**Cornet Player 2** – She recalled meeting Rolf Harris and being allowed to go up on stage. She said, "He was on the side of the stage sitting down. I remember standing next to him whilst he was writing in my autograph book that I carried around with me all the time. There were a few people there, but I do not remember who. He put his arm around my waist and said hello, and probably asked me my name. I may have ended up sitting on the arm of his chair, but I cannot remember, except I was very excited. He drew a little picture – a cartoon sketch self-portrait.

I think all of this happened after the proceedings. I have been asked by the police if I know of anything of concern or anything inappropriate and the answer is no. When Mr Harris put his arm around me, I must stress that it was not inappropriate.

**Trombone Player** – She recalled seeing Rolf Harris on stage whilst she and the other band members ate lunch after their performance. She said she had no interaction with him and she was not aware of any issues. She has no memory of anyone being distressed or crying.

**Other Band Members** – None of the other band members we managed to speak with had heard or seen anything inappropriate happening at the Lyceum. Their overall recollection of the trip was a rushed affair, travelling there and back in one day. They left in the dark and apart from two hours of free time after their performance, they saw nothing of London. For many of them it was a 'big thing' for the band to go to London and for most members of the band it was their first trip away. On the way back they did not sleep but talked all night and there was no mention of an assault on Victoria.

## THE AUTOGRAPH

When Victoria made her first statement to the police, in August 2014, she produced a scrapbook, a programme and two photographs. One of the photographs was of her standing next to Rolf.

The trial was scheduled to commence on 9th January 2017. In mid to late 2016 my team and I were busy interviewing and gathering evidence for the defence regarding this allegation and seven others. It was during these ongoing investigations that Mike Kelly spoke to Victoria's older brother, Peter. This was the meeting in September 2016 that I mentioned previously.

Shortly after this contact, Victoria got in touch with the police and produced what appeared to be a page torn out of an autograph book. On it was Rolf's signature along with his trademark 'Rolf-a-roo' – a cartoon sketch of himself. She told the police, and later the court, that her brother had found the autograph when they were clearing out their mother's room and that he had given it to her, saying, "You might need this."

This story just did not add up. Victoria had never mentioned to the police anything about her older brother being at the Lyceum in 1971, and in the absence of her parents, her aunt and her uncle he would have been her only key witness. Not only did she not mention him, he was also reluctant to become involved. According to Victoria's testimony he produced this autograph a week or two after we had located and interviewed him and brought to his attention that we knew he was with the band at the Lyceum in 1971.

Two years after making her complaint and producing the scrapbook for the police investigation, Victoria had produced this page that appeared to have been torn out of an autograph book and which had Rolf's signature on it. Later, at the trial and during cross-examination, Victoria was asked how she had managed to get Rolf's autograph when she had got up and left immediately after Rolf had allegedly pulled her onto his lap. She answered that this was one of a number of pre-signed autographs that were on the table where Rolf was signing them, and it was taken from this bundle.

In order to have an understanding of the inaccuracy of Victoria's statement, one has to know more about Rolf and his philosophy on celebrities providing autographs for fans. Of course, Victoria would not have been aware of this, and she therefore made an assumption that Rolf followed the same procedure as many other celebrities who provide autographs.

Rolf has over the years shown a high level of consistency and style when signing autographs. His characteristic 'Rolf-a-roo' is unique, and he takes great pride in this. An article in the *Telegraph* (Brisbane) dated 1st April 1970, which covered Rolf's visit to perform at the Brisbane City Hall, highlighted his attitude towards signing autographs.

He told the reporter, Ted Croft, "Entertainers by and large should be prepared to accept autograph signing. I had a summer season show in England a couple of summers ago. Some people on the bill refused to sign autographs at the door. I feel this is part of their job. I felt that if ever I had another show like that, I'd like to get written into the contract that entertainers sign a reasonable number of autographs at the door. Because that is part of it after all. If a guy is popular, people pay money to come and see him. They wait in the rain to get his autograph."

I spoke to several people who were very close to Rolf in a professional capacity and whose association with him spanned the years from 1966 to the present. The information they gave me backed up what Rolf had told reporter Ted Croft in 1970.

Rolf's PA, Lisa Ratcliff, who has held this position since the late 1990s, said that Rolf would never have left a pile of pre-signed autographs for fans. He would sign his autograph in their presence and add his 'Rolf-a-roo' selfie sketch. This was confirmed by Jan Kennedy, Rolf's managing agent for 38 years from the mid-1970s until 2014.

Barry Booth, who was Rolf's musical director from 1970 to 1996, made a full statement covering his years with Rolf. One of the subjects he covered was Rolf's love of his fans. He said,

*"Rolf was very attentive to his fans and autograph signing has always been very important to him. Autograph signing would sometimes take longer than the actual performance. Rolf always made time to have a photograph taken with someone and draw a small sketch of a 'Rolf-a-roo'. On many occasions this would go on for hours and I would find it quite tedious. Often by the time he had finished, the bar would be shut. I found this frustrating because, unlike Rolf, I do like to enjoy a drink, particularly after a concert."*

Ken Jeacle, Rolf's tour manager for a decade from the mid-1980s, testified along the same lines. He said that the signing sessions and meeting and greeting fans would sometimes exceed two hours. Mr Jeacle would endeavour to shorten the sessions, but Rolf would plough on. Mr Jeacle also said in court that he was 99.9 per cent certain that no autographs were ever pre-signed and stacked up prior to sessions.

Bruna Zanelli, who was Rolf's managing agent from 1966 to 1976, was of immense importance as a witness as she gave evidence at the second trial in relation to complainant Wendy Rosher. She was also able to shed light on how meticulous Rolf was about the signing of autographs. She told me that Rolf always took the time to sign autographs and she had never seen a bundle of pre-signed autographs left for fans. Rolf would never have allowed such a thing to occur.

Victoria's description of being pulled on to Rolf's lap and her immediate retreat suggests that she did not have the opportunity to get Rolf's autograph. The evidence provided by his close associates tends to rule out her explanation that the autograph she handed to the police was one of a number in a bundle on a table next to where Rolf was signing them.

One must question why Victoria's mother would have kept Rolf's autograph for 45 years if Victoria had told her father at the event that Rolf Harris had touched her in some way.

The autograph was allegedly found by Victoria's brother, who refused to provide a statement to support his sister even though he was at the Lyceum in 1971. Yet he was happy to give her the autograph when he apparently found it at their mother's home, when they were clearing it out after she left to go into a care home.

Was this autograph obtained to add support to Victoria's complaint and perhaps take the heat off her brother, who had made it clear that he did not want to be involved? This is the question that the defence legal team were asking.

Investigations online revealed that autographs from celebrities are bought and sold all the time, so it was very easy to locate Rolf's autograph with the 'Rolf-a-roo'. As you will note from the sample below, this is an original that has been removed from an autograph book.

The possible purchase of a Rolf Harris autograph was put to Victoria during the trial and of course she denied it. As her brother, Peter, was not called as a witness, he was never cross-examined on this point. The history of this autograph remains a mystery.

*Rolf Harris's Trademark Autograph*

## SEX ON THE FARM

The Pringles were tenant farmers. In the eyes of their friends and acquaintances the Pringles were an affluent family but in truth the farm was not owned by them. At the time of the trial Mr Pringle was deceased and Mrs Pringle was in a care home.

The farm had been sold a few years earlier. As tenant farmers the Pringles did not benefit from the sale of the farm.

I focused my investigations on the two witnesses who had given evidence in support of Victoria. Neither claimed that they had witnessed the alleged indecent assault, nor were they told of it by Victoria at the time.

The witness Geoffrey was a person of particular interest to us in our investigations.

In their evidence to the court both Victoria and Geoffrey admitted that they were friends. However, during my investigations I became aware that there was more to their relationship and that they were intimately involved, which is something that they did not tell the court. Perhaps that was because Geoffrey was 18½ and Victoria was only 14.

Geoffrey is two years older than Victoria's brother Peter Pringle, who was 16 at the time. He was no longer at school but out working. He said in evidence that he spent a lot of his spare time helping out on the farm because he was friends with Peter.

When making enquiries with former band members I used two investigators who worked as a pair. This was because of the sensitive nature of the questions we were having to ask and the fact that we could not divulge the name of the complainant.

As part of our enquiries, we interviewed the man previously referred to as Cornet Player 1. His wife, who had a wealth of local knowledge, was present during the two interviews we had with him. She had been brought up in the town and, whilst she was not a member of the youth band, she knew Victoria, her former boyfriend Geoffrey and Geoffrey's ex-wife. She showed me a group photo taken some years ago and pointed out Geoffrey, who was standing next to her and her husband.

She described Geoffrey as 'a ladies' man but in a nice way'. He was unfaithful in his marriage and was known to have had affairs with at least three women. We were not advised of any details other than to be told the name of the first of the women linked to his affairs.

My fellow investigator and I located the woman late one evening. After explaining the purpose of our visit we arranged to return the following day, at a more hospitable hour. I will call her Barbara, which is not her real name. Barbara is a professional who holds a responsible position in the town. Understandably she was concerned about becoming involved but did promise to answer truthfully any questions we put to her. Her actual words were, "You ask the questions and I will answer them truthfully."

I could not help noticing a wry little smile and a twinkle in her eye when she said this. It was clear that Barbara wanted to tell the truth but in such a way that she couldn't be accused of spilling the beans on her friends. Although Barbara had been in the youth band at some point, she had not been on the trip to the Lyceum.

Barbara described Geoffrey in almost exactly the same way as Cornet Player 1's wife had: "He was a ladies' man but in a nice way." She told us that she had had a sexual relationship with him commencing when she was 15, at which time he was around 25 or 26. He had been married for two or three years at that time.

Barbara said she was aware that Victoria had been in a sexual relationship with Geoffrey when she (Victoria) was about 14 or 15, and that this was common knowledge among the band members. Barbara told us that Victoria had telephoned her a couple of times when she (Barbara) was having a sexual relationship with Geoffrey and discussed this with her, saying that Geoffrey had now passed her (Victoria) over and that she (Barbara) was his new chosen one.

Geoffrey was known to have been involved with other women during his marriage and as someone who had underage sex with girls. This apparently was also well known by other members of the band. Both he and Victoria misled the court when they claimed they were not boyfriend and girlfriend in 1971.

During this phase of our enquiries we became aware of another woman who had not been located or interviewed by the police. I will refer to her as Deborah.

Deborah told us that she went to school with Victoria, and they have been friends ever since. She showed us a photograph of three teenaged girls in swimsuits and said it was taken on their first holiday together. She and Victoria were two of the girls in the photograph. The third girl had moved overseas but remained a friend.

Deborah still lives in the same town. She is now in her late fifties, the same age as Victoria. Deborah had no hesitation in telling us that at the time of the incident at the Lyceum she was the girlfriend of Victoria's older brother, Peter. She was not a member of the band but was on the coach as Peter's girlfriend. Peter was 16 and she was 14 at the time. She was never told of any incident occurring between Victoria and Rolf Harris and she could not recall Mr and Mrs Pringle being on the coach.

As a result of our enquiries around the town and with former band members, we established that there was far more going on at the farm in 1971 than voluntary farm work.

## THE TRIALS

The information about the various relationships had not been gathered prior to the second trial. Victoria had made no mention of her older brother, Peter, being at the Lyceum. The jury was unable to reach a verdict on this count and a further trial was ordered.

By the time the third trial commenced we were aware of Peter being at the Lyceum, and he knew this. He would also have known that we were aware of what had been going on at the farm in 1971, and that this was more than likely the reason why he did his best to avoid getting involved. Additionally, he had commented on the likelihood of his father not having been at the Lyceum. If he had been required to give evidence at the trials, and had told the truth, he would have been of no assistance to his sister.

What had to be evaluated by the defence QC is whether Peter would tell the truth in court, as along with Geoffrey they could both have been facing charges relating to having underage sex with girls aged from 13 to 15 years. In 1971 a person convicted of this type of crime could well have been sentenced to a term of imprisonment.

Geoffrey, on the other hand, was not aware of our enquiries so he appeared willingly as a witness for Victoria, without knowing that at any time the QC for the defence could have questioned him about having had sex with girls who were underage, including Victoria.

As it happened, the defence QC made the tactical decision not to attack Geoffrey, as to do so may well have alienated some members of the jury. Jurors are prone to feel sympathy for a witness who is being hung out to dry. The QC running the defence is the best judge of when to use evidence that I gather and present to him. In this case Geoffrey's evidence under oath fell far short of what Victoria had wanted him to say in order to back up her allegations.

At the third trial it was made clear that Victoria's brother Peter was one of the members of the band who was with Victoria at the Lyceum in 1971. The fact that he had refused to get involved, and to provide witness evidence in court on behalf of his sister, was in itself telling.

Under oath and during cross-examination Victoria told the court during both trials how the alleged indecent assault occurred.

Victoria claimed that she was standing with other young people when she was pulled from behind on to Rolf Harris's lap. She was wearing a short dress, which was very much the fashion at that time, and underneath she had tights on over her pants. When she was pulled onto his lap, she stood up immediately. To use her words, "It was very, very short and I don't know whether his hand was there as I sat or as I got up. I just don't like being pulled down [on] to somebody's lap."

According to Victoria, as she landed on Rolf's lap she felt his hand touch her around her vaginal area but over her pants and tights. It stands to reason that if she was wearing a short dress then her pants and tights could well have been showing. She said that he did not attempt to put his hand inside her pants or under her tights. After she jumped up she went to tell her father but she did not tell him where she alleged Rolf had touched her and she did not tell anyone else.

No-one else witnessed the alleged indecent assault. As Victoria did not tell anyone, the question is, was she indecently assaulted, or did she just take exception to being pulled onto Rolf's lap? Her friend Patricia testified that she had witnessed her being pulled onto Rolf's lap but nothing else. Geoffrey, who was supposed to have been a star witness, could only tell the court that he saw her crying at some stage after she had returned from seeing Rolf Harris. She did not tell him what she now claims to have happened.

What did come out during the second and third trials, and which is worthy of comment, is that a photograph of Victoria with Rolf – and, we were led to believe, his autograph – had been kept for over 45 years at the Pringle home. As her parents were supposed to have been aware of the alleged assault on their daughter one might question why they chose to keep the autograph, or why Victoria herself had chosen to keep the photo. As I have mentioned previously, we were unable to interview her parents as her father was deceased and her mother had dementia. The only person who might have been able to shed some light on why these items were kept was her brother, Peter, who had refused to become involved.

Victoria could not provide a believable explanation as to why the photograph had not been thrown away many years ago, other than it had been in a scrapbook kept by her mother. The autograph that suddenly appeared from nowhere had not been in the scrapbook, so this was even less credible.

## THE VERDICT

So, what did happen at the Lyceum back in 1971?

Being tactile was quite the norm back in the 1960s and 1970s.

One of the band members, who I have referred to as Cornet Player 2, said she was quite happy for Rolf to put his arm around her. She thinks she may have sat on the arm of the chair whilst he signed his autograph and drew his 'Rolf-a-roo'. She saw nothing inappropriate in this and was very excited to meet Rolf.

Victoria, who was described in interviews with other band members as very attractive, was in a relationship with an older man. It is likely that as a result she was more tuned in to adult concepts of sensual and physical contact. If Rolf had pulled her on to his lap, she would arguably have been more likely to have taken exception to it. That was, of course, her right but there is a difference between light-hearted fun and indecent assault, and there is no corroborating evidence whatsoever that the latter had occurred.

Similarly, if what Victoria's friend Patricia told the court is correct, it is possible that Rolf did pull Victoria onto his lap. In 1971 it would not have been seen as inappropriate for a celebrity like Rolf to have a child sitting on his lap whilst he gave them his autograph. If he did in fact do this then the evidence does not show that there was an indecent assault. This appears to have been added many years later when Victoria made her complaint to the police.

Following the third trial, the jury, in an outcome reflecting that of the second trial, was unable to reach a verdict. The Crown Prosecution Service advised Judge Deborah Taylor that they would not be pursuing this complaint any further. The judge ruled that the charge had not been proven and Rolf Harris was found not guilty.

As an investigator I try to remain impartial, but this becomes difficult when the evidence used by the police to prosecute someone falls far short of what is required to prove the crime. As a stand-alone charge there was insufficient evidence to prove that Rolf Harris had indecently assaulted this woman 45 years previously.

She waited until Rolf was found guilty of the first group of charges before allowing her then boyfriend to contact the NSPCC on her behalf, at which point her complaint was referred to the police.

It is the hypocrisy of all this that goes against everything I was taught as a young police officer in New Zealand. I am sure there are many people who share my annoyance.

Did Rolf pull this young woman on to his lap 45 years ago and, if he did, was that an indecent assault in 1971?

Now compare this to the two people who were involved in this complaint – Victoria and her then boyfriend Geoffrey, both of whom are hiding behind anonymity. It is my view that Geoffrey was the sexual predator, not Rolf Harris. Other members of the band and one of Geoffrey's ex-girlfriends advised me that Victoria was sexually active at 14 years of age with Geoffrey, who was four years her senior. If this information is correct then it should have been Geoffrey who stood trial for a sexual offence, rather than supporting Victoria in her complaint against Rolf Harris.

This arrogance and hypocrisy saw no limits.

# CHAPTER 4
# THE ROLF-A-ROO

Portsmouth, on the south coast of England, is about six miles from Leigh Park, where Wendy Rosher claimed to have been indecently assaulted by Rolf Harris around the time of her eighth birthday. It is a city known for its naval heritage and one of the Royal Navy's most famous warships, HMS Victory, which is located at No. 2 Dry Dock in the Historic Dockyard. HMS Victory, launched in 1765, is a proud memorial to Vice-Admiral Horatio Nelson, one of Britain's greatest naval heroes. Nelson died on the Victory during the Battle of Trafalgar after being shot by a French sniper.

In view of Portsmouth's long-standing association with HMS Victory it was not surprising that when an independent radio station was launched in Portsmouth on 14th October 1975 it was called Radio Victory. The radio station operated for 11 years until 1986 from its base at 247 Fratton Road, Southsea.

Radio Victory provided the backdrop for Count 2 at the second trial. A woman in her early fifties had alleged that she had been indecently assaulted by Rolf Harris in 1977, when she was aged 12 or 13. She said that at the time of the alleged assault she had been outside the Radio Victory building with her mother.

The complainant has anonymity so I will refer to her as Christina Newton. During the court case she gave her evidence via a video link, so she did not have to appear in person.

*Radio Victory: how the building would have looked in 1977*

## THE ALLEGATION

Christina alleged that in 1977 she was living in Portsmouth with her family. Their home was within walking distance of the Radio Victory building. On one particular occasion, when she was listening to the radio station with her mother, a live interview with Rolf Harris was being broadcast. She said that her mother was a keen autograph collector, so they decided to go to the radio station to try to meet Rolf Harris and get his autograph.

According to Christina, when they arrived at the radio station it was about 8.00 pm. It was a warm evening, so she was wearing a skirt and a short-sleeved top, which suggests that it was summertime. She recalled the song 'All I Need Is the Air That I Breathe' by the Hollies, which was released in 1974, playing at the radio station.

Her various accounts of standing outside the radio station with her mother differ. She said initially that they had to wait a long time before Rolf Harris came out of the building. Later she changed this to having had to wait only five to ten minutes.

According to Christina, she and her mother were the only people waiting outside. Rolf, who was accompanied by another man, approached Christina's mother first and signed her autograph book. Her mother was giggling at the time. Rolf wrote, 'To [her name] with love Rolf Harris - Stop laughing!' and added his 'Rolf-a-roo' caricature. Christina said that Rolf then approached her and gave her a cuddle. As he cuddled her, he put his hand down her skirt and into her knickers, touching what she described as the outside of her 'hole', but he did not penetrate her. She later clarified this somewhat vulgar term as referring to her vagina.

Christina said that she pulled away as she knew that what Rolf Harris was doing was wrong. He then signed her autograph book, 'To [Christina] with love Rolf Harris' and added a 'Rolf a-roo'. When the autograph book was produced as evidence it was noted that '1977' had been written underneath Rolf's autograph in small print, whereas her mother's Rolf Harris autograph was undated.

Even though Christina's mother was standing just inches away, according to Christina, she did not see what Rolf had allegedly done to her. Christina made no mention of what the mystery man accompanying Rolf did. She does not describe any reaction from him. This suggests that the man, if he existed, didn't see what allegedly happened either. Christina claimed that a couple of days later she told her mother what had happened, but her mother did not believe her, and she never mentioned it again.

Christina's mother is deceased. The man who Christina claimed was accompanying Rolf has never been identified. The only evidence that she was able to produce to support her allegation was her autograph book, inside of which were autographs from several celebrities – including the one from Rolf Harris. Rolf's autograph was on a page opposite an autograph from Cliff Richard, which although not conclusive seems to suggest that both of these signatures had been obtained around the same time.

Christina's mother worked at a venue that at the time attracted many famous names. She was in a position to obtain autographs and acquired these not only for herself but for her daughter as well, which is how Christina came to have such an impressive collection. The question arises as to whether her mother had at some point met Rolf Harris in the course of her work and had obtained the autographs then. As she was by then deceased, there was no way of establishing whether this was the case.

## RED FLAGS

This term is commonly used to identify facets of a complaint that require closer scrutiny. Even in the early stages of this investigation there were numerous red flag indicators that raised suspicions as to whether the information provided by Christina in support of her allegation reflected the true situation.

Christina had said initially that she thought she had been only eight years old when the alleged indecent assault occurred, which meant that the estimated year of the incident was 1973. However, when she looked up Radio Victory on the internet, she realised that the station hadn't started transmitting until 1975 and was surprised to find that she must have been older than she had remembered. This comment was quite extraordinary when at that stage she was still in possession of the autograph book because she hadn't yet handed it over to the police. If the year 1977 had been written beside the 'Rolf-a-roo' at the time that Christina had obtained Rolf's autograph, she would have known the year and there would have been no need for her to carry out any internet research to determine when Radio Victory first started transmitting.

This flagged up the suspicion that Christina may have written the date on the autograph when she had become aware of Radio Victory's history.

Christina's mother obtained Rolf's autograph at the same time, according to Christina, but her mother's autograph differed in that there was no date. It was interesting that Christina's autograph was dated, whereas all the other Rolf Harris autographs I had seen in the course of the investigation did not have the date written on them. I will not go as far as saying that Rolf never put the date on his autographs, but I had never seen this before and would consider it to be a rarity.

Rolf Harris's first trial would have been of particular interest to people in the Portsmouth area because of the allegation made by Wendy Rosher that Rolf Harris had indecently assaulted her at the Leigh Park Community Centre in nearby Havant. There was extensive local media coverage that had gone into considerable detail as to how Rolf Harris had carried out the alleged assault.

In early June 2014, when the first trial was ongoing, Christina started having counselling sessions and undergoing therapy for reasons unconnected to Rolf Harris. Almost immediately after he was sentenced, she told her counsellor, her brother, and a close friend about what Rolf had allegedly done to her 37 years previously.

She claimed that this was the first time she had mentioned being indecently assaulted by Rolf to anyone, although she had also claimed that she had mentioned it to her mother the day after it happened and had been ignored.

Both Christina's brother and her close friend encouraged her to speak with the NSPCC, which she did. The NSPCC referred the matter to the police. Christina provided a statement to the police on 22nd July 2014 and at the same time gave the police her autograph book.

There were remarkable similarities between Christina's complaint and the earlier allegation made by Wendy Rosher. Christina's allegation might be viewed as a 'variant copycat' of this allegation.

| Wendy Rosher | Christina Newton |
|---|---|
| It was a chilly morning. | It was a warm evening. |
| She was 7 or 8. | Initially thought she had been only eight years old at the time, then:<br>*'I saw that Radio Victory didn't actually launch until 1975, which would have made me 10 years old and not 8.'*<br>*'It would have been around the summer of 1977'* [when she was 12] |
| She went to get his autograph. | |
| Marker song: *Two Little Boys* | Marker song: *The Air That I Breathe* playing in the background |
| His hand went between her legs. | |
| It was expertly done. | It felt like it was something he was experienced at doing. |
| Carried out in public but no one noticed, not even her friend/ sister. | Her own mother was standing right next to her and did not even notice. |

## DATE OF THE ALLEGED OFFENCE

George East was a key figure at Radio Victory from its launch in 1975 until 1980. In 1977, when he was a programme coordinator, his duties included meeting and greeting visiting celebrities. He recalled many celebrities visiting the radio station but not Rolf Harris.

George told us that it was very unlikely in his view that Rolf would have visited Portsmouth for the sole purpose of an interview with Radio Victory. It was a very small local radio station, very low down in the pecking order. Radio Victory would pick up the crumbs from the likes of Southern Television, Portsmouth News and Radio Solent. Celebrities would visit these media outlets and if they were going to Radio Victory it would be their last port of call.

Our investigation concentrated initially on identifying events in 1977 that Rolf had attended with a view to identifying a visit to Portsmouth when he could have included a visit to Radio Victory.

I have included examples of the timelines to illustrate the fastidious work that the researchers completed for my investigators to assist them in ensuring that no stones were left unturned. The same methodology was applied to every allegation where there was doubt as to whether Rolf had been at a particular venue.

*The News* (Portsmouth) was reviewed for the period 16th May 1977 to the end of September 1977, as Christina had described the alleged incident as having happened on a 'warm evening'. There was *no* evidence of a visit to the area by Rolf Harris. We catalogued appearances by national figures to the Portsmouth area for that period and his name did not show up anywhere.

We developed a timeline for Rolf Harris covering 1977. This did not reveal any windows of opportunity when a visit to Portsmouth might have taken place.

## APPEARANCE OF ROLF HARRIS AT RADIO VICTORY

Operation Yewtree officers had interviewed ten past employees of Radio Victory and found two witnesses who stated that they could remember Rolf having visited the radio station in the late 1970s. Having just completed the Rosher investigation, during which the farce that

Operation Yewtree had called a fair investigation was uncovered, I was not prepared to accept their findings.

Locating and interviewing the remaining past employees was the perfect assignment for the intrepid Doug Quade, ably assisted by our Australian investigator, Mike Kelly. I had been reliably informed that Doug was an expert on HMS Victory, Vice-Admiral Nelson and the Battle of Trafalgar. Portsmouth was his old stomping ground, so he was the obvious choice.

Between them, Doug Quade and Mike Kelly located and interviewed a further 20 past employees of Radio Victory in addition to the 10 interviewed by the police. The former employees named below were able to provide information that was particularly useful.

**David Gamblen** was at Radio Victory between 1977 and 1980. His son Darren also worked at Radio Victory. David has a clear memory of saying to Darren on a Friday that Rolf Harris was visiting the next day to appear on the Wonderful Wobbly Wireless Show, which was aimed at, and presented by, children. He says he recalls seeing Rolf Harris on the Saturday and shaking his hand. He could not date the occasion other than it being the late 1970s.

**Paul Robbins** was a sound engineer at Radio Victory between its inception and May 1981. He has a very clear recollection of meeting Rolf on a Saturday, on Wonderful Wobbly Wireless. He recalls speaking with Rolf outside the studio, where Rolf was using a nasal spray, and they exchanged a joke about it not being drugs. Again, he could not recall the date.

**Darren Gamblen** worked on a Saturday on children's programmes between 1977 and 1983. He had a very clear memory of Rolf Harris's visit. He recalls it being for a recording session rather than a live transmission and is quite adamant that it was for a show called Young Victory, which was the successor to Wonderful Wobbly Wireless. He was certain of this because Rolf stayed on after the session and recorded some jingles, one of which remains in his memory. It was "Hey ho, tiddly dee, here's Young

Victory, splonge!" – which might be described as a typical Rolf Harris ditty. Once again, he could not recall dates.

We made every effort to date accurately the demise of Wonderful Wobbly Wireless and the commencement of Young Victory, though a lack of programming details made this problematic. As the principal presenter of Wonderful Wobbly Wireless had died in the late 1970s, we had to locate other people who had presented the show on a regular basis.

One of the presenters of Wonderful Wobbly Wireless declined to speak to our investigator other than to acknowledge the difficulties that Rolf faced in having a fair trial. Whilst this was unfortunate from our point of view, it was not at all unusual. Many people were concerned about how their involvement in the case would be perceived by others if they were called to be a witness for the defence, given that Rolf had been found guilty on all counts at the first trial. This was an issue that we had to deal with in order to ensure that the evidence presented to a jury was fair and balanced.

To summarise:

**1977**

No records of Rolf Harris appearing in Portsmouth in 1977 were located. A considerable amount of research was completed before we reached this conclusion. An appearance by Rolf Harris was newsworthy on a local level and often on a national level. It would be fair to conclude that if he had been in Portsmouth in 1977 it would have been reported. Our researchers would have found a record of this visit. Over 30 people who were connected to Radio Victory in the 1970s and 1980s were located and interviewed, some by the police and others by my team. No-one was able to confirm that Rolf had visited Radio Victory in 1977.

**March 1978**

As a result of further research and investigations we established that Rolf had been in Portsmouth during the week commencing 6th March 1978. His *Rolf on Saturday, O.K.?* television show was being filmed on HMS Victory. During this particular week he rehearsed with the children of Alexandra Middle School, Portsmouth who were appearing on the show.

Doug Quade contacted Mr Peter Hoade, who was the headmaster of Alexandra Middle School in 1978. He remembered the visit well. He told Doug that Rolf Harris came to the school to meet the children and on another day they had a rehearsal in a nearby secondary school. The show was filmed on HMS Victory on Friday, 10th March 1978, and the children finished at 6.00 pm.

Doug also spoke with Jim Moir, who produced the programme. Jim confirmed that Rolf would have been in Portsmouth during the week of production and that none of it would have taken place on the Saturday.

It is highly probable therefore that if Rolf had been at Radio Victory as a guest on the Wonderful Wobbly Wireless Show or its successor, Young Victory, it would have been on Saturday, 11th March 1978.

# AUTOGRAPH

Having turned over every stone we could find, it was time to look more closely at the autograph and whether Rolf did write the date alongside his 'Rolf-a-roo'. Getting access to Rolf – who, of course, was in Stafford Prison – was not easy owing to all of the security procedures in place.

Only Rolf's solicitor could take writing materials and correspondence into the prison and then bring them back out. Phillip Barlow of LHS Solicitors was representing Rolf and I worked closely with him during this time. The police had the autograph book, which meant that Phillip had to refer to a photocopy. However, following a prison visit to Rolf he was able to advise me that his basic tests of Rolf's writing of numbers revealed that the sevens in '1977' were not written by him.

While this may sound simple it is not that easy, as the CPS could quite easily have put it to the jury that Rolf was an experienced artist and as such disguising his writing would be easy for him. With the assistance of Rolf's secretary/PA we searched through his previous writings.

Although we were convinced that he did not write the date on the autograph there was still room for doubt, and where Rolf and the waiting tabloids were concerned, we had to have proof well beyond any doubt.

Handwriting experts were considered but their evidence can be contested by other handwriting experts, so we decided that the best course of action was to use the services of a forensic laboratory to complete an analysis of the ink used in the signature and the date 1977. This was my department. I chose Cellmark Forensic Services, a firm based in Abingdon, Oxfordshire that was also used by the police.

## INK COMPARISON

Cellmark were unable to carry out this work at their laboratory. They informed me that they contracted out specialist work such as this. After various referrals I was given the name of Dr Jürgen Bügler of the Institute of Forensic Sciences in Munich. Emails sent to Dr Bügler did not elicit a response, so I attempted to locate a telephone number or find some other form of contact. I was unsuccessful in making contact with him.

Ink dating using thermal desorption and gas

chromatography / mass spectrometry:

Comparison of results obtained in two laboratories

Agnès Koenig[1,3], M.Sc, Jürgen Bugler[2], Ph.D, Dieter Kirsch[3], Ph.D, Fritz Köhler[3], Ph.D, Céline Weyermann[1], Ph.D.

I made further enquiries with Cellmark to see if they could assist. After searching through their various scientific registers, they were not able to provide any more details for Dr Bügler. However, Cellmark's Business Development Manager, Elaine Higgins, told me that she had spoken with her colleague Hilary regarding the ink comparison work that Dr Bügler had documented. Hilary said that having read his paper she could advise that the ink comparison was able to be done only on samples up to about 18 months old – and that the techniques used were destructive to the paper.

Cellmark did not know of any non-destructive ways in which we could establish the age of or compare inks. It seemed that we had reached the end of the road with this line of enquiry. Then we received that little bit of luck that one dreams of in a difficult and complicated investigation. I refer to it as tapping into the top three inches – by far the most conclusive science.

It took Operation Yewtree and the CPS two and a half years to gather evidence against Rolf Harris in readiness for his second trial, which was scheduled to commence on 9th January 2017. There were seven complainants, including Christina, and eight allegations. For most of this time Rolf was in Stafford Prison. I was not involved with the first trial. I came on board prior to the second.

Christina made her complaint to Operation Yewtree officers on 22nd July 2014 – three weeks after the guilty verdicts had been returned at the first trial. At the same time, she handed over her autograph book. By the time I had received the information from Cellmark that the ink comparison tests could not be completed it was December 2016 and there was only a month before the trial commenced. For the entire two and a half years that the police had been in possession of her autograph book, Christina had led us all to believe that Rolf had written the date on the autograph.

For Phillip Barlow to have access to the original autograph in the book he had to liaise with Operation Yewtree. This meant that they became aware that we had identified an expert who, as far as they were concerned, could analyse the ink. What they didn't know was that the expert couldn't actually do this. In fairness to us, we did not know either until late December 2016.

By this time someone at Operation Yewtree had spoken with Christina, who confessed that she had written the date. Having finally admitted this she then insisted that she had written it only a few days after Rolf had given her his autograph – in other words, it had still been written in the summer of 1977.

If indeed she had written '1977' just a few days after Rolf had signed her autograph book, she would have been definite about the year, and there would have not been any confusion as to when this alleged incident occurred. Neither would there have been any doubt in her mind about how old she was at the time.

As you have probably realised, if you didn't already know, the top three inches is the intelligence network between one's ears – or, in other words, the brain. Christina's probably went into overdrive when she heard that the ink was going to be analysed.

She would have thought that the police would be informed that the autograph and date had been written by different people at different times, and with a different pen. I suspect it was not just the top three inches of Christina that went into overdrive. I also suspect that the Operation Yewtree officers thought they had better re-interview Christina about the date on the autograph.

## THE TRIAL

As a professional investigator I was disappointed by the next move by Operation Yewtree and the Crown Prosecution Service. They decided to continue with the charge, even though they knew that the complainant had been misleading them about the date on the autograph. I can only speculate that they were confident a jury would find Rolf Harris guilty based on the outcome of the first trial.

Well, fortunately they were wrong. The jury saw right through this false allegation. The verdict was Not Guilty.

This was significant as it was the first time that a jury had returned a Not Guilty verdict in a trial involving Rolf Harris. It showed that the jury was prepared to listen to the evidence and not be swayed by the vociferous condemnation of Rolf by the tabloids.

What this court case showed was the necessity for an accused person to employ their own detectives to gather evidence to create an equilibrium that would lead to a fair trial. The problem is that most accused people cannot afford to employ their own detectives and they must rely on the police to investigate a complaint in a fair and balanced manner. This is something that Operation Yewtree officers did not do.

Finally, you may be wondering what happened to Christina. The answer to that is **nothing**. Remember the promise, **come forward and you will be believed**.

# CHAPTER 5
# I SWEAR TO GOD

The enquiries into the additional eight counts were going well until I encountered Count 3. I can still remember vividly the thoughts that went through my mind when I heard about the complainant and read the circumstances of her complaint. I had this sinking feeling deep within me and I chastised myself for my negative thinking. But there it was in black and white. My mind raced at full speed. Had I got it wrong, I thought, but surely not, because the evidence in the Wendy Rosher case and the others I had investigated thus far was overwhelmingly in support of Rolf's innocence.

Count 3 was a complaint by a woman who was described in media reports prior to the trial as 'a blind, disabled woman'. She had lost her sight as a teenager and had cerebral palsy that was severe enough for her to need a wheelchair. She has anonymity, so I will refer to her as Jane Hatfield.

If anything could have been guaranteed to induce a sense of public revulsion, this was it. The message implied by some of the pre-trial media coverage was clear: Rolf Harris had taken advantage of a vulnerable woman who had been in no position to fight him off. He was the lowest of the low.

Jane said in evidence that she was 27 when Rolf Harris was a guest at the hospital radio station where she volunteered as a presenter. The radio station was operating from a small room within the hospital, and Rolf was carrying out one of his many charitable engagements.

Jane's over-the-top narrative of the alleged encounter read like a parody of a titillating novel. On 11th January 2017 *The Guardian* reported Jane's claim that Rolf Harris had begun to 'caress and cup her breasts over her clothing, squeezing her nipples between his fingers', and that the alleged assaults included 'slipping a hand up her skirt to touch the vaginal area'.

This extract from Jane's account was published in *The Sun* on 16th January 2017:

> *"He [Rolf Harris] said there was no problem, and he got his fingers spread across breasts [sic] so my nipples were between his fingers, and he was squeezing them, so they became pumped.*

> *"My legs were going like rigid boards; my muscles were going so tight because the next thing he's going to do is put his hands on my private parts. I couldn't escape."*

The alleged sexual attack as described by Jane was not a brief encounter. The impression she gave was that it lasted for some time and started from the moment Rolf entered the room and first greeted her.

The problem I was faced with was how I was going to investigate this complaint by a woman who suffered from such severe disabilities without being accused by the media of attempting to denigrate her.

The press had already claimed that Rolf's defence had hired private investigators to 'dig up dirt' on the complainants. Of course, nothing could be further from the truth. I tend to ignore such comments as normally they come from journalists who have no idea how a professional investigator operates. Their thought processes are therefore limited to thinking that we operate at the same low and untruthful level as they do. What does annoy me is when they use the term 'investigative journalist' to describe themselves, when the truth is that they can't be bothered to investigate but rely instead on clickbait headlines, which are often inaccurate.

As a professional investigator I had only one choice, and that was to start making enquiries. Hopefully, by treading carefully I would be able to avoid any adverse criticism and pull out of the enquiry if it seemed like we were trying to dig up dirt, so to speak. It was with much trepidation that I embarked on this investigation.

My concerns were short lived. Instead of digging up the dirt, as journalists often accuse us of doing, I had to put on my largest waders to navigate my way through the very muddy waters that Jane had left in her wake.

Open-source research is always the safest place to commence an investigation of this nature, and this is where my enquiries started.

My research team discovered that some years earlier Jane had lodged a sizeable claim against a service provider for an injury she claimed to have sustained. She alleged that she had suffered injuries to her legs and upper body when she had been 'manhandled' into a seat.

Jane is a rather large woman, so it is not inconceivable that she could well have had difficulty in fitting into the confines of a standard seat. The organisation concerned, which I cannot name for legal reasons, settled out of court rather than face the inevitable bad publicity that a trial would bring with it.

This was my first clue that all may not be as it appeared. Perhaps Jane was not averse to making compensation claims, or was I being a bit unfair? I continued my investigations and very soon this decision proved to be the right move.

In the course of my research and investigations, I acquired photographs of Jane enjoying a special occasion at a highly prestigious venue. In one photograph she is seated, drinking champagne and smiling. It was noticeable that the seat she was sitting in appeared to have the same confines and dimensions as the seat at the other venue at which she claimed to have sustained injuries. A further photo showed that Jane had needed to be carried – some might say 'manhandled' – by company employees to enable her to access this particular seat.

I completed my own investigations into the size of the seats and without giving away the details of where these venues were located, I am satisfied that the difference in the width of the seats was minimal.

I do not know the actual date of the joyous occasion but from Jane's appearance it would have been close to the time when she had made the claim against the other organisation. To my knowledge there was never any complaint made by her that she had been publicly humiliated by having to be manhandled into the seat at the more prestigious venue.

As our research continued, we encountered many references to Jane's struggle to be able to fund her 24/7 care. There was little doubt that her personal circumstances were most unfortunate, and some may say tragic.

I had to ignore this side of things and concentrate on whether Rolf Harris was guilty of the sexual abuse that Jane had complained about or whether he was a target through whom she could source the funds she seemed to need so desperately.

My investigations turned to locating and speaking with people who had encountered Jane over the years. I had to be careful not to mention the reason for my enquiries, and this required some skilful questioning to avoid alerting them to the fact that Jane had made an allegation of indecent assault against Rolf Harris. At the same time, I had to ascertain whether they had ever heard Jane speak of Rolf Harris or the allegations.

I found no-one, although I did locate one woman who was very close to Jane who had put two and two together and realised that Jane was one of the complainants in the new charges that Rolf Harris had to answer to.

I will call her April, although this isn't her real name. April told me that she had been Jane's carer for five years. When I asked about her relationship with Jane, she replied that she did not like her at all. "I don't like her. That's the nicest thing I can say about her."

When it was explained to April that this was a serious enquiry and that it was of a sensitive nature, she replied, "If this is about her being interfered with by Rolf Harris, I don't believe her as she has made allegations against two previous male carers."

After April had revealed that she knew Jane was one of the new complainants, I conducted a formal interview with her and wrote out a statement in which she revealed everything she knew about Jane. April was a key witness for the defence.

In April's statement, matters we had previously suspected were confirmed. It also contained other interesting information.

April said that Jane had made no secret of her expectation that she was going to receive some compensation in the coming January, but she did not say where this was coming from. The coming January coincided with the start of Rolf's second trial, at which Jane was scheduled to appear as one of the complainants. April knew this, and along with other comments Jane had made she was left in no doubt that Jane was once again making an allegation of sexual assault.

Unfortunately, April could not remember the names of the two male carers against whom Jane had made the complaints, but she did know the name of the agency that had employed them.

When we made enquiries with the agency we were met with a 'no comment' response and asked to leave. All we were asking was to have the opportunity to speak with the two men involved to ascertain if the complaints were similar to the complaint against Rolf Harris and whether compensation had been paid. According to April, the agency did not want any bad publicity, so they offered a financial settlement, which Jane accepted.

April directed me to relatives who were able to confirm the information she had provided. They had distanced themselves from Jane since the death of a family member who had been close to Jane. They did not have anything nice to say about her. They told me that they considered her to be a people user and had used her disabilities to the maximum for personal financial gain.

The impression I gained was that all the people close to Jane were good hard-working people who had just had enough of being used and seeing her manipulate others. April came from a religious background; her father was a minister of religion. April was in her mid-seventies when I interviewed her. She was caring for her partner and was often called on to care for Jane as well. April's partner has since died, and she is no longer in contact with Jane.

Even at this stage of my investigation I felt a tinge of sadness that anyone with the disabilities that Jane had suffered with for most of her life had to resort to these measures in order to get enough money to pay for the 24/7 care she required. It was an unpleasant investigation to be involved in because I kept being drawn back to how I would cope if I were in her position.

Fortunately, I had others around me who made it quite clear that two wrongs don't make a right, and for Jane to use her disability in this way, as a means of generating income, was dishonest. Such actions can serve to make fundraising for disability-related causes more difficult.

I suppose that, armed with the above background information, most investigators would feel that it was job done and pass the information and evidence to the defence team. However, I was not satisfied that we had done enough. I could still hear the words of the doubters and the media ringing in my ears: Investigators hired to dig up dirt on the complainants – or, to use their term, victims.

So, it was not job done.

Several people had provided us with a lot of good background information, so it was now time to find some solid stand-alone evidence that could be used in court.

Over the years I have given evidence in front of a jury on many occasions, and I have listened to numerous cases before a jury. This experience and working closely with learned men, such as Stephen Vullo QC, meant that I was aware of how a jury of 12 people can think very differently from each other. There was always a danger that, if too much bad character evidence was disclosed, some members of the jury would sympathise with the complainant and start looking at them as a victim. The actual real evidence could be lost, and the verdict might go against the accused.

I knew that Stephen Vullo QC expected far more, so it was my job to find out if other evidence was out there to find.

My investigations moved from background bad character evidence on to the radio broadcast at the hospital. This required a site visit and seeking the co-operation of the hospital officials to allow us to inspect the room from where the programme featuring Rolf Harris was broadcast. We received full co-operation from the officials at the hospital. If there was still a sour taste in my mouth resulting from the appalling attitude of the employment agency that managed the two carers assigned to Jane, and whom she subsequently accused of assaulting her, it soon dissipated and my faith in human nature was restored.

During the conversations my team and I had with the hospital it was made clear that they would not take sides on this matter but, in the interests of justice, they were prepared to cooperate with both the prosecution (police) and the defence (investigators) and assist where possible. No-one can ask for more than this. If others in the UK followed this lead, there would be far fewer injustices.

The room where the alleged assault occurred in 1977 was no longer being used as a hospital radio studio. However, the staff member who assisted us knew the room when it had been used for this purpose, and he was able to describe it as it was in 1977.

The room is now being used as a counselling suite. I was surprised at just how small it was. It is located on the ground floor opposite the lifts, and although there have been recent cosmetic changes to the inside of the room, basically it remains the same size.

The internal measurements of the room confirmed that at the time of the alleged incident it would have been approximately 14ft long by 9ft wide. This is about the size of a typical single bedroom. There was only one door into the room. Inside was a mixing desk, a round table with chairs and a cupboard that was used as a record library.

Enquiries confirmed that at the time of the alleged assault there were three people inside this room: Jane, the technical sound engineer who I will refer to as Peter, and Rolf Harris. Rolf was met by Peter and told where to park, and then he was taken into the studio. Peter assisted Rolf with his luggage, which included a didgeridoo and a wobble board.

With the assistance of a retired BBC music producer, who in 1977 was a sound engineer and knew the equipment Peter had been using, I established that there would have been nothing blocking Peter's view of Rolf and Jane, who were seated a few feet from him at the round table. Even with light background music playing, Peter would have been able to hear anything that was being said between Rolf and Jane. Therefore, if anything such as Jane described had occurred, Peter would have been aware of it. Jane claimed that she had cried out at one point during the alleged assault.

Our research located not only the recording of the show in 1977 but also comments Jane had once made in a media interview.

I have read the transcript of the audio tape of the broadcast, which lasted over an hour. All three participated, with Peter describing the wobble board and digeridoo to Jane and commenting on various matters throughout. There is no question that Peter would have been fully aware of anything untoward going on in the studio. If Rolf had sexually assaulted Jane, Peter would have had to have seen it.

There was nothing that suggested the three participants were not having fun on the show and there was lots of laughter. It appears that Jane enjoyed her meeting with Rolf, as she revealed in an interview that she gave years later.

This extract is from the interview referred to above.

*"There was one time when I managed to get Rolf Harris to do a programme with me, and he got me playing the 'digeridoo' and he did interviews with, sorry, autographs for the patients, and they'd come down and get his autograph, and all that kind of thing, and we had this wonderful bit, where he was telling us about the story of the record, Two Little Boys, and he's got this Aboriginal gentleman, who's singing and talking the words of Two Little Boys, over the telephone line, to Rolf, from Australia, and what we managed to, was feed in exactly the music, so that you got the man's voice, and the music of Two Little Boys, playing in absolute sync. And I think that was a, a brilliant piece of radio broadcasting, and I'm really chuffed about that, 'cause it worked so well".*

For clarification, the Aboriginal man Jane refers to as singing and talking the words of 'Two Little Boys' over the telephone was on one of the tapes that Rolf had brought to the studio with him. It was not a live telephone call at the time of the broadcast.

Armed with the evidence my team of investigators and I had uncovered, I felt far more comfortable with this investigation. Even though the evidence we gathered was disclosed to the prosecution, Jane was still called to testify. Why this occurred I do not know, but it soon became clear that the prosecution and the police had not re-interviewed Jane and/or kept her informed of the new evidence we had uncovered that would severely undermine her complaint.

# THE TRIAL

Jane's imparting of her evidence in court was not the solemn affair that one normally associates with a courtroom. While one can appreciate that most people are not familiar with giving evidence, and it is often given with a cautious or nervous tone, Jane invoked God – loudly – and, once into her stride, rambled on, unable to respond to visual signals to stop.

But it seems that Jane thought she was on safe ground, as when Peter's name came up, she confidently informed the court that he would be 'dead by now' as he had been overweight. She was then told that Peter had been located and he was very much alive. In fact, he was the next witness on.

The revelation that Peter was alive was just too much for the over-confident Jane. She turned towards where the jury was seated and shouted, "Ladies and gentlemen of the jury, I swear to God that I am telling the truth." She was clearly rattled. The jury sat in stunned silence looking at her.

When Peter gave his evidence, he told the court that nothing untoward had occurred in the studio and he had neither heard nor seen any of the things that Jane had alleged.

None of the bad character evidence we had gathered was presented to the court and Stephen Vullo QC decided that no other defence witnesses needed to be called. This was a skilful move on his part because there was no need to risk alienating any of the members of the jury by pointedly cross-examining a severely disabled woman. She had self-destructed and by now everyone in the courtroom, including the jury, knew the complaint was false.

On 8th February 2017 Rolf Harris was found not guilty on this charge.

# THE MOTIVE

What was Jane's motive for accusing Rolf Harris of indecently assaulting her?

One didn't have to look far to find a likely motive for the allegation. Jane's multiple disabilities meant that she was reliant on carers. Although the local authority was meeting some of the costs, when other factors were taken into account, she was finding it difficult to make ends meet.

My own view is that having been buoyed by the previous out-of-court settlements, Jane realised that she had nothing to lose by making further allegations that might lead to substantial compensation payments, not to mention the financial windfall she stood to receive by selling her story to the media.

This would go a long way towards making her life more comfortable. When Rolf Harris – with whom she had enjoyed 'a brilliant piece of radio broadcasting' many years ago – became headline news for all the wrong reasons, the jackpot was in sight.

Had we not been given the opportunity to complete a very extensive investigation, Rolf's lawyers would have had to rely on the police investigation, which had its limitations, and I am sure he would have been wrongly convicted.

# CHAPTER 6
# SATURDAY SUPERSTORE

S aturday Superstore was a children's television series comprising 142 episodes that was broadcast on BBC1 from 1982 until 1987. It was centred around an imaginary department store. The studio presenters were Mike Read and Sarah Greene, with Keith Chegwin as the roving reporter outside the studio.

Each week there were different guests. Various departments within the store were featured, for example the sports department, the fashion department, and the cafeteria. Children were invited to phone in and speak with the guests, whereupon gifts from various departments within the store were given away.

Children could apply to be in the studio audience, which gave them the opportunity to meet the presenters and their guests.

A woman now in her early fifties alleged that she was indecently assaulted by Rolf Harris when he was a guest on the show. She claimed that this occurred in 1983, when she was 13 years of age. Count 5 at Rolf Harris's second trial resulted from this allegation.

The programme of interest was recorded and shown on 31st December 1983 – New Year's Eve. The woman who made the allegation has anonymity, so I will call her Naomi Smith.

Naomi said there were eight children from the close where she lived who had attended this episode of Saturday Superstore. The trip had been arranged by one of the boys who also lived there. (For overseas readers who might be unfamiliar with the term, a close is a residential street without through access, also known as a cul-de-sac.) There were adults in attendance, although she could recall the surname of only one male adult.

The show was being recorded at the BBC studios in White City, London. Naomi was in the audience with her sister, who was older by two years, some other children from the close, and school friends.

There were breaks in the filming during which the hosts and celebrities would talk to the children. Naomi had forgotten her autograph book, so she used some scraps of paper for autographs, which included an autograph from Rolf Harris. She testified in court that at a later date she had glued the autographs she had collected that day into her autograph book.

During the morning Rolf was mixing with the children on and off, entertaining them and drawing with them. Naomi was included in the drawing group that Rolf was involved in, as she was interested in art. She had a few conversations with Rolf, as did the other children.

At midday they went to the Green Room, where drinks and light food had been laid on for the children, guests, and celebrities. Naomi said she recalled the Green Room as being not very big – it was 18 feet long by 12 feet wide – and she remembered thinking, 'It's not green.' She went to the Green Room with her sister. Celebrities, including Rolf Harris, were coming and going from the room.

Naomi testified that whilst her sister was talking to another attendee, she went up to the table to get a can of drink. According to her account, Rolf came over and stood next to her. He was on her right and there was a wall to her left. It was then that she alleged that Rolf slid his right hand under her breast and said, "Do you often get molested on a Saturday morning?"

Naomi said it was her right breast that he had touched, in a kind of cupping manner, over the top of her clothing. She said that she was fairly well developed and was wearing a bra and that this was the last thing she had expected to happen. She didn't really know what to do. She couldn't move and she was in shock.

According to Naomi, Rolf left quite quickly afterwards. Although there were people milling about, she could not recall anyone standing as close to her as Rolf had, even though her sister was nearby.

Initially, Naomi said she had told her sister that Rolf Harris had touched her inappropriately. However, during the trial, when both Naomi and her sister were cross-examined, it transpired that Naomi had not told her sister at the time, nor in the intervening years. She had told her that Rolf Harris had said something to her, but that was all. Her sister agreed under cross-examination that she had been told by Naomi that Rolf Harris had touched her only after the complaint had been made to the police, over 30 years later.

They left the studios about half an hour to an hour after this alleged incident. Naomi said she could not recall seeing Rolf Harris again. When they arrived home, she told her parents what she claimed Rolf had said to her. Her sister played it down and said what Naomi was telling them was wrong. Her parents took her sister's word for it. As they have both since died, there was no way of verifying if such a conversation ever took place.

Naomi said that over the ensuing years she had spoken about the incident involving Rolf Harris 'fairly constantly'. She said that whenever he appeared on TV she told people about the incident and what she alleged Rolf had said to her. She told her husband and others but she did not consider telling the police because the reaction she got from everyone was of sheer disbelief. If her friends did not believe her, the police wouldn't believe her either.

What she did not tell anyone, until after she had made the complaint to the police in 2014, was that Rolf had touched her. All she had ever said was that she thought he was a pervert and that he had said something to her that she didn't like, which was asking her if she had ever been molested on a Saturday morning.

## SUPPORTING WITNESSES

The police called Naomi's husband and her sister as witnesses to support her allegation. However, all they were able to do was tell the court that Naomi had referred to Rolf as a pervert because he had made the 'molesting' comment to her.

## INVESTIGATION

As with all investigations, there is a lot more evidence gathered than the legal team will use in a court case. The QC will make the final decision on the day of the trial as to what evidence is used, so when I carry out an investigation I do not know what evidence will be selected. When I work with Stephen Vullo QC he usually provides me with more definitive targets to keep me in the know, but even then he plays his cards close to his chest and only he and his court legal team know what evidence will be used for the defence case.

According to the reports made available to the court, the Green Room was 18 feet long by 12 feet wide. It was set up for a lunch buffet, with tables for the food and drink and seating for the guests and celebrities. The size of the room meant that there wasn't a lot of room for too many people at one time, so they were all close to each other. There were others in the room and, given that it was the lunch time break, one would expect the room to be full. It seems unlikely that the alleged assault or what Naomi claimed that Rolf had said to her would have gone unnoticed.

One thought that played on my mind during this investigation was whether in a crowded room Rolf did bump into Naomi and she became wedged between him and the wall. Perhaps he may well have said something similar to what she claims, but as a joke, and as a precocious 13-year-old she took it to mean something more sinister. That could explain why her sister was so dismissive.

It should be noted that that the term 'molested' has more than one meaning. Current usage relates to sexual abuse or assault. However, there is another meaning, which is now dated, that refers to pestering or harassing someone in an aggressive or persistent manner.

It seems likely that if Rolf did use this word, he would have meant it in the old-fashioned context, albeit with an element of humour thrown in, given his age at the time. The Latin and Old French origins of 'molest' have no connection whatsoever to sexual assault: they translate as 'to annoy' or 'to cause trouble to'.

Some of those who had attended the Saturday Superstore event, who at the time were young teenagers, commented that Rolf had sometimes acted in a way that would have appealed more to a younger audience – though to be fair, most of the viewers would have fallen into that category. It was also ascertained that the type of comments he made fitted the description of what those who know him refer to as 'Rolfisms'.

Our job as investigators was to ascertain if Rolf did make such a comment to Naomi and, if so, whether it had been taken out of context. We were of course also looking for corroborative evidence for her allegation that Rolf had assaulted her by placing his cupped hand on her breast, over her clothing. My team and I were instructed to investigate the integrity of the evidence being provided by Naomi and the prosecution witnesses.

By far the most difficult and lengthy part of our investigation was identifying and locating the other people who had attended Saturday Superstore with Naomi on the day that she alleged Rolf had assaulted her. Naomi had provided very sketchy information on the others who were there. One might be forgiven for suspecting that this was deliberate as she had continued to live in the close for 12 years after this visit to Saturday Superstore in 1983.

## ATTENDEES

In her evidence Naomi said that there were about eight children from the close where she lived who were at Saturday Superstore. There were also three adults. The evidence later provided to the court established that the live audience consisted of around 30 children who were accompanied by an undisclosed number of adults. Most of the attendees were located and interviewed. So were the presenters.

There is no need to identify any of the attendees, as this would not add anything of value, and it could lead inadvertently to the revealing of the real identity of Naomi. Below I will summarise some of the comments made by the attendees, presenters and adults who were at the filming of Saturday Superstore on this day in 1983.

### Presenters

None of the presenters had seen or heard anything inappropriate or untoward.

### Parents

The father of two of the children present recalls Rolf showing them to the Green Room after the show and getting into the lift with them. He recalls thinking that Rolf was a perfect gentleman. He heard no allegations about Rolf at the event, on the way home or at any subsequent time.

None of the other adults recalled hearing any complaints about Rolf, and they all said it was a most enjoyable day.

## Children

Naomi and the children who attended Saturday Superstore were all in their mid-to-late forties when Naomi first made her complaint in 2014.

The man who had organised the trip to Saturday Superstore was 15 years old in 1983. He had been doing work experience at the BBC and was told that he had to bring along 15 other children, as this was the minimum number required to get an invitation to the filming. He arranged to bring eight from the close where he lived. The others were from the school they all attended. He invited Naomi and her sister, as they were friends who lived in the close, and he also took along his 11-year-old brother.

At the time the complaint was made he was in his late forties so, like the others, he had to call on his distant memory to remember what had happened over 30 years previously. To make it even harder for him he did later work at the BBC, where he met many entertainers, so the Saturday Superstore event was not exactly imprinted on his memory.

When we finally located and interviewed him we were surprised, as were the defence team, to learn that he had already been interviewed by the police. He told us that he had provided them with a signed statement. He was able to confirm only that the event did take place and that he had arranged it. Other than this his memory was vague, though he had certainly never heard anything bad about Rolf Harris.

The police are required by law to disclose to the defence the names of people they have interviewed and taken statements from. Sadly, they do not always comply and in this case there was no excuse for such behaviour. This man was a key witness owing to the fact that he had arranged the event and invited all the children. He told us that he was reluctant to become involved and, had he known before that he did not have to speak with the police, he wouldn't have. He made it quite clear that he wanted nothing to do with the matter. The Crown Prosecution Service chose not to use him as a witness.

The younger brother of the teenager who had arranged the event was 11 years old in 1983. At the time the complaint was made he was 45 years of age. He said that he recalled Rolf Harris sitting next to all the children in the audience area. He actually sat on Rolf's knee when Rolf was chatting to them. They all received goody bags and were very happy. He found Rolf to be charming, fun, engaging and very personable. He had never heard of anything inappropriate happening between Rolf and Naomi, who he knew because she lived in their close. He was called as a police witness for the sole purpose of confirming that Rolf did attend the event.

A close friend of the young man who organised the trip was also around 15 years old in 1983. He said he had never heard of anything inappropriate happening at the event. He remembered Rolf Harris being at the filming of Saturday Superstore. Rolf had his wobble board with him and he sang a song.

One of the women from the close who attended Saturday Superstore said she did not recall anything untoward happening. She remembered Rolf being in the lift with them after the filming. She found him to be a pleasant person.

A man who was in his mid-teens at the time said he was living in the close and knew Naomi. He saw nothing of, and heard nothing about, the alleged incident. He considered Rolf to be a lovely person and he believed the allegations were 'a load of crap'. It was his belief that Naomi 'saw money signs'. He said that during one of the breaks in filming, Rolf had all the children marching to the lift singing. It was a great day.

Another woman said she was one of the children from the close who went to Saturday Superstore. She saw nothing untoward and recalled that Rolf Harris was fun. She remembered being in the lift with him.

A woman who was part of the group said she remembered bumping into Rolf Harris. He was joking around and making funny noises. When he took them into the lift he used his arms to make sweeping gestures to usher them all in. He was friendly and entertaining. She added that she knew Naomi and her sister and described Naomi as being one of the 'tough nuts' at school. She described her as a bully and said she had been a bit scared of her.

In the opinion of the defence team, this was one of the weaker counts faced by Rolf. There were no witnesses to the alleged assault, it was not mentioned to any of the other attendees in the train on the way home and no such incident was discussed between them at any later date.

Over 30 years later, when hearing about the allegation made by Naomi, there were seeds of doubt raised by others who had attended the event about the possibility of there being a financial motive behind the allegation.

Of all the people traced and interviewed – film crew, presenters and attendees – only Naomi and her sister recalled anything about an alleged incident. Even then Naomi had told her sister only that Rolf had made a comment to her about being molested on a Saturday morning and she thought he was a pervert. Naomi did not tell her sister that Rolf had indecently assaulted her.

Over 30 years on, Naomi, who was now in her mid-forties, was far more tuned in to the business of making a complaint. She had a job as a media manager. Part of her job was to deal with communications and public relations, and to manage a busy press office.

From an investigative point of view, all our enquiries were complete. We had located a large number of people, which had been achieved mainly through canvassing Naomi's former neighbours and we had found no-one who had been told of the assault. The picture that formed was of an event where children and teenagers were entertained by Rolf Harris. It was vintage Rolf, with him singing, playing his wobble board, drawing, lining them up and making funny animal noises and the like. The kids loved it.

It seems that there was only one among them who took exception to his fun and jokes, and she branded him a pervert. It was this type of attitude that had allowed an overzealous prosecutor at Rolf's first trial to present him to the jury, and indirectly to the public through media reports, as a Jekyll and Hyde character.

The investigative process was complete, and it was now over to Rolf's defence team, led by Stephen Vullo QC.

## THE TRIAL

The timeline leading to Naomi's complaint to Operation Yewtree revealed the following:

Rolf was convicted at his first trial on Monday, 30th June 2014 and was sentenced on Friday, 4th July 2014. The *Daily Star* posted an article on Monday, 7th July 2014 stating that Rolf's 'victims' (their description) could get £200,000 in compensation.

At midday on that same day, Naomi sent an email to Operation Yewtree in which she alleged that Rolf Harris had indecently assaulted her in 1983.

In her evidence Naomi tried to play down her public relations/media manager position, which required her to have up-to-date knowledge of local and national news. Her protestations under cross-examination by defence counsel regarding having only limited knowledge of what had happened at Rolf's first trial, along with all the adverse publicity that had surrounded it, made her account even less believable. If, as she alleged, she was a victim, then one would certainly have expected her to have been interested in the progress of the first trial.

Rolf's autograph was a contentious issue in at least two of the other charges that he faced, and this charge was no different.

It was established through the testimony of others who attended Saturday Superstore that Rolf signed autographs for them at the end of the filming, when they were in the Green Room following the buffet lunch, and shortly before they went home. Naomi received an autograph from Rolf, so if the assault had occurred in the Green Room, as she alleged, it would have occurred shortly before he had signed the autograph for her.

It appears that even though Naomi was traumatised and shaken, according to her testimony, she still had the presence of mind, and desire, to collect Rolf's autograph. When Stephen Vullo QC asked her about this, her memory seemed to desert her, as her reply was that she had no recollection of when she obtained the autograph. She added that she did not have an autograph book with her, so she presented Rolf with a piece of paper, on which he signed his autograph. She said that she later stuck it in her autograph book with the others she obtained whilst at Saturday Superstore. The autograph book had no other signatures in it – only those from the Saturday Superstore event.

Despite claiming that she had been indecently assaulted by Rolf, and being left traumatised and shaken, she still took his autograph home and pasted it into an autograph book, which she kept for the next 30 years.

Asked why she would keep a memento of something that had left her traumatised and shaken, she answered that she was quite confused after the incident and the reaction from other people made her think it wasn't quite as serious as it was. It was part of the day, so she kept it.

There are thought-provoking parallels between Chapter 3 – *Bold as Brass*, Chapter 4 – *The Rolf-a-roo* and now Chapter 6 – *Saturday Superstore*, namely that the complainants all decided to keep Rolf's autograph. Whilst this was useful in being able to convince the police that they had had contact with Rolf so many years previously, no-one questioned them as to why they would want to keep anything that had been given to them by a man who they claimed had indecently assaulted them.

No-one, that is, until Stephen Vullo QC asked this question. All three of them floundered when asked. Not one of them could provide a logical and reasonable explanation.

Naomi was no shrinking violet. Those who knew her said they would have expected her to have said something at the time of the alleged assault. Add to this the timing of the complaint – on the same day as the *Daily Star*'s '£200,000 in compensation' headline – and it is no wonder that some members of the jury were satisfied that the charge against Rolf had not been proven.

The jury could not reach a verdict so Judge Alistair McCreath dismissed the jurors and ordered a retrial, with a new jury, which would focus on the undecided counts.

At the retrial, the same impasse was reached. This time the Crown Prosecution Service decided that they did not have any more evidence to offer and they advised the judge that they would not be pursuing the case.

On 30th May 2017, Judge Deborah Taylor formally found Rolf Harris not guilty of indecently assaulting Naomi Smith. He was also found not guilty on the other three counts.

## POSTSCRIPT

So, what did happen in the Green Room after the filming of this episode of Saturday Superstore in December 1983?

The verdict was that Rolf Harris did not indecently assault Naomi Smith. Everyone, except Naomi, and possibly her sister and husband, accepted this. But did Rolf inadvertently say or do something that triggered the attitude that Naomi appears to have adopted towards him? Something that left her, without conscience, to pursue a conviction against him over 30 years later, which – if he had been found guilty – would then have allowed her to claim compensation?

Or was the fact that she had met Rolf Harris simply convenient in terms of launching a compensation claim – as was the case for the disabled complainant, Jane Hatfield.

I did mention earlier that I wondered if Rolf might have made the comment to Naomi, "Do you often get molested on a Saturday morning?" albeit as a throwaway remark broadly consistent with the banter of the times and with no sexual intent.

When giving her evidence Naomi said that the children were dressed up for the occasion and she wore a shirt with epaulettes. It also came out in court that Naomi and a group of other children, including her sister, were in a lift with Rolf, at which point they were all laughing and joking. Furthermore, it was pointed out that the shirt she was wearing had a large rope tassel on it. It was suggested by defence counsel that Rolf may have pulled at this and possibly commented, "Do you often get molested on a Saturday morning?"

This is the type of comment that Rolf would have made back in the 1980s, when such comments were generally considered to be more acceptable than they are now. Naomi's answer to the suggestion that Rolf might have pulled at the rope tassel on her shirt was that she did not remember being in a lift with Rolf Harris.

If Rolf did say to Naomi, "Do you often get molested on a Saturday morning?" and we have only her word for it that he did say this to her, is this an indecent assault? Furthermore, did it warrant him being prosecuted over 30 years later, for which the not inconsequential financial burden was borne by the taxpayer?

## CATCHPHRASES

As with many good past and present entertainers, Rolf had his trademark catchphrases and through these he created his own identity. One well-known phrase when painting was, "Can you tell what it is yet?" This was probably the best known of all of them.

# 'ROLFISMS'

I have listed below various 'Rolfisms' and mannerisms that those close to him came to know well. These were put together by the women who were instrumental in managing his career over the years. No-one outside of the family got to know him better than they did.

He always likes to make people feel good about themselves.

He often pays people compliments to give them confidence.

He looks at everything from a creative perspective.

If someone is wearing a good colour, he picks up on it straight away and tells that person.

If someone is standing where the sunlight catches their hair, he will often take a photo of that person bathed in that light or with a shadow across their face, contrasting with the background. He would say to that person "You should always travel with that light around you all the time."

He would frequently take photos of people, wherever he was. As a passenger being driven to his various work destinations, he would often take photos from the car. Many of these photos have been the inspiration for his paintings of real-life scenes.

Rolf loved giving women compliments. They would openly giggle, flirt, throw themselves at him, show excitement, express delight, and laugh, loving the attention. What Rolf would say was almost 'scripted' to him, knowing the reactions he used to see from everyone.

Rolf would often kiss a woman on the back of her hand or arm when he was introduced. He did it in a fun and joking way, and the reaction was amusement and delight. A not uncommon reaction was for the woman to say, "I'm never washing my hand or arm again!"

The following are examples of some of Rolf's throwaway comments. These would be said in front of anyone who happened to be present, including his wife Alwen, other family members or friends, or people he had just met. They would always be well received and were often met with a laugh:

"Do you know how attractive you are?"

"Do you know you are very attractive to the older man?"

"Gosh ... don't you look stunning in that colour!"

"Stay right where you are! You should always stand in that light."

"Gosh ... you're looking good today!" or "Don't you look good today!" (These were often said by Rolf when he was on the phone.)

"That's a lovely jacket. Would you like me to help you off with that?" People would react by laughing and replying, "Yes, please!" or "No thanks." If he met a fan he would often say, "Don't you look good in that jacket/top/blouse!" which was said to get a laugh.

"Have you ever been molested on a [for example, Saturday morning]?" which was said to get a laugh and in front of other people.

These were standard old vaudeville comedy lines and a reflection of Rolf's decades-long 'routine' as an entertainer.

"Has anyone told you how good you look today?"

"Has anyone told you how attractive you are?"

"Gosh ... what an attractive woman you are! Has anyone ever told you?" Women of all ages would giggle and take it as a compliment.

"Did you know you've got spots/stripes all over your shirt?" This was said in a humorous way to anyone wearing a spotty or striped shirt.

"So delighted to meet you." As Rolf said this, he would sometimes kiss the back of the woman's hand, and he would in a fun and joking way plant exaggerated kisses up her arm to her neck. This would be taken in the spirit in which it was intended, and it did appeal to many women who met Rolf on a night out.

Social attitudes change over time and maybe this would not be so acceptable now. But back in the day it was all part of the fun.

### Eeffing and Eiffing

This was Rolf's name for his vocal trick that involved breathing in and out frantically. He recorded and performed a song by the same name. He would demonstrate this technique all the time, during interviews on TV, radio, at public events, on the phone and so on. Sometimes he would demonstrate it personally to people. If he gave a fan a hug, and if they were shrieking with delight, as often happened, he would sometimes 'eef and eif' in their ear.

### Hot Potatoes

One of Rolf's party tricks was the 'hot potato'. If someone told Rolf that they felt cold, he would offer to give them a 'hot potato', which involved cupping his hands on their back and blowing into them to warm the person up. It was done in the context of fooling around in a social situation. Many willing fans found themselves on the receiving end of a 'hot potato'.

### Stairway to Heaven - Miss Given

During Rolf's live concerts he would sometimes perform his version of the Led Zeppelin classic 'Stairway to Heaven'. During the song he would require an assistant, who he nicknamed 'Miss Given'. The role would entail going on stage with Rolf and his band for a couple of minutes, during which time they would be walking or dancing on the stage to give Rolf his didgeridoo, taking away his wobble board and returning to centre stage after another minute or so. 'Miss Given' would always get a big cheer from the audience. Whoever did this guest appearance enjoyed every minute. Rolf would kiss that person on stage in an exaggerated, comical way.

The participant would be asked before the performance if they were willing to partake in this routine. Rolf's PA and/or stage assistants would arrange this and explain clearly what it entailed. All the women who agreed to do this 'guest spot' were extremely excited at having the opportunity to go on stage with Rolf.

One particular 'Miss Given' occasion stood out. At the Eastleigh Festival in Hampshire, a woman wearing a T-shirt whilst showing her midriff did the spot on the stage. Embroidered lettering on the T-shirt said, 'Dip me in chocolate and feed me to Rolf Harris,' It was difficult to get her off the stage as she was enjoying herself so much and she kept trying to kiss and hug him.

# CHAPTER 7
# THE TATTOO

I n the summer of 2002, a rehearsal studio in central London was being used by a well-known ex-sportsman-turned-commentator to rehearse a set of songs for a charity gig. For ease of reference, I will refer to him as 'the sportsman'. A band made up of five male musicians and a 19-year-old female backing singer, who was just starting out on a professional singing career, had assembled to assist him at the rehearsal.

Twelve years later, the backing singer made a complaint to the police that she had been indecently assaulted by Rolf Harris whilst at the venue. Her complaint was Count 6 of the new charges. As she has anonymity, I will call her Monica Jackson.

On the same day that the sportsman and the band were rehearsing, Rolf Harris was rehearsing in another part of the studio in preparation for an appearance at Glastonbury. About two hours into the practice session, Rolf walked into the studio unannounced and greeted the sportsman, whom he knew.

After greeting the sportsman, Rolf saw Monica. He made a comment along the lines of, "You didn't tell me you had a beautiful girl in the room." Everyone laughed. The mood in the studio was jovial. Monica admitted in evidence that she thought she felt slightly flattered but was also shocked at Rolf's comment.

Monica is taller than average, about five feet nine. On the day of the alleged assault she was wearing white trainers, flared hipster jeans and a crop top.

Rolf walked over to where Monica was standing and stood next to her. He ran his fingers over her lower back as if he were drawing. According to Monica he said, 'You're gorgeous' or 'You're really gorgeous'.

She alleged that Rolf continued to run his fingers over her back from the middle and going lower down, but not to her bottom. He didn't put his hand inside her clothes. His hand was moving and stroking her back in circular, up and down movements. It lasted about five to seven seconds, maybe a bit longer.

According to Monica, when he was doing this he used the word 'gorgeous' and said, "Do you know what I find really attractive about women? If you were to join up the two dimples on a woman's back to her bum crack it would make the shape of a diamond." Then he said, "I find that really attractive, really sexy."

Monica said she started to feel uncomfortable. She was really shocked that it was happening. It was like some sort of weird dream.

When Rolf had finished speaking with Monica, he walked back to the sportsman, spoke with him a bit more and then he left. According to Monica, the other members of the band were just looking on in disbelief and surprise. They didn't say or do anything.

This was the only charge that Rolf Harris faced where there were eyewitnesses present at the time of the alleged offence. The rehearsal carried on for another hour or two. When it finished, Monica went to the local pub with the band. Despite calling her mother to tell her what had happened, Monica didn't contact the police, presumably because she considered the encounter wasn't serious enough to warrant police involvement at that time. However, when Rolf Harris was on trial for other alleged offences 12 years later, she saw the coverage in the media and this led her to decide to tell the police.

## WITNESSES

The police had five witnesses for the trial, namely Monica's parents, who she told about the incident, and three members of the band. Interestingly, the sportsman refused to co-operate with the police and did not want to get involved. He said that he could not remember anything and declined to make a statement.

The three members of the band described Rolf speaking with Monica and touching her back. Although the studio was quiet and everything said could be clearly heard, none of the band members had heard Rolf talk about the dimples on her back, and nor did they hear him use the words 'bum crack'. They did hear him say that she was a beautiful girl.

Monica made her complaint to the police and gave a statement in August 2014. The other prosecution witnesses gave their statements to the police later in 2014, except for her father, who did not make his statement until early 2016.

During our research we found a social media post of interest from Monica's father. This had been posted six days after Rolf had been found guilty at the first trial, and a month before Monica made her complaint. It would appear that he had been following the trial closely as his comment referred to Rolf Harris having 'pissed off' a lot of women and questioning whether he might find 'two little boys' while he was in 'the nick'.

The question arises as to whether Monica might have been encouraged by her father's thinking to lodge this complaint against Rolf.

# INVESTIGATION

The studio where this alleged assault occurred is no longer there. With the help of Rolf's PA, and his diary, we were able to narrow down the date of this allegation to Friday 28th June 2002, two days before Rolf left for Glastonbury. Rolf had a knee operation on 16th May 2002 and had remained in hospital for 7-10 days. On his release he walked with a limp for some weeks and used a walking stick, which he was still using when he performed at Glastonbury.

The sportsman declined to cooperate with the police over this complaint, so I decided not to contact him. This decision was made after much deliberation about his personal situation.

As the band members were potential prosecution witnesses, I could not approach any of them to clarify a point that was concerning me. I could not understand why Rolf would spend time touching someone's bare back with at least six others looking on. Rolf could remember meeting the sportsman but no-one else and certainly not Monica.

My suspicion was that Monica may have had a tattoo on her lower back. To an artist like Rolf this would have been like a red rag to a bull. He would simply not have been able to refrain from commenting on it. Anyone who has ever seen Rolf perform will understand just how passionate he is about drawing and painting.

To an artist, a well-designed tattoo is a work of art. A tattoo would be of interest to a visual and performing artist like Rolf. Whilst tracing one's finger along the lines of a tattoo is still touching, it is not sexual touching. It is an expression of interest and appreciation of the skill of the artist, and in the case of Monica it was initially treated that way.

The problem I had was that no-one had mentioned a tattoo. I would have thought that if Monica had a tattoo on her back where Rolf had traced an outline, she would have mentioned this.

I asked my researchers to check every photo of Monica they could find to see if any of them showed the lower part of her back. This did not produce any results because we could not locate such a photo. I then located the names of venues where she was performing and instructed one of my team to visit each venue to see if Monica was wearing a dress or top that showed the lower part of her back. Unfortunately it was winter, and Monica was not wearing summer attire, so this line of enquiry also failed.

As for the term 'bum crack', none of the people close to Rolf had ever heard him use this term. It is also worth pointing out that not one of the band members had heard Rolf say this.

## THE TRIAL

Count 6, which related to Monica Jackson's complaint, was heard at Southwark Crown Court on 17th January 2017.

As indecent assaults go, it is at the 'less serious' end of the spectrum. I am sure that most people would agree that pursuing through the courts the tracing of a finger on someone's back would be a waste of taxpayers' money. Needless to say, it was still a charge that Rolf was having to answer, 12 years after it allegedly occurred.

I was disappointed that I had not managed to confirm whether Monica had a tattoo on her lower back, as this would have provided a reason as to why Rolf had shown the level of interest that she had alleged.

During the trial the band members who were called gave varying accounts of what they had seen and heard, but there was one point in their evidence that was consistent – Rolf had been seen running his hand or fingers over the middle and lower part of Monica's bare back.

When Monica gave her testimony, she made no mention of a tattoo on her lower back. Then one of the band members, whose testimony was very revealing, was called to the witness box.

The band member testified that he had never met Monica before the rehearsal, which took place in the morning after they had loaded their equipment into the venue. After they had been rehearsing for about an hour, Rolf Harris entered the studio with an assistant. This was not a surprise as it was known he was in the building, and they were aware that Rolf knew the former sportsman with whom they were working.

The band member said that Rolf had a pronounced limp and was using a walking stick or a crutch. His recollection was that Rolf shook hands with the sportsman and then went over to Monica, who was at the microphone, at which point he said something like, "Well, you're a lovely little thing, aren't you?" According to the band member, Rolf patted her on the bottom, although under cross-examination he admitted that Rolf might have touched her lower back.

He was cross-examined by the defence barrister:

Q. *Do you find it difficult to remember the details?*

A. *I find it difficult to remember because I do hundreds of rehearsals, but I have a recollection of this one because I remember clearly him saying, "Look at that lovely tattoo."*

This was the first time anyone had said that Monica had a tattoo on her lower back. It confirmed my suspicions.

Q. *Are you sure it was on the bum that Rolf patted her?*

A. *No, it could possibly have been her very lower back. It wasn't her upper back.*

Q. *You said Rolf Harris didn't appear to think he was doing anything inappropriate?*

A.   *He wasn't trying to hide it. It was certainly mentioned*
     *again that day in a break. It wasn't mentioned in front of*
     *[the sportsman]. It may have been mentioned in the pub.*
     *There was no point where she was demonstrably upset in his*
     *presence. All she said was, "That was weird."*

At the conclusion of the trial the jury could not decide on Rolf's guilt or innocence. The issue wasn't so much that he had touched her back, but whether he had indecently assaulted her by doing so. This impasse meant that no verdict was handed down. Following subsequent deliberations, the Crown Prosecution Service advised the judge that they would not be pursuing a retrial on this count. The judge found that the charge had not been proven and he found Rolf Harris not guilty.

## REASON FOR NOT PURSUING THIS CHARGE

No reason was given by either the complainant or the Crown Prosecution Service for dropping the charge of indecent assault against Rolf. If there had been a retrial Monica would certainly have been questioned about the tattoo and why she had not mentioned this important fact. The disclosure of the tattoo on Monica's lower back came to light only when one of the band members confirmed this. This was after Monica had given her evidence in court. He also claimed to have heard Rolf referring to the tattoo when he was speaking to Monica.

Maybe that is why Monica and the Crown Prosecution Service decided not to seek a retrial?

Following the trial, I understand that pressure was put on Monica from the musician witnesses, who were concerned that their musical careers might be adversely affected, especially after the information about Monica having a tattoo on her lower back was revealed during the trial.

I am sure there will be differing viewpoints on Rolf's actions. Some will argue that no man has the right to touch a woman without her consent, even if he was tracing the tattoo with his fingers briefly whilst admiring it. This is probably why the jury could not decide on this charge.

What is not disputed is that Rolf was a tactile person, and an artist. The evidence leans heavily towards his interest being in the tattoo, which he combined with the usual off-the-cuff 'Rolf flattery' that was part of his make-up.

Many people who have tattoos like to show them off as an art form. It would be interesting to hear how they would react if a world-renowned celebrity artist had shown the same interest in one of their tattoos.

# CHAPTER 8
# GET WITH THE PROGRAMME

C ounts 7 and 8 at the second trial related to an alleged incident at a wrap party at the BBC Television Centre in White City, West London, in May 2004. For those unfamiliar with film industry terminology, a 'wrap party' is a social event held to celebrate the completion of filming.

Rolf Harris and his co-host, Kate Humble, were the presenters of a television programme called Test Your Pet. This programme should not be confused with Animal Hospital, in which Rolf starred between 1994 and 2004. Test Your Pet consisted of two episodes that were broadcast to coincide with National Pet Week, which was held from 1st May to 9th May 2004.

On 2nd July 2014, a complaint against Rolf Harris was made to the NSPCC helpline by a 53-year-old woman. As she has anonymity, for ease of reading I will refer to her as Patricia Morgan.

Patricia Morgan said that in 2004, when she was 42, she was employed by the BBC as a researcher. The county where she was living, and where her BBC office was located, is some distance from London. She said in evidence that she was seconded to work on a TV programme called Test Your Pet.

Patricia stated that her contribution to the programme had been pre-recorded and that she was not involved with the live transmission of either of the two episodes, both of which had been broadcast in early May 2004. She had not attended the first show but had attended the second, which she recalled had been broadcast from a studio at the BBC Television Centre at White City between 7.00 pm and 8.00 pm on a Saturday night. According to Patricia, she had been there for the rehearsal and watched with the studio audience during the live broadcast.

Patricia alleged that she had been indecently assaulted by Rolf Harris shortly after entering the room where the wrap party was being held following the live transmission of the second episode of Test Your Pet. According to her testimony, Rolf Harris had grabbed her breasts and thrust his crotch into her. She said that everyone was gathering for the wrap party, so it was quite crowded and there were between 50 and 100 people in the room. The room being used for the event was a studio that had been set aside for this purpose.

Patricia claimed that there was a screen covering a wall on her left as she entered the studio where the party was being held. Along the line of the screen was a temporary walkway that ran through and past the crowded area. She was in a line of people following this walkway. Between 25 and 30 feet into the room she saw Rolf Harris coming towards her from her right. Almost immediately he pushed her into the screen with his body.

Patricia said that she did not think Rolf had anything in his hands because as he pinned her to the wall his hands grabbed hold of her breasts. His right hand went onto her left breast and his left hand went onto her right breast. She was wearing a bra, but she could not recall what other clothes she was wearing.

According to Patricia the move was deliberate, and not at all an accident. With his hands on her breasts, she maintained, he was pushing them and thrusting his crotch into her. His crotch was coming into contact just above her crotch, and he thrusted twice. She said she was looking him in the face and eye to eye, though she was looking up slightly as he was taller. His expression was blank, vacant even, and she thinks he was wearing glasses, but she was not sure.

Apparently, Rolf did not say anything. She slid away from him and moved away to join the crowd of people. No-one reacted to what had taken place. Patricia described herself as being 5' 2" tall. At the time of the alleged incident, Rolf was 5' 10".

After moving away from Rolf, Patricia saw three women she knew who were in positions of authority within the production team. According to her testimony, when she told them what had happened to her, they all laughed and one of them said, "Oh [Patricia], get with the programme. We make sure that no woman on her own goes into a lift with him."

When Rolf was questioned by the police over this allegation, more than ten years had passed. He said he had a vague memory of doing the programme, but he could not recall many details about it, and he could not bring the format to mind. This was not surprising given his heavy work schedule. Rolf did remember working with Kate Humble on a few programmes and he said they had always got on well.

Rolf could not remember a wrap party after the filming of Test Your Pet, and he certainly did not know Patricia Morgan. He maintained that everything she had said in her statement to the police was totally untrue and a complete mystery to him.

In her complaint Patricia named the three more senior women to whom she had complained shortly after the alleged incident had occurred. The women, along with other people who were members of the production crew, were subsequently located by my team and interviewed.

# INVESTIGATION

The first step in our investigation was to familiarise ourselves with the programme Test Your Pet and then to identify the production crew and anyone else who may have been connected with the programme. IMDb – the Internet Movie Database – is the best open-source research mechanism as this lists the times, dates, and places when the programmes were recorded and broadcast.

**TEST YOUR PET: SYNOPSIS**

> **BBC One London, 1st May 2004 18.00**
> Programme 1 of 2: Synopsis
>
> *Rolf Harris and Kate Humble join an audience of pets and their owners to find out just how smart our animal companions are. Using a series of tasks devised by experts, studio participants – and viewers at home – can gain an insight into their pets' intelligence. There is a comparison of results from across the country in next week's show, plus more on animal IQ on Tuesday to Friday at 4.35pm.*
>
> **BBC One London, 8th May 2004 18.00**
> Programme 2 of 2: Synopsis
>
> *Which animal is best at problem solving? What is the most popular breed of dog? Which animal is Britain's cleverest pet? Rolf Harris and Kate Humble announce the results of a revealing survey carried out last week designed to test the intelligence of your pet and put some of the UK's smartest pets through their paces in the studio.*

When we delved a little further, we discovered that the first episode of Test Your Pet had been filmed in front of a studio audience during the week and transmitted on the Saturday evening. This format was repeated the following week for the second episode. The reason for this was that the show featured several animals and one can never predict how an animal is going to behave or react on live television.

We obtained a copy of the breakdown of the filming schedule for the second episode, as it was after the Saturday night broadcasting of this episode that the indecent assault allegedly occurred. This provided us with some interesting information.

The filming of the second episode of Test Your Pet had not taken place at the BBC Television Centre in White City as had originally been planned, but at Fountain Studios in Wembley. Apparently there had been a clash between Test Your Pet and another production in terms of using the studio, so Test Your Pet was moved.

From the filming schedule we were able to establish the time frame for the second episode. This shows that it was filmed in front of a studio audience on Thursday, 6th May, and that this recording was broadcast on Saturday, 8th May. Patricia Morgan had stated correctly that the show had been broadcast on Saturday, 8th May, but she had understood it to be a live broadcast.

## The Filming Schedule

**Tuesday 4th May 08:00 – 14:00**
Set up of sound rig and lighting rig.

**Wednesday 5th May 08:00 – 20:00**
Completing set up of sound, camera and autocue call.
After lunch, a run through and then a studio stagger through with Rolf, Kate, Tim & Collette.
Rehearse

**Thursday 6th May**
Morning – rehearsals
Afternoon – set up and dress rehearsal

18:30 – 19:00 – audience in
19:00 – 21:30 – recording of show
21:30 – Wrap & Strike

'Wrap' is a word used to signal the end of filming. 'Strike' is a term used for turning on the lights, as one experiences in a cinema when the film has finished.

## SATURDAY 8TH MAY 2004

The second of the two programmes, which had been filmed at Fountain Studios in Wembley, was broadcast at 6.00 pm from the BBC Television Centre at White City. The presenters, most of the production crew and the audience were not involved, as the programme had been recorded two days earlier.

Patricia seemed to be under the impression that the show had been broadcast live in front of a studio audience on the Saturday night, which clearly it was not. She was also under the impression that the filming had taken place at the BBC Television Centre, as had been the case with the first episode, rather than at Fountain Studios.

This threw doubt on how involved she had been in the production of the programme. Her work did not require her to be in London, nor did it require her to be present during the filming. Therefore, she would not have been aware that the location for the filming of the second episode had been changed from the BBC Television Centre in White City to Fountain Studios in Wembley, unless a member of the production team had told her. Similarly, there is no reason to believe that she would have known that the programme had been recorded instead of being broadcast live unless someone had informed her of this.

The next and most obvious phase of the investigation was to interview as many members of the production team as possible. The police had already interviewed some individuals. My team completed these enquiries, while at the same time seeking potential witnesses.

Well over 25 people were interviewed. As it turned out, only one knew Patricia. She could not recall her being at the filming at Fountain Studios in Wembley on Thursday, 6th May. None of the three women to whom Patricia claimed she had reported the alleged incident, at which time she had been told to 'get with the programme', had any recollection of this discussion. The production team had not been required to be at the BBC Television Centre in White City on Saturday, 8th May.

As Patricia was based elsewhere, and a long way from London, it seems that she was not known to most of the production team. Her role did not include being involved with the filming of the programme and this may explain why she was not known. None of those interviewed could remember a wrap party, although one or two seemed to recall having a quick drink and some sandwiches afterwards, which was certainly nothing like Patricia had described. All except one gave glowing reports about Rolf and his behaviour.

The exception was a woman who said that she thought Rolf was a bit creepy, but she also acknowledged that he had never touched her or done anything inappropriate. No-one else had heard of or witnessed Rolf doing anything that gave rise to concern.

Further research reinforced our suspicions that Patricia had not been at the recording in Wembley. We were able to access the expenses, details of transport arrangements and the other logistical data for the programme. Patricia was not mentioned, so if she did travel to London, it was not on the transport provided by the BBC and she was not catered for at either of the two venues.

## ROLF'S SUPPORT STAFF

As this complaint was not as historic as the other allegations made against Rolf in that it related to an alleged event only 10 years earlier, there were more potential witnesses available to interview. This included three particularly important witnesses, who at the time of the filming of Test Your Pet were part of Rolf's support team.

I know that previously I have criticised the handling of cases by Operation Yewtree officers. To the uninitiated, this could be construed as an attack on the Metropolitan Police. Not so, and anyone who knows me would certainly be very clear on that point. In fact, I was head coach of the London Metropolitan Police Rugby Team between 2002 and 2004. I still have my Met Police rugby tie.

I am an avid supporter of the police. What I am highly critical of is the way in which certain police officers, and those retired police officers who were brought in as civilian investigators, conducted themselves whilst they were attached to Operation Yewtree.

In the case of Patricia Morgan, the investigations conducted by Operation Yewtree officers entailed taking a statement from the complainant, speaking with some members of the production team and interviewing Rolf, whom they had identified as their suspect.

If the officers had conducted a truly unbiased and independent investigation, the story provided by the complainant should have been verified with the documentary evidence that was available. Had the Operation Yewtree officers done this they would have discovered what we did. Patricia Morgan could not have been at the BBC Television Centre during the 'live' broadcast on Saturday, 8th May because Test Your Pet had not been broadcast live. Furthermore, the show had been recorded two days earlier at a different venue entirely.

Now, on to the unbiased investigation point I have alluded to.

An entertainer as popular as Rolf Harris was in 2004 would have been surrounded by support staff. Why, then, did the police not speak with any of his staff when they were unable to find anyone in the production team who could verify Patricia's story? Perhaps they did not want to find out that Patricia's story was fabricated, or that she had been mistaken. Or am I being too hard on these officers? Surely, Scotland

Yard officers receive the same training as the rest of the police forces in the UK.

Well, we did what the Operation Yewtree officers should have done. That is, we identified, located and interviewed the three women who were supporting Rolf during the production of this programme.

In 2004 Lisa Ratcliff was an entertainers' agent working with Jan Kennedy, the owner of Billy Marsh Associates. This renowned entertainment agency, based in London, was at that time representing Rolf Harris. In May 2004, when Patricia Morgan was allegedly assaulted by Rolf Harris, arranging Rolf's schedule took up around 90 per cent of Lisa's time.

Lisa, who had been made aware of the allegation, said that she had never heard of Patricia Morgan. However, she did have a good recollection of the programme Test Your Pet as she is a dog owner, and Rolf had two dogs at the time.

On a day-to-day basis it was Lisa's responsibility to deal with Rolf's diary and everything that pertained to his work commitments, which included liaising with production teams and event organisers, coordinating and managing his time, and accompanying him at events and appearances. Rolf had his own diary at home, which often appeared disorganised purely because he had so much work on. Lisa worked from a diary system on her computer in the office, which was detailed and well organised.

Lisa recalled that the first of the two episodes of Test Your Pet was filmed at the BBC Television Centre in White City. This was confirmed by an entry in one of Rolf's diaries that she had located amongst the many files at his home. The diary entry referred to the filming of the second programme having been moved from the BBC Television Centre to Fountain Studios in Wembley. Lisa remembered this but not why the venue was changed. This was an arrangement made by the BBC.

There were three support staff with Rolf at Fountain Studios – Lisa, Jan Kennedy and Rolf's personal assistant at the time, Annette

McQuarrie. Jan and Lisa arrived together between 3.00 pm and 4.00 pm on Thursday 6th May 2004, the day on which the show was to be recorded in front of a studio audience. They were not required beforehand.

I spoke to both Jan and Annette. They verified the account given by Lisa in signed statements that were presented in court. Annette is now living in Australia. She had had no contact in recent years with either Lisa or Jan, so the statement I obtained from her was totally independent and confirmed everything that Lisa and Jan had told me.

In addition to Jan, Lisa and Annette, Rolf's wife Alwen and their two dogs, Summer the poodle and Cadge the Weimaraner, were also there. Summer and Cadge were included as part of the show.

The reason why Rolf always had to be accompanied by at least one of his support staff was to ensure that he was looked after on both a professional and a personal level. Their role was to advise him on his appearance, posture, clothing, hair and so on. They would keep an eye on his energy levels and general wellbeing as studio days can be very exhausting and demanding. He needed rest periods and personal time in his dressing room for a power nap.

In May 2004 Rolf was 74 years old. He had recently returned from a very demanding film shoot in Lapland for the BBC as well as working on another BBC show, Star Portraits. According to Rolf's support staff, his diabetes was causing him some health problems and, as he was a workaholic, he needed to have someone on hand who he could rely on.

People would want to see Rolf, even when he wasn't on set, for production discussions, personal meetings, signing of books and autographs or just to meet him to say hello. Rolf was the type of person who would never say no, so he always needed shielding when he was at the studio.

Jan Kennedy told me that on the night of the filming she walked with Rolf to the set, waited for him to finish filming and then walked him back to his dressing room as quickly as possible. Lisa and Annette gave him a change of clothes and shoes, a cup of tea and some fruit. Alwen and their two dogs joined Rolf in the dressing room. They recall that the production executives popped in to speak with Rolf about the show.

No-one can remember a party after the filming. If there had been some drinks or something to eat, and Rolf had gone along, he would have been accompanied by Jan, Lisa, Annette, Alwen and the two dogs. They are firmly of the belief that this party didn't happen.

Following the conclusion of the filming their main objective was to get Rolf home, as he was very tired. A car was arranged to take Rolf, Alwen and the dogs home to Berkshire. They couldn't remember who the driver was or whether this was a hire vehicle or someone driving Rolf's car. Once Rolf, Alwen and the dogs had left, they were then able to relax and make their own way to their respective homes.

The scenario related by Patricia Morgan just could not have happened. Rolf would not have been on his own without any of the support people. It is inconceivable that no-one in his support team, which included his wife, nor any of the 50 to 100 people that Patricia claimed were at a post-event wrap party, saw the alleged indecent assault. It appears that the only person who witnessed this was Patricia Morgan.

So, yet again, it's back to the criticism of Operation Yewtree. Why could they not have completed the same enquiries that my team and I made? Had they done so there would never have been a trial in relation to this accusation, which came at a significant cost to the taxpayer.

The jury found Rolf Harris not guilty on Count 7 and Count 8, which were the two charges that had arisen from Patricia Morgan's complaint.

# MOTIVE

The question I am sure most readers will ask is why Patricia Morgan came forward with this story about being at the live show and being indecently assaulted by Rolf Harris, when surely she would have known that it could be checked out and found to be a fabrication, or at the very least a case of mistaken identity.

Let us go back to when she made the accusation. As with many of the other complainants she contacted the NSPCC in the first instance – in July 2014, shortly after Rolf had been found guilty on all 12 counts at the first trial. Was she just jumping on the bandwagon? If so, why? And why Rolf Harris?

In the wake of the furore surrounding former DJ Jimmy Savile, gossip about male celebrities was rife. Any celebrity who was known to be tactile risked being a target. My investigations confirmed that Rolf sometimes tended to be a bit enthusiastic when it came to demonstrative acts such as hugging, but not in a sexual way or in a manner that was intended to cause alarm. Most of the women said they loved this affection, but as with everything, there are those who will disapprove, some very strongly.

I realise, of course, that some people are uncomfortable with over-familiarity, especially when it involves physical contact. I cannot blame them for feeling this way. However, an issue that can arise is that what is entirely natural behaviour for some people, in that it is a personality trait, can be interpreted as offensive by others.

I don't consider myself to be a tactile person, but this does not mean that I am incapable of showing affection. I was raised in New Zealand at a time when it was not the done thing to be openly affectionate towards a woman in public. To do so would elicit a negative reaction from the woman involved or, worse still, from her other half.

When I arrived in London in 2000, I would shy away from any woman to whom I was introduced if she leaned forward to hug me or give me a peck on the cheek. Needless to say, this was regarded with some amusement by others, including the rugby team that I was coaching at the time. I just could not get used to this cultural difference and even now, after 21 years of living in England, I am still a bit awkward with it.

I understand therefore how some women might take exception to being given an unexpected bear hug by a celebrity. Others, as I have said before, have said how much they enjoyed Rolf's exuberant displays of affection.

Patricia alleged that she had been told by someone at the BBC that Rolf Harris had wandering hands, so she probably felt safe making this complaint. Rolf had been found guilty on all 12 counts at the first trial and women were being urged to come forward on the basis that "**You will be believed**." Patricia had no reason to think that there would be an in-depth investigation as there had been no evidence of this at the first trial.

I do not know if Patricia intended claiming compensation. This information was not disclosed and would not have been unless Rolf had been found guilty. Once he was found not guilty it would have been far harder for her to make a civil claim given the complete lack of any evidence to support her allegation. She would have struggled to get anyone to take her seriously.

As with all investigations I supervise, I arrange for my research team to complete background checks on persons of interest. Owing to court restrictions on publishing anything that might disclose Patricia's identity, I cannot go any further into what we discovered, as to do so would probably include information that could identify her. However, I can say in a general sense that there were indications that Patricia's life had not been without its difficulties.

My brief was to investigate the strength of the allegation, and my investigations revealed that there was no substance to them, so my team and I had completed our task satisfactorily.

Sadly, once again the basic right of the accused to be presumed innocent until proven guilty was ignored. Rolf had to employ his own investigators to prove that he was innocent of this additional charge that was brought against him by the Crown Prosecution Service.

# CHAPTER 9
# FAKE NEWS

I have deliberately left Count 4 of the second trial, and Counts 2 and 3 of the third trial, to the last. That is because the motive of the woman who made three allegations of indecent assault appeared to differ from that of the others in that money was not her primary objective.

When Rolf Harris said in court at the first trial that he hadn't been to Cambridge until 2010, Jackie Daniels, a journalist and local radio broadcaster, contacted police to say that she remembered him having visited Cambridge in either 1977 or 1978. Rolf had simply forgotten that he had been to Cambridge in the mid-1970s and his legal team at the time had not uncovered anything to place him there. However, Jackie Daniels remembered that he had taken part in Star Games, a television show that had been produced by Thames Television. She brought this to the attention of the police. It seems likely that her motive in doing so was either to put the record straight or to 'prove' that Rolf Harris had lied about not having been to Cambridge – something that was likely to benefit the complainants – or maybe it was a combination of both.

Jackie Daniels is a pseudonym, as are the names given to certain other individuals mentioned in this chapter.

## THE COMPLAINANT

Jackie Daniels went to the police during the first trial. Her evidence formed part of the prosecution case. After the trial had ended, she appeared on television and in newspaper reports giving her views on Rolf Harris's convictions.

One of the complainants at the first trial had alleged that in 1975, when she was 13 or 14, Rolf Harris had indecently assaulted her when she had been working as a waitress to earn pocket money at the filming of the BBC's game show It's a Knockout in Cambridge. This woman has anonymity so I will refer to her as Miss Cambridge.

After Miss Cambridge had given her evidence and it was the turn of the defence, documentary evidence was produced to show that Rolf Harris had been in Toronto, Canada at the time It's a Knockout had taken place, so he was never there. He then made a mistake that many believe led to the jury deciding that he was a liar, by stating under oath that he had not been to Cambridge prior to 2010.

Jackie Daniels claimed that she had not been following the reporting of the trial, even though she was a working journalist. She claimed that it was a family member who had brought to her attention an article in the *Daily Mail* stating that the defence had claimed that Rolf Harris had not been in Cambridge in 1975. She said she knew that he had been in Cambridge, but it was later than 1975. When she checked she found a photo that had been taken at Thames Television's Star Games in 1978, so she contacted the police to advise them that Rolf Harris had appeared as a celebrity on Star Games – three years later, in 1978.

A video of the event was obtained and, sure enough, Rolf Harris was there. The Crown Prosecutor, Sasha Wass, played on this point throughout the trial and managed to convince the jury that Rolf had lied. Furthermore, if he had lied on this important point then his assertion that he had never met Wendy Rosher could not be believed either, and his denials in respect of the other two complainants could not be believed. He should be found guilty.

I will discuss Miss Cambridge in Chapter 12, which covers the first trial. However, one thing is certain: Rolf did not lie. He simply had no recollection of having been to Cambridge prior to 2010. His lawyers in the first trial had completed their own research without using experienced investigators, and they had concluded that Rolf Harris had not been to Cambridge prior to 2010. Rolf was simply stating what he had been told.

It is all very well to have the benefit of hindsight, but many believe that if Rolf had said, "I don't remember being in Cambridge, and my solicitor has told me I was not there prior to 2010", it is highly likely that he would not have been found guilty of this charge.

The first trial finished on 30th June 2014. On 4th July 2014, Rolf Harris was sentenced to a term of imprisonment of five years and nine months.

Three days after advising the police by telephone of the date on which Rolf Harris had been in Cambridge, Jackie Daniels made a statement in which she claimed that she had been indecently assaulted by him. The Crown Prosecution Service decided to add Jackie Daniels' complaint to the new charges. On 9th January 2017, almost three years later, Jackie Daniels' complaint was listed as Count 4 at the second trial.

## THE CHARGE

Jackie Daniels alleged that in 1978 she had attended the filming of a television programme called Star Games, which had taken place at Jesus Green, Cambridge over two consecutive weekends. She said that on one of the days during which it had taken place she had been tasked with looking after Rolf Harris.

Jackie Daniels claimed that, on three separate occasions during the day, Rolf Harris had indecently assaulted her. The first two assaults, she alleged, had consisted of Rolf Harris placing his arm around her and touching her breast. On the other occasion she was joined by Rolf Harris in a taxi, whereupon he touched her inner thigh and then attempted to move his hand up towards her groin before she pushed him away. Rolf Harris was eventually charged with two counts of indecent assault in relation to Jackie Daniels, which included the one that allegedly took place in the taxi.

When she arrived home her father had asked about her day and who she had met. According to Jackie Daniels, she had replied that Rolf Harris was a dirty old man, to which her father said, in reference to the tight jumper that she had worn on the day, "I'm not surprised, in that jumper." Her father had long since died so we were unable to verify that this conversation had taken place. Jackie Daniels did say that she remembered the day as being warm and sunny and she wore a pink fluffy polo neck jumper, jeans and glitzy trainers.

## INVESTIGATIONS

Rolf had no recollection of appearing at Star Games. It follows therefore that he had no memory of ever having met Jackie Daniels. It was only when he was shown the video of Star Games that he recalled the swimming event. Rolf had been a competitive swimmer in his younger days. As a schoolboy in Australia, he had represented Western Australia in swimming, and in 1946 he was the Australian junior backstroke champion.

# WA's Rolf. Harris Wins Title

MELBOURNE, Today: Rolf Harris continued WA's winning sequence in back-stroke swimming events when he swam away with Australian junior back-stroke championship this afternoon in Victorian record time of 80sec.

Percy Oliver in pre-war days was outstanding in the same stroke for the State, and last year Vernon Oliver, his younger brother, won the event. Harris, coached this year by the elder Oliver, carried on the sequence in delightfully smooth style.

Garrick Agnew, WA free-style champion, filled 3rd place.

*From the Australian publication The Mirror, 2nd February 1946. Rolf Harris was 15 when this article appeared.*

During my investigations I discovered that it was not unusual for celebrities to have difficulty in remembering events and places they had visited, unless a visit had been particularly memorable. Their diaries were so full that they could not possibly have been expected to recall an insignificant event 30 to 40 years later.

Michael Aspel was the host of Star Games over the weekends of 1st and 2nd July and 8th and 9th July 1978. When interviewed, Michael Aspel said he remembered being the host of Star Games, which had run for one series in the early to mid-1970s (it was actually the late 1970s). He could not recall the venue for the show, nor could he recall Rolf Harris appearing in it. He had no recollection of most of the other celebrities.

Having memories of places visited is the norm for most people. However, this is not necessarily the case for celebrities, some of whom make hundreds of appearances every year. It is impossible for them to keep an accurate year-by-year tally of every venue at which they have appeared, and often they don't remember more general details such as which cities they visited.

Sue Cook, a former BBC presenter, gave evidence at Rolf's first trial. She could not recall many of the places she had visited. Often, she said, they were loaded onto a coach, taken to the venue and then transported home. Unless she was visiting a place of interest to her, she wouldn't remember many of the towns and cities she visited, let alone when.

Colin Baker, who was later to find fame as Doctor Who, was one of the celebrities who appeared at Star Games. He recalled that he had appeared in Star Games but had no idea where the venue was. He could not remember any specifics about the event, nor Rolf Harris being there. He could not remember ever having met Rolf Harris. He summed up his busy life in much the same way as all the other celebrities we spoke to:

*In my profession, and in my experience, it is not unusual that a person cannot remember the location of where they have made a programme. For example, I was in Houston, Texas last week and*

*I thought I had never been there before, but I was told that I had
in fact been there in 1985.*

It must be very difficult for members of the jury, who may take one
or two trips a year away from their homes and jobs, to understand what
it would be like to be a celebrity who visits hundreds of venues each year
and meets many tens of thousands of people. Everything is arranged
for them – transport, venue, accommodation, performances, interviews
and so on. It is no wonder that they forget many of the cities, towns and
venues where their profession has taken them.

Why then was the prosecution permitted to call Rolf Harris a liar
when he was in exactly the same position as all the other celebrities I
had spoken to? Are they all liars? I think not. Sasha Wass QC, who was
the Crown prosecutor in the first trial, had before her a jury who did
not understand the busy life of a celebrity, and in my view, she took full
advantage of this.

It is stated in the IMDb, the internet movie database, that Rolf Harris
appeared at Star Games on both weekends, but it was finally agreed in
court that he made an appearance only in the final. The evidence to
support this was a written record by the organisers, which read 'Whilst
other members of the theatre team were paid £200.00, Rolf Harris was
paid £100.00, as he only appeared in the final.' The final was held on
Saturday, 8th July 1978 and the grand final on Sunday 9th July 1978.
Witnesses referred to the day on which Rolf was present as the Saturday,
which was the day of the final.

In her evidence Jackie Daniels told the court that in the 1970s she
was attending a secondary school in Cambridge. In either 1977 or 1978
she had put her name down to take part in an event called Star Games.
According to her evidence, there was an advertisement posted on the
sixth form notice board at the school asking for volunteers to help out
at Star Games.

She was selected to take part in the event, which included Radio 1 DJs Peter Powell and Bruno Brooks. She said that she had initially thought that Star Games had been held in June or July 1977 or 1978, but she had found a photo of her at the event and on the reverse of the photo was written the date: July 1978. She continued by saying that the venue for Star Games was Jesus Green, Cambridge – a large public open space with an outdoor swimming pool. There were playing fields and swings, and a nearby pub called the Fort St George.

An important omission in Jackie Daniels' account was the testimony provided by one of her two younger sisters, who was 15 at the time of Star Games. She had also helped at the event – and she gave a different version of how she came to be there.

Her sister said in evidence that their mother had been working for the council at the time on the entertainment and publicity side. She said that her mother had asked her to help, and she acted as a 'fetch and carry' for the celebrities. She would carry their bags, get them a drink and so on. She was not assigned to look after any particular celebrity. She recalled the presenter being Michael Aspel and she also remembered Rolf Harris, the actor and singer Dennis Waterman and the actress Rula Lenska being there. Her mother and her younger sister, who was five at the time, were also at Star Games. She said they were all dropped off and picked up together.

The evidence of Jackie Daniels' sister gave us cause for concern as we wondered why Jackie had not mentioned that her mother and two sisters had also been at Star Games, and that one of her younger sisters had been carrying out the same duties as she had. Her sister had described the role she had been given at Star Games as that of a 'gopher' – in other words, she would have been expected to run errands and perform tasks as directed. The helpers had received their instructions from the officials who had been looking after the celebrities.

Jackie Daniels had left everyone with the impression that she was the only member of her family at Star Games. This was an omission in her evidence, which on its own could be thought of as being along the lines of, "Well, you didn't actually ask me this, did you?" How often have we heard that?

The most obvious person to speak to was Jackie Daniels' mother, but that wasn't going to be easy because Jackie Daniels had told the police that her mother had health issues and was a vulnerable person. In the circumstances the police decided not to approach Jackie Daniels' mother.

There is no record, as far as I am aware, showing that the police asked for a medical certificate to confirm what Jackie Daniels had told them. They just decided not to pursue this line of inquiry.

When the police asked Jackie Daniels for names of possible witnesses, she insisted on contacting the witnesses first, speaking with them and only then providing their contact details to the police. The way in which she appeared to control certain aspects of the police investigation was astonishing. It was something I would never have believed could happen.

In the years leading up to the three Rolf Harris trials there had been considerable media coverage of celebrities who had been accused of historic crimes of a sexual nature. As so many years had passed, there was often little or no corroborative evidence to support the allegations, and people who might have been able to throw some light on them had died. This meant that the police focused on trying to find people who had been told about the alleged assault by the complainant. Whilst this is hearsay evidence, which is usually inadmissible, in cases of indecent assault and other crimes of a sexual nature it is admissible, whether historic or not.

Jackie Daniels had done her homework. She nominated relatives, a business associate, and a friend to provide this evidence. This left it open for her to contact her nominated witnesses and speak with them before they were interviewed by the police, so one might reasonably assume that they were primed and ready.

# THE TRIAL

When giving her evidence at the second trial, Jackie Daniels presented herself as a confident person who was in control of the situation. Her job as a radio presenter and journalist meant that she was accustomed to delivering presentations to an audience, so she did not appear the slightest bit fazed by having to face a judge and jury. But as her testimony progressed, and under skilful cross-examination by Stephen Vullo QC, cracks started to appear.

It soon became apparent that the version of events she had given to the police in 2014 had potentially been exaggerated to some extent. Had a hug from Rolf, who as a tactile person had a tendency to hug people, turned into an accusation of groping her breast?

In her evidence, Jackie Daniels said that Rolf Harris had spent a lot of time at Star Games playing to the crowd. Whenever he saw a group of people he would approach them, sign autographs and play the fool, which often included making physical contact by hugging people.

Jackie Daniels alleged that she had been hugged by Rolf when he had been speaking to her in front of the crowd and that this had made her feel uncomfortable. She told the court that she began to form the view that he wasn't the man she thought he was in terms of his show business profile.

When she first made her complaint to the police, she said that Rolf had put his arm around her after an official had come over to hurry him up, as he had spent far too long mixing with admirers.

She alleged that Rolf Harris had told the official 'that it wasn't [Jackie's] fault' and had given her a hug. She said that his hand had brushed against the side of her breast. According to Jackie this had happened to her on other occasions with men, and they had been apologetic and embarrassed. Rolf Harris hadn't been, and this had made her feel quite peculiar as 'he was an old man' – even though at the time he was only 48.

She alleged that there had been another occasion when Rolf had put his arm around her. This time, she said, he had cupped her breast with his other hand.

Despite this apparent unwanted attention, Jackie Daniels claimed that she had remained with Rolf Harris for the rest of the day. She said that it had been later in the day that she had accompanied him in a taxi to the swimming pool area. When she gave her initial statement to the police, she alleged that when they had been sitting in the back seat of the taxi Rolf Harris slid over to her and told her that she had worked so hard and she was lovely. When he said this, he put his hand on the inside of her knee. As his hand was sliding up her thigh, she pushed it away. She said that she had been wearing jeans and his sweaty hands had left marks on them. The jeans had to be thrown away.

This rang a few alarm bells. Even if someone with sweaty hands were to touch someone's jeans briefly, they are not going to leave sweat marks to such an extent that the jeans are permanently damaged.

As it happened, by the time this matter got to court her story had changed. The hand on the thigh became, "He said something about me being irresistible and he put his left hand on the inside of my right knee. I put my legs together and he forced his hand up between my legs until it made contact with my crotch. I pulled it off and I told him to fuck off."

Her performance on the witness stand involved her showing the judge and jury how Rolf had allegedly groped her breasts. This led one woman who had been in the gallery to comment later, "I still have PTSD from watching her in the witness box, grabbing both breasts and jiggling them up and down to the amazement of the startled old judge."

It didn't work so well in the retrial – the third trial – when the judge was a woman.

I suspected that Jackie Daniels had exaggerated her account. The evidence did not support her claim of having been put in charge of a celebrity for the day. This description of what had been involved in her volunteering role seemed to have been put forward to explain why she would have been in Rolf's company long enough for him to have committed the assaults that she alleged.

Jackie Daniels contacted relatives, business associates and a friend to support her allegations, but all they could tell the court was what she had told them, namely that Rolf had groped her, and she thought he was a dirty old man. She admitted in court that the first time she had disclosed to her supporting witnesses what Rolf had allegedly done to her at Star Games in 1978 was when she had made a statement to the police on 27th May 2014 during a three-hour interview at her home.

Judge McCreath asked her about the depth of discussions she had had with her friends, relatives and business associates before she had given the police their names and contact details. She admitted to pre-warning them and telling them, "The police may come and see you because of something I said to you about Rolf Harris. Are you happy for them to do that?" She added that she had explained to them that the police were looking for corroborating evidence, but she said that she had not discussed any details with them.

At the conclusion of the second trial the jury was undecided on this count, as well as on three of the others. The judge dismissed the jury and ordered a retrial, which was scheduled to commence on 15th May 2017.

Despite having just over three months to prepare for the third trial, which was not a lot of time considering how much work had to be done, it was to our advantage that only three of the seven charges from the second trial were to be re-heard. Rolf had been found not guilty of the charges laid in respect of three of the complainants, and the other complainant whose charge would have been brought forward to the third trial had decided not to proceed. However, the Crown Prosecution Service did add an additional charge of indecent assault in relation to Jackie Daniels' complaint, making a total of four charges for Rolf to answer at the third trial.

Meanwhile, there had been a reshuffle at the law firm that was representing Rolf, with solicitor Dan Berke taking back control. This allowed me to have direct contact with Dan Berke and Stephen Vullo QC. Most of the difficult and tedious research work had been completed prior to the second trial and we also had the evidence transcripts from the second trial to refer to. The transcripts of evidence, which are the typed records of the testimonies given by all the witnesses, the complainants, and the accused, were useful as they identified some further lines of inquiry that needed to be explored.

## SCHOOL FRIENDS

It seemed unlikely that Jackie Daniels had been the only girl from her school who had volunteered to be a helper at Star Games. She had not disclosed that her sister had been helping at Star Games, and she had said that only one of her friends had been at Star Games and that this friend had died in 1999.

Stephen Vullo QC, in cross-examination, questioned her about other people she knew who had attended Star Games. She was also reexamined by the prosecutor Jonathan Rees QC.

**Stephen Vullo QC (Defence)**

Q  *In respect of other potential people. You attended this event, I think, with other girls from your school?*

A.  *One girl from my school and some girls from the local convent who were in my friendship group.*

Q  *Okay. Did you ever give the police the names of any of those people?*

A.  *No.*

*Q  Are you in contact with any of those people?*

*A.  No, no.*

*Q  Would you remember any of the names of those people if you were asked to recall them?*

*A.  Well, the only one who – it was my best friend [name redacted], who didn't work but came to the event a couple of times while I was there, and unfortunately, she died in 1999. The other girls – I can't really remember. There was a crowd of us.*

**Jonathan Rees QC (Prosecution)**

*Q  You were asked questions about whether or not school friends accompanied you or were present at Jesus Green at the time, and you told us there was one school friend who sadly has since died and a number of other girls.*

*A.  Yes, [she] wasn't helping, she just came over to see me whilst I was there.*

*Q  Yes, quite, and I think some other girls within your friendship group who went to a different school, a convent? Is that right?*

*A.  Yes. There wasn't anyone from my immediate friends. It was just a crowd, but we weren't together during the day. We were sent off for different celebrities, so we didn't really spend time together during the day.*

I decided to extend my investigations to the school that Jackie Daniels had attended in 1978 to establish if there was any information that could confirm or otherwise clarify her story about having been selected to assist at Star Games through an appeal for volunteers posted on the sixth form notice board. I was also interested in finding out if the school friend who had died was her only friend helping at the Games.

This meant hours of trawling through news reports covering 1978, in part for the purpose of locating references to alumni and making enquiries at the school. I found no record of the school having had any involvement with Star Games in 1978.

The next course of action was to identify and locate other girls who had been in the same year as Jackie Daniels to ascertain if they recalled the school advertising for helpers at Star Games – and, if so, whether these other girls were volunteers.

This meant that my hard-working research team had to try to identify and locate these girls. This was no easy task because 37 years had passed and many of the former pupils had married at least once and had changed their names. Others had left the country and could no longer be traced.

We identified 72 of the girls who were in the same year as Jackie Daniels and then set about trying to find out what names they were now using and where they were living. I drew the short straw on this one, which meant some old-fashioned gumshoe work. Essentially this meant knocking on doors, which in some cases were in remote areas.

I sorted my door knocking enquiries into two-to-three-day stretches, staying overnight at hotels so I could resume enquiries early the following morning. This enabled me to avoid long periods of commuting. In between I would return to the office, catch up on the other investigations and then repeat the exercise until everyone we had identified had been accounted for.

I covered many miles and met a lot of women who had attended Jackie Daniels' former school. They were polite and friendly and helped me as much as they could with my enquiries.

Towards the end of one of the three-day stretches I was feeling very tired. I was about to give up and return to the office for a well-earned rest. I had one further house call on my list before calling it a day. In fact, I had all but convinced myself not to make that final call, but something made me keep going and that is when I had my first breakthrough.

I was in Cambridgeshire. The woman who was on my list was a former pupil at the school that Jackie Daniels had attended. I will call her Bridget to protect her identity.

Bridget was at home on her own when I called in March 2017. The house was undergoing renovation work. She did not invite me inside, but she was courteous and polite. After identifying myself I asked her if she had been a volunteer at Star Games in 1978, which had been held on Jesus Green, Cambridge. This question prompted her to ask me if this was about Jackie Smith, who is now Jackie Daniels. She said she was aware of the complaint that Jackie had made against Rolf Harris, as Jackie was a close friend. She said that they had both been volunteers at the 1978 Star Games.

Bridget said she thought that they had worked at Star Games over both weekends, but she could not be certain. She knew that she was there when Jackie was and that they had both definitely worked on a Saturday and a Sunday on at least one weekend, probably both. She said she was one of a number of girls from their school who had volunteered to work at Star Games. She could not recall how she came to hear about the opportunity to work at the event.

Bridget recalled that there was a refreshment tent within walking distance of where Star Games was being held and that she spent a lot of time in there serving drinks and providing towels and anything else that the celebrities taking part in Star Games required.

Bridget told me that none of the girls were assigned to look after any celebrities. They were directed by officials and told what to do. Bridget also used the word 'gophers' to describe their role at the games.

I asked Bridget if taxis had been used to transport the celebrities or anyone else around the site. She could not recall any taxis and questioned why they would need taxis because everything was so close together, and the type of celebrities who had taken part would have had no problem with walking around because they had to be fit to take part in the various activities.

I asked Bridget if she had heard of any unacceptable behaviour whilst volunteering at Star Games. She said that none of the girls, including Jackie, had ever told her that they had been assaulted in any way. She had become aware of the allegation that Jackie had made against Rolf Harris only when Jackie had appeared on national television a couple of years previously.

I made notes of my interview and asked Bridget if she was prepared to make a formal statement. She told me that she wanted to speak with her husband and Jackie Daniels before coming to a decision. I informed her that I would formulate a statement and return at a later date, when we could discuss it further with a view to her signing it.

Despite three further visits I found no-one at home, so I posted a copy of the statement, with an accompanying letter, through the front door. This was on 8th May 2017, a week before the start of the third trial.

The following day, which was 9th May 2017, I received an email from Bridget, which read:

*Dear Mr Merritt,*

*After receiving your correspondence yesterday, I felt I should inform you that I have already provided the police with a statement after our discussion on 17th March, and therefore I have decided that I will not be signing anything further.*

*This statement was made after much more careful thought and consideration, as I had the time to try and get a better recollection of the day in July 1978, rather than try to grasp some memories from a long-forgotten event, suddenly brought up on my doorstep.*

*As I have nothing further to add to this final statement, I would be grateful if you could refrain from making further contact.*

The police never disclosed Bridget's statement, nor did they call her as a witness. From this I assumed that the statement had not been helpful to Jackie Daniels. Bridget had telephoned Jackie Daniels after I had left her home and the police were contacted. An officer from Operation Yewtree had taken a statement from her. This is a tactic that some police officers use in an attempt to nullify evidence uncovered by an investigator that contradicts information that has been supplied to the police by a complainant. It doesn't always work, particularly when an honest witness is involved.

Bridget had provided significant information about the circumstances of Jackie Daniels' volunteering role at Star Games. Jackie Daniels had testified that there was only one girl from her school who was at Star Games, and she was her best friend who had died. She was not in contact with any of the other girls from a local convent who were volunteers at the games, nor did she know their names. She had not mentioned her close friend, Bridget.

Bridget had confirmed that to the best of her knowledge there were no taxis used at Star Games. We had not found any evidence in the accounts for Star Games of taxis having been hired, and no-one else recalled seeing taxis. The area of Jesus Green that was being used for Star Games was so small that taxis would have been more of a hindrance than a help.

Bridget had also confirmed that none of the girls had been put in charge of looking after celebrities. Jackie Daniels' sister had said the same thing and so had the officials who were contacted.

The official comment from the organisers of the event was that schoolgirl volunteers would never have been given the responsibility of looking after celebrities.

Stephen Vullo QC had the option of calling Bridget as a defence witness. He was considering this, even if she had to be declared a hostile witness. I did assure him that in my opinion Bridget would be reliable, but she had found herself in a difficult position. I did not think she would lie under oath, so to call her as a defence witness was a risk worth taking.

This option was still being considered when the third trial started on 15th May 2017.

The next breakthrough was totally unexpected. The police had provided photographs of Jackie Daniels at Star Games. In some she was on her own and in others she was with other girls. The photographs were copies, not originals. However, at the trial the original photos were produced to the court. One of the defence team was looking through the photos, and when turning one of them over, noticed that written on the back was *Avec [Sara]* – 'avec' being French for 'with'.

We were so intrigued by this that we revisited the list of alumni from Jackie Daniels' school. We identified a girl named Sara in the same year as both Jackie Daniels and Bridget. What we didn't know at the time was that in 1978 there was only one girl at the school with this Christian name. As with Bridget I have used a pseudonym to protect the real identity of Sara.

Further investigations identified a woman named Sara who appeared to be the person we were looking for. She had married, her surname had changed, and she was living in Kent. The trial was in progress so I caught up with the legal team during a recess and told them that I believed I may have found an important witness. This was received as very good news and I can still recall Stephen Vullo QC's reaction. He told me in so many words to ensure that Sara made it to the court.

The following day I drove down to Kent and knocked on the front door of the house where I believed Sara lived with her husband. The door was opened by a petite woman who fitted the age group of the Sara in question. I was holding the copy of the photograph in my hand, and as I started to introduce myself, she said, "What are you doing with a photograph of me?" It was job done; I had found her.

I explained to Sara how I had come to have a copy of her photograph, and immediately she told me that she was aware of the complaint that Jackie Daniels had made against Rolf Harris. Jackie had been a school friend of hers and they had kept in contact. She further told me that she had been a volunteer at Star Games in Cambridge in 1978, along with her three school friends – Bridget, Jackie and the friend who had died. Sara invited me inside and we had a long discussion about Star Games.

What Sara told me produced another breakthrough in this case and just reward for all the hard work we had put into identifying other girls from Jackie Daniels' school in our efforts to locate volunteers at Star Games in 1978.

The salient points of what Sara told me during our conversation are summarised below.

*"I remember this photograph being taken. I was with a close friend of mine, [Jackie Smith], who is now known as [Jackie Daniels]. We have been friends since I was about 13 and we both attended [the same secondary school]. The photograph was taken by one of the photographers who was at Star Games. I still have this photograph and a programme from Star Games.*

*I cannot remember how many days the Games were held over, but I think I went to all of them. I have looked at the programme and it shows that Star Games was held over two weekends in July 1978 and there were four days. I believe I did go to all four. I was a volunteer with three friends from [her old school] – [Jackie Daniels], [Bridget] and [name redacted], who died in 1999.*

*I was working on the day that Rolf Harris was at Star Games, and I worked at both the swimming pool and the area where the running and field events were being held. I recall there was a tent with refreshments, and I was used as a volunteer to serve drinks and provide towels and anything else that the celebrities taking part in the Games required.*

*None of us were assigned to look after any of the celebrities. We were directed by officials and told what to do. We were used as gophers. There was a lot of down time, and we spent a lot of time sitting around and watching the Games. I did spend time with Jackie, and I remember her younger sister and her mother were also there. I was with them all on some occasions.*

*I have been asked if there were any taxis used to transport the celebrities around. I do not recall seeing any taxis. The area of Jesus Green that was used for Star Games, including the swimming pool, was not very large and it was easy to walk from one event to the other.*

*I have been asked if I can remember an area near the swimming pool that was set aside for celebrities. I cannot remember any such area, although I suppose the celebrities needed somewhere to change into their swimming costumes.*

*I am aware that Jackie made a complaint against Rolf Harris because I saw her on the television about two years ago. I do not know anything about the complaint and even though I have seen Jackie since, we have never spoken about it.*

*I neither heard of nor witnessed any unacceptable behaviour whilst I was working at Star Games and none of the other girls, including Jackie, ever told me that they had been assaulted in any way. I did not have any direct contact with Rolf Harris."*

In mid-2016 Jackie Daniels invited Bridget and Sara to dinner. Their husbands also attended. Sara told me that there had been no talk about the pending Rolf Harris trial. A few months later, in September 2016, Jackie invited Bridget and Sara to lunch and once again the pending trial was not discussed. I asked Sara why it was not discussed, and she said that although she knew, she didn't think Jackie would want to talk about it, so she did not mention it.

When I analysed these two meetings, I suspected that Jackie Daniels had arranged these get-togethers to see if either of her friends was aware that she was a complainant at the second trial, which was due to commence in January 2017. She would probably have known that they knew about her appearance on national television in 2014, but not that she was a new complainant.

When the case was not mentioned during their get-togethers it is likely that she would have assumed that they did not know, so she was safe in not mentioning her friends to either the police or the court. To have done so could well have made her account far less convincing because the friends could have given the police details of the Star Games set-up that contradicted hers.

I asked Sara if she would be willing to attend court and provide evidence for the defence. She was reluctant to do this because Jackie was a friend, but she said she would speak with her husband, who was currently away on business. I told her I would speak with legal counsel and call her to let her know if she was required to attend court as a witness.

After speaking with the legal team, it was apparent that they would prefer to have Sara as a witness rather than Bridget, so I was instructed to contact her and ask her to appear as a witness. The next day I called her home phone and her husband answered. He had returned hastily from his business trip and told me that his wife would not be appearing as a witness for the defence. I informed him that we may have to summon her, and he challenged me to do this.

Sara had qualifications in the legal field and her husband was a senior insurance executive. Their next-door neighbour, according to what they told me, was a barrister and he had given them advice. It was time to take a gamble. Stephen Vullo QC trusted my judgement and decided to summon Sara. I had told him that Sara had impressed me and I had no doubt that she would be a reliable witness. She had been put in a very awkward position and was reluctant to testify against her school friend. This is something that none of us would want to do.

The court case was well under way when the defence applied for a witness summons. It was my job to serve the summons as I could identify Sara if difficulties arose. However, it was decided that Rolf's solicitor, Dan Berke, should accompany me and serve the witness summons. In the event of any contentious issues, a witness summons served by a solicitor should be almost watertight.

So off we went to Kent, not knowing what we were going to encounter.

When we arrived, Sara answered the door and accepted the summons from Dan Berke without any protest. She was to attend Southwark Crown Court the following day and agreed to do so.

Sure enough, the following day Sara, who was unaccompanied, arrived at Southwark Crown Court. She was spoken to by the defence team and duly summoned into the witness box.

Sara's evidence was consistent with what she had told me a few days previously, but she was reluctant to admit that she had spent time with Jackie Daniels and her other friends during the day of the Star Games final. She said that she had been busy working and could not recall them meeting up during the day. It was clear to me and the defence legal team that she was doing her best to protect her friend Jackie Daniels, who had already told the court that only one of her friends had been there on that day.

One of the more tedious jobs we had undertaken was to check the video of Star Games on a frame-by-frame basis. This job was given to one of the researchers who assisted us on a voluntary basis. As a result, the officials were identified and so were some of the volunteers, including Jackie Daniels, and other girls whom we had not identified prior to the trial. The officials were much older than the volunteers, and they were always near to the celebrities.

Stephen Vullo QC had several photos of Star Games. Some were stills that had been extracted from the video and others had been taken by photographers. The photos showed a young woman, who we knew was Sara, at various times during the day sitting with Jackie and Bridget and with Jackie's mother and sisters. This was unsurprising as Sara had told me that there had been a lot of down time. As a result, the volunteers had spent some time sitting around and watching the Games.

One can only imagine the conversations that must have taken place since I made my visit to Sara's home. I very much doubt that Jackie Daniels would have wanted yet another of her close friends located and providing testimony in court. I did feel sorry for Sara, but the truth had to come out.

It was at this stage that the QC's experience came to the fore. Stephen Vullo QC showed Sara a number of photographs of her sitting at various times with Jackie Daniels and her sister and mother, as well as with the other girls. As she was shown each photo, Sara responded by saying that she could not recognise herself, and she was unsure whether one of the girls in the photo, who was pointed out by Stephen Vullo QC, was her. I cannot now recall the exact number of photos shown to her but there were at least six.

When Sara was shown the last photo, which was the photo that I had shown her, she agreed that it was her in the photo. Stephen Vullo QC then discussed with her the coat she was wearing in the photo. Sara told him that it was her favourite coat. After a bit of banter about favourite clothes, Stephen Vullo QC reverted to the previous photo and asked Sara if the girl in the photo was wearing her favourite coat. She agreed and also agreed that it was her in the photo.

Each of the photos was shown to her in reverse order. In each photo the young woman, whom Sara had a few minutes earlier said she couldn't recognise, was wearing her favourite coat.

As Stephen Vullo QC pointed this out to her, you could feel the atmosphere in the court room change. It became very tense. I could sense the sinking feeling that Sara must have been experiencing. She looked very embarrassed and uncomfortable as each photo was shown to her again, one after the other. Sara finally had no option but to agree it was her in all the photos. It was a master class in cross-examination.

The evidence we had uncovered revealed that:

- Rolf was his normal tactile self at Star Games; he did play to the crowd, which included hugging fans and having photos taken with them.
- Jackie Daniels, by her own admission, took exception to Rolf playing to the crowd in this manner and it seems that she may have been on the receiving end of one of Rolf's hugs. We don't know, but it seems highly likely.
- She said that she was wearing a tight jumper. I have seen photos of her in the crowd that show her wearing a jumper that was very noticeably tight-fitting. If Rolf had put his arm around her and given her a hug it is unlikely that he could have avoided brushing against one of her breasts.
- Jackie Daniels never mentioned this alleged assault to her close friends. This seems rather strange, with her being the confident person that she is, and why would she mention something to her father, and not her close friends?

- Her claim that she was sexually assaulted in a taxi later in the day does not pass muster.

  (a) There is no corroborating evidence that taxis were used at this event.

  (b) The swimming events were in the morning so she would not have been travelling in a taxi to the swimming pool late in the day.

  (c) All celebrities were looked after by officials who were fully paid members of the production team. Schoolgirl volunteers would never have been asked to look after a celebrity. They were used as 'gophers' and were under the control of the officials.

At the conclusion of the third trial, and after five hours of deliberations, the jury was unable to reach verdicts on any of the charges. When the Crown Prosecution Service advised Judge Deborah Taylor that they would not be seeking a further retrial, a not guilty verdict was returned on all the charges.

The question remains as to why the jury could not reach a verdict in the second and third trials. I think it is likely that the media's labelling of Rolf Harris as a paedophile played its part. At the conclusion of the third trial, in May 2017, his conviction for indecently assaulting the then eight-year-old Wendy Rosher had not been overturned. It was finally overturned in November 2017, almost six months after the third trial had ended.

Jackie Daniels seemed unable to accept that Rolf Harris had been found not guilty of indecently assaulting her and was quite vocal in this regard. She also appeared to be unable to accept that a convicted person should be able to instruct private investigators to seek out further evidence that would enable them to lodge an appeal, a point that she made quite forcefully in a national newspaper.

However, Jackie Daniels did not provide a full picture to the police and the court regarding her two close friends who were with her at the Games. There is also the question of whether she had any influence over some of the witnesses the police were wanting to interview. She denied having influenced any witnesses when it was put to her during cross-examination. It would seem that her perspective of a fair trial differs greatly from mine.

I should make it clear that finding new evidence to put right a miscarriage of justice is not 'digging up dirt'. Had I and my team not searched for new evidence in the case of Wendy Rosher, her lies would never have been exposed and Rolf Harris's conviction would not have been overturned on appeal. Likewise, the incomplete picture provided by Jackie Daniels would never have been rectified if we had not been involved, and there is every prospect that without this Rolf may well have been found guilty.

It is worth noting that not one, but two juries failed to find Rolf Harris guilty of indecently assaulting Jackie Daniels.

# CHAPTER 10
# BAD CHARACTER EVIDENCE

I t is not uncommon for the accused to call witnesses to provide evidence of good character. This is much like nominating referees when applying for a job. A good character witness could be an employer, relative, friend or associate who has known the accused for many years and who can testify that he or she is not someone who would commit the type of crime of which they had been accused, or any type of crime or wrongdoing.

Bad character evidence can be called by the Crown Prosecution Service to counter good character evidence. It is normally in the form of recounting similar unlawful activities that the accused has been involved in and shows that he or she has the propensity to commit the type of crime he or she has been accused of.

In some instances, bad character evidence is important in a trial, particularly when there is an absence of evidence to support the accusations made by the complainant, and especially when the complainant is not a strong witness, and it is his or her word against the accused. The danger is when the Crown Prosecution Service relies too heavily on bad character evidence, and actively recruits people to come forward. This can attract the wrong kind of witness, for example:

- An individual who has a grudge against the accused and sees this as an opportunity to seek retribution for some past disagreement.
- Someone who sees the pound signs and the trial as a means of climbing onto the compensation ladder.
- An individual prone to confabulation, which according to experts in human behaviour is far more common when people are trying to recall historic events.

Confabulation is when a person plugs gaps in their memory with imaginary experiences to the extent that they come to believe that the event happened. To give an example, the complainant, who might appear obviously upset, truly believes that the accused has assaulted them, or holds the accused responsible for something unpleasant that happened to them as a child or young person. It goes without saying that this can have serious repercussions for an accused person who has never met the complainant, let alone assaulted them. Papers and articles have been written by members of the legal fraternity who have recognised this as a problem, and they have asked for juries to receive more guidance in recognising that some mental health conditions make confabulation more likely.

If a police detective intends using similar fact evidence to show the bad character of the accused, it is the detective's civil duty to ensure that the witness does not have an ulterior motive for coming forward. Some straightforward detective work is all that is required to satisfy this criterion. Unfortunately, this was sadly lacking with the officers of Operation Yewtree, who were willing to accept evidence of bad character without carrying out some basic checks and investigations into the accuracy of the evidence. This is unforgivable as there is little doubt that the jurors in Rolf Harris's first trial were heavily influenced by the bad character evidence that the Crown Prosecution Service produced during the trial.

As Rolf Harris did not have an investigator working for him during the first trial, his defence team had to rely on the police investigation. They were entitled to believe that the police had checked out the information supplied to them by the individuals providing bad character evidence. They did nothing of the sort. Because of this lack of attention to detail, evidence was presented to the jury without verification of the source of this evidence.

It might appear that I am continually criticising the police but, as I have already explained, it is not the police I am criticising. It is the officers who worked on and ran the Operation Yewtree team who were at fault. If this lack of attention to detail were to become the norm, it would compromise the integrity of British justice.

From an investigative viewpoint it was disappointing that I was not involved in the first trial when so much bad character evidence was produced by the Crown Prosecution Service. There was none produced in the second and third trials, probably because the Crown Prosecution Service believed that the convictions from the first trial were going to be sufficient bad character evidence. They were presuming, of course, that Rolf Harris's new defence team was going to be a pushover. How wrong could they have been? What they didn't expect was that the new legal team would be backed up by a small team of experienced investigators who would locate the evidence that the Operation Yewtree detectives and their civilian investigators either ignored or couldn't find.

I did get the opportunity to complete a full investigation into the evidence of one of the bad character witnesses from Rolf Harris's first trial because after giving her evidence she instructed the 'no win, no fee' firm of solicitors Slater and Gordon to lodge a civil claim against Rolf Harris. At the point when I was instructed by the Harris family, one year after Rolf Harris had been convicted, the compensation negotiations were well under way, and I was asked by the Harris team to assist the firm of lawyers handling the defence of this compensation claim.

The woman in question provided witness testimony to the court that Rolf Harris had indecently assaulted her in a beachside bar in Malta in 1970. Owing to Malta being outside the jurisdiction of the British legal system, Rolf Harris could not be charged with the alleged offence.

The Malta Police Force was not interested in pursuing the complaint. Therefore, the woman's testimony was used as bad character evidence against Rolf Harris at his first trial.

The Malta investigation was both interesting and rewarding. Much of the information in the next chapter, which I have called 'The Malta Mystery', has never been reported as Rolf Harris was not charged with assaulting the woman concerned and for this reason media coverage was limited. As details of the settlement are confidential, they were never reported by the media either. The investigation, which encompassed England and Malta, was so involved that I just had to recount it in its own chapter.

During the course of my investigations into the complainants who appeared at the second trial and the circumstances surrounding Rolf Harris's conviction for assaulting Wendy Rosher, some unexpected circumstances led to my finding out some information about two of the other bad character witnesses called by the Crown Prosecution Service.

I was unable to complete full investigations owing to time and budget constraints but the limited information I did obtain is worthy of inclusion as it provides an overview of just how far the police were prepared to go in order to prop up a weak case with anyone who was prepared to provide evidence of bad character against Rolf Harris.

## BAD CHARACTER WITNESS TONY PORTER

Tony Porter is a retired Australian actor. He appeared in a number of Australian television dramas and in three international feature films –

Blue Heelers (1994), Knowing (2009) and Killer Elite (2011) – and was also a radio and television news reporter. He appeared on variety and game shows as well as being involved with acting workshops.

Porter was a last-minute addition to the prosecution case. He contacted the Metropolitan Police following articles in the Australian press about the Rolf Harris case. The front page of the *Sydney Morning Herald* of Thursday, 20th March 2014 had summarised the directions hearing at Southwark Crown Court held on Tuesday, 18th March 2014 and listed the 'untested' allegations in detail.

Porter appeared at Southwark Crown Court on Wednesday, 21st May 2014 as a bad character witness.

## Porter's Claim

According to Porter he was engaged on a weekly ABC TV variety show called 'ROLF!' to co-star with Rolf Harris in various comedy sketches. Ten programmes were recorded.

Porter said that on *one* occasion, in the make-up department, he was beside Rolf Harris, who was being made up for his next 'take' by a female make-up artist. He described the make-up artist as white Australian, aged from late 20s to mid-30s, 160 cm to 170 cm tall and of slight build. Porter could not recall her name.

Porter alleged that the make-up artist was facing Rolf, who was seated, and that as she leaned forward to 'dust' his face, "Rolf Harris reached out with both hands and fiddled with her breasts. He made lascivious noises while he tickled her up." He said that Rolf Harris, who appeared to regard the incident as harmless fun, did not speak to the make-up artist or to Porter. Neither the make-up artist nor Porter made any comment or objection. Porter said that from his viewpoint the make-up artist had found the attention unwelcome.

He described the incident as being over in a matter of seconds. Porter was startled by the brazenness of it. He commented, "As dressing rooms are universally rife with sexual innuendo and horseplay it didn't seem to be my place to make an issue of it at the time."

Porter further stated, "In the 1970s and 1980s it was considered fair game for anyone - usually male, and especially those with status - to engage in such shenanigans in dressing rooms and make-up departments."

Porter did not make a complaint to anyone at the ABC. He said, "I suspect I would have been told to grow up – and may even have lost my job into the bargain."

# ROLF!

ROLF! was a series of ten shows produced at the ABC studios in Melbourne, Victoria in late 1983.

The shows featured Rolf Harris in the roles of singer, comedian, raconteur, interviewer and painter. Rolf's regular guests were the singers Jane Scali and Patrick McMahon. Bruce Rowland was the musical director. The show was directed by Lindsay Dresden.

The ABC archive records for the show do not mention Tony Porter. Footage of a clip from an episode of the programme ROLF! featuring Rolf Harris and Porter was shown to the court. There was no indication of the date of the episode, the timing of the clip or where the footage was obtained. Rolf had no recollection of Tony Porter at all.

ROLF! was recorded before a studio audience. Porter clowned around during the delays in shooting to keep the studio audience entertained, so he was more like a warm-up artist, rather than the co-star he claimed to have been. He testified that Rolf Harris had come up to him after one such interlude and quietly said, "Mate, I'll do the funny stuff." He continued, "That's when I realised Rolf wasn't simply aloof or shy, that there was this totally self-absorbed and self-interested side to him. To put it bluntly, he was an arsehole – and that's the very word other friends and contacts have used since to describe their experiences with him."

According to Porter, Rolf barely spoke to him during the entire series. Porter turned up for the recordings, delivered his lines and left. His status on the show was relatively insignificant; he appeared in occasional comedy sketches in a few of the televised programmes.

Porter said that he had never previously worked with Rolf Harris, and he never worked with Rolf Harris again.

Porter told the court that he had never heard any rumours about Rolf, which contradicted what he had said previously. He said that he had found Rolf to be affable and professional. Porter was not a co-host; he was a 'junior member of the team'. Rolf communicated with Porter only when he was on set.

The make-up artist was not identified, and she never came forward. Another make-up artist contacted the police with a similar complaint, and she was also used as a bad character witness against Rolf Harris. After the trial, a number of other make-up artists went to the media with similar stories of inappropriate touching by celebrities. As far as I know, no further complaints by make-up artists about Rolf were made to the police. It seems that inappropriate touching was considered an occupational hazard associated with make-up rooms in television studios at that time.

Sasha Wass QC told the court that Rolf Harris could not be prosecuted in relation to some of the complaints on the basis that they had happened outside the jurisdiction of the British legal system or because they were 'borderline in their criminality'.

Rolf Harris, she continued, had a long history of groping young girls and women, confident that he would get away with it. "The defendant was using his celebrity status to approach them in the knowledge that nobody would be likely to complain about his misconduct."

These were speculative comments with no substance. They were very damaging, yet when the allegations of groping (her word) were properly tested, they were found wanting.

Tony Porter said that he had come forward to support the make-up artist who the police did use as a bad character witness, although he did not know her, and he knew nothing about her allegation.

It should be noted that Rolf was often concerned about his make-up. Make-up is required to ensure a consistent and blemish-free appearance under the harsh studio lighting and to ensure that the person looks the same even when scenes are shot at different times during the day. Rolf is allergic to powder and was sometimes upset that make-up artists did not appreciate his objections to having his face powdered. He always carried a personal Max Factor pancake make-up kit to ensure that he was properly catered for. This sometimes caused tensions or irritation when make-up artists thought that Rolf was being critical of their professional expertise.

The alleged incident that Tony Porter said he had witnessed occurred over 30 years previously. At the time he did not make any comment about what he claims to have seen, and neither did the make-up artist complain. No complaint to the organisers of the show was ever made. There is no record of the police having contacted the organisers of the ROLF! show.

Was supporting the unknown make-up artist Tony Porter's motive for coming forward, or did he see this as an opportunity to exact revenge on the man who had once chastised him for over-stepping his role on the ROLF! show? Porter seems to have felt slighted and ignored by Rolf Harris during the ten episodes of ROLF! The question arises as to whether the extensive news coverage of the allegations against Rolf Harris revived memories of this and motivated him to make a complaint to the police 31 years later. The prospect of an all-expenses-paid trip to London as promised by visiting Metropolitan Police officers could also have been a key motivation for his involvement.

After the trial Tony Porter had a brief flirtation with fame as a star in the documentary episode on Rolf Harris in the series Crimes that Shook Britain. This documentary was released for broadcast in the UK in September 2015.

Going back to Porter's comment about shenanigans, I have no doubt that shenanigans occurred in make-up departments and dressing rooms in the 1970s and 1980s. It was not just backstage where the sexual innuendoes and horseplay occurred. They were a staple of television shows and films such as The Benny Hill Show and the 'Carry On' films, to name only two of many. Did Rolf Harris become involved in shenanigans? I am sure he did as it was part of his persona to act the fool and engage in horseplay, and it would have fitted in with the culture that prevailed at the time. He was also very tactile, as has been mentioned on many occasions.

The question one must ask is how far this horseplay and the sexual innuendoes went. In the case of the make-up artist that Tony Porter mentioned, it was "over in a matter of seconds."

Why was this man flown over to London on an all-expenses-paid trip to give evidence about something that happened in thousands of workplaces in the 1970s and 1980s? What has this got to do with Rolf Harris allegedly being a paedophile? Surely the 'station stamp', which was the initiation ceremony carried out by some senior British policemen on new female recruits, was a far more serious crime than what Tony Porter alleged he saw Rolf Harris do to a make-up artist? I have covered the 'station stamp' in more detail in Chapter 1 – Operation Yewtree.

## NEW ZEALAND BAD CHARACTER WITNESS

Shortly after the news broke that Rolf Harris had been arrested, Operation Yewtree officers made a heavily publicised visit to Australia. The Australian media reported that Scotland Yard detectives were visiting the country and were looking for any witnesses who could provide evidence of having been touched inappropriately by Rolf Harris.

A New Zealander, who I will call Fiona Meekle, contacted the police via a newspaper and alleged that in 1970 in New Zealand, when she was aged 16 or 17, Rolf Harris had indecently assaulted her when they were dancing at a function that he had attended as a celebrity. She claimed that he had assaulted her by sliding his hand down her back and placing it on her bottom, after which he had placed his hand on her crotch, under her dress but over her underwear. She produced photos of herself with Rolf Harris at the event.

The event had been held in Hamilton, which is a city about one and a half hours' drive south of Auckland on State Highway 1. It had been sponsored by a wine company. Rolf Harris had no recollection of the event or Fiona Meekle but he conceded that it was him in the photograph dancing with her. Fiona had been working part-time as a hostess on the night of the event.

Another photo was produced that showed four people – Fiona Meekle, Rolf Harris, another young woman and an unknown man. Both women were wearing sashes advertising the wine company. The man seems to have been either a representative of the wine company or one of the organisers. As far as I can ascertain, the police did not attempt to speak with this man or to the other young woman. They were happy to take what Fiona Meekle had said at face value.

Fiona did not make a complaint about this alleged indecent assault at the time, and she testified that she had not told her co-worker hostess friend, or anyone else, about it – although according to her husband, she did mention it to him in later years, and her son also got to know about it. At least that is what they said.

There is no record of Fiona Meekle having sought compensation in relation to this 44-year-old allegation. Not having sought compensation would have strengthened her evidence in the eyes of the British public and media as she would have been seen as 'not being in it for the money', but an Antipodean would have seen it differently. Something even more important to a New Zealander, especially one who has British or Irish ancestry, is the chance to travel to the land of their forebears. In this case, an all-expenses-paid trip to London was being offered by the Crown Prosecution Service via the Australian media.

I was not able to complete a full investigation into the allegation made by Fiona Meekle. This was most frustrating as I would have liked very much to have located the unknown man in the photograph and the young woman who was the co-hostess on the night in question.

I had instructed a New Zealand investigator to complete some preliminary enquiries and as a result he located a woman who had recently returned to the area of Northland where Fiona was living and working. This woman, who I will call Summer to protect her identity, had been living in England and she had followed the Rolf Harris trials closely. She was at Southwark Crown Court when Fiona gave her evidence and was later able to identify Fiona from her occupation.

Summer was one of the many Rolf Harris supporters who believed Rolf did not receive a fair trial. She had taken it upon herself to speak with Fiona and she passed on to the New Zealand investigator what Fiona had told her.

Summer told the investigator that Fiona was not difficult to find owing to her occupation.  She readily engaged in a conversation when Summer revealed her own occupation and said that she had just returned from living in England.

Fiona told Summer that she had visited England about 18 months previously and the trip had included two weeks in London. She was able to take her husband and adult son with her and she had loved it. They had visited tourist sites, had travelled on the Eurostar to Paris for the day, where they had been on a guided tour, and everyone was lovely. They had stayed in Dubai on the way over and in an expensive hotel in Singapore on the way back.

She said that she had planned on going to the UK when she was young and had bought the ticket. She then met her husband, who was about to get married to someone else, so she had cancelled the trip and eventually married him. The all-expenses-paid trip to London had finally provided her with the opportunity to do what she had planned to do when she was young. Whilst it was much later than planned, she considered herself fortunate because she had been able to take her family with her.

When Summer asked Fiona how she managed to arrange this trip, she was a bit hesitant at first but then said it was to attend to some business. She did not mention the real reason for the trip but as the date of the trip coincided with her giving evidence at the first trial of Rolf Harris, it was evident to Summer that her business was to give bad character evidence at Rolf's trial.

The trip to the UK that Fiona said she had missed out on as a young woman is known in New Zealand and Australia as The Big OE – 'OE' being the abbreviation for Overseas Experience. Even today it is a big part of the lives of young people in New Zealand and Australia and many see it as being important in their life qualifications for future work. It is similar to the gap year in the UK when students take a year out before starting university.

If someone misses out on their OE, they generally have a need to have the experience later in life. I make this comment based on the countless conversations I have had with New Zealanders who didn't get to do it for whatever reason.

I grew up in New Zealand and missed out on my OE because I married young and then joined the police. My older brother did get to do his OE and spent a couple of years based in London, where he worked in different jobs before touring Europe with his friends in a VW Kombi campervan over the summer months. I am sure this image will bring back memories for so many New Zealanders and Australians who are reading this and who will recall the great times they had, and the challenges they faced, on their own OE.

I finally got to do my OE when I was in my early fifties. I was able to stay on in the UK, which was not the case for many New Zealanders, because I was born in England, and I hold dual citizenship.

So, for Fiona to finally get the opportunity to visit London and Paris, this was better than seeking compensation. No questions asked, just a matter of appearing in court, being given name suppression, which she insisted on as part of her agreement to testify, and then telling her story.

Another point that I consider to be worthy of comment is this. When testifying in court, Fiona was especially vocal about what Rolf had written when he was giving her his autograph. He had written on the front of an airmail envelope, 'To Fiona with my love, Rolf Harris' and he had included his standard 'Rolf-a-roo' sketch. She was outraged that he had written the words, 'with my love' and she virtually screamed that he was being over-familiar, and he had no right to use such a term of endearment to a woman he had only just met.

This is one of those cultural differences that I have discussed previously, for example the hug and peck on the cheek that are part of the European, and now English, culture when meeting someone. This certainly did not occur in 1970s New Zealand. I recall how my ex-wife, who was a policewoman, would get very upset if someone referred to her as 'love'. In later years she spent time in England and her attitude changed because over here the word 'love' is a commonly used word in some regions.

Fiona had lived in rural areas of New Zealand. She was still locked away in that small town mindset and unable to see that what Rolf Harris had written was nothing like how she was interpreting it. 'Love' is a friendly and well-used word in the UK. Many celebrity autographs that I viewed during this investigation contained the words 'love from' or 'with love'. I am surprised that the harmless nature of the wording was not pointed out to both Fiona and the jury by Rolf's defence team.

The testimony that Fiona gave in court was uncontested, which gave her carte blanche to relate her story without fear of being challenged. Even without conducting a full investigation I have picked up on things that do not ring true.

In 1970 Rolf Harris was a huge international star and was well known in New Zealand. The venue where Fiona claims the event took place was The Chelsea Rooms, a restaurant inside the Federated Farmers Building at 169 London Street, Hamilton. The venue hosted events such as receptions and dinner and dance evenings. These days the building comprises office accommodation and a private health clinic. The restaurant was of medium size, so it would be fair to assume that a star like Rolf Harris would have been the focus of much attention.

Fiona produced two photos of her dancing with Rolf. In the background one can see people standing around looking towards where Rolf was. It is therefore safe to assume that all eyes would have been on Rolf Harris and anyone with him.

Fiona was one of four or five hostesses. She was wearing a wide sash that went around her neck to below her waist and which covered her bottom. The dress she was wearing was above the knee but fairly tight. In one of the photos Rolf is pulling a funny face. Fiona is smiling and is holding on to Rolf, who has one hand holding hers and the other over the sash just below her hip, which is the position one would expect if a couple had just stopped dancing and were posing for a photograph. Fiona said it was just after this photo had been taken that Rolf had lifted her dress and touched her bottom over her knickers.

For this to have occurred, Rolf would have had to bend and lift her dress and the sash, which would have exposed her knickers to everyone in the room. I cannot see how anyone would have missed seeing this.

From the way in which Fiona had reacted to what Rolf had written on the airmail envelope, one would surely have expected her to have reacted strongly if he had even attempted to do to her what she claimed he did in front of the people at the venue, yet it appears that she did nothing. Had she made a complaint at the time, it seems reasonable to assume that she would have mentioned this in her evidence.

It is unforgivable that more enquiries were not made, and that Fiona's version of events was all that was provided to the court. Rolf would have given many autographs during the evening, so I am sure there would still be a number of people in New Zealand, and probably in Hamilton, who were at that event and who could have provided useful information.

We have all been guilty of embellishing stories, particularly the old ones, in order to make them sound more dramatic. Would Fiona still have been provided with her all-expenses-paid family two-week holiday to London and Paris if she had told the police that Rolf Harris had placed his hand on her bottom, over her dress and a sash, and provided her with an autograph that said 'with my love' on it?

The final point I would like to make is that if Fiona did not like what she alleges Rolf Harris did to her, and given her indignation about what he had written when he gave her his autograph, why did she keep his autograph for 44 years? Why also did she keep three photographs of a man she detested and who she alleged had indecently assaulted her?

## FOOD FOR THOUGHT?

In any high-profile case there is the likelihood that people who claim to be victims will jump on the bandwagon with allegations that are either false or so weak that they are borderline in their criminality or don't fall within the definition of what constitutes a crime at all. The Rolf Harris trials were no exception. Those who appeared in court as complainants were the tip of the iceberg. Some of the women whose complaints were rejected by the Crown Prosecution Service later went public but to my knowledge none claimed civil compensation.

Vanessa Feltz of television fame came forward during the course of the first trial to claim that Rolf Harris had assaulted her on live television in front of millions of viewers. The Crown Prosecution Service did not add her allegation to the list of charges against Rolf Harris. She later went public on the matter, following which footage emerged of her groping comedian Freddie Starr's bottom on 'An Audience with Freddie Starr'.

*Vanessa Feltz (right) on An Audience with Freddie Starr.*

In the next chapter I will relate the story about the only bad character witness complaint that I was instructed to investigate fully.

# CHAPTER 11
# THE MALTA MYSTERY

## SHEILA CLARKE

Sheila Clarke was called as a bad character witness by the Crown Prosecution Service at Rolf Harris's first trial. This meant that although she was not a complainant, she was in court to give an account of an alleged encounter with Rolf Harris during which she claimed that he had indecently assaulted her. The purpose of her testimony, along with those of other individuals who were called as bad character witnesses, was to bolster the accounts of the complainants and in doing so to aid the prosecution in convincing the jury that there was a pattern of offending on the part of the accused. The use of bad character witnesses was particularly important to the prosecution as the evidence against Rolf Harris was decidedly weak.

Sheila Clarke testified at Southwark Crown Court on 15th May 2014. In her evidence she alleged that she had been indecently assaulted by Rolf Harris in September 1970, when she was 18, whilst on holiday in

Malta with her boyfriend.

Sheila Clarke is a pseudonym, as are the names given to her family members and certain other individuals mentioned in this chapter.

## ALLEGATIONS

Sheila Clarke described how she had been sitting outside a bar in Malta watching Keith, her then boyfriend, making his way into the sea for a swim when he had cut his toe badly on some rocks. She said she went into the bar seeking assistance and was given a hand towel, which she used to stop the bleeding coming from the cut on Keith's toe.

Sheila Clarke claimed that while they were sitting outside, Rolf Harris came out of the bar. She said that Rolf directed them to a doctor's surgery, which wasn't too far away. They made their way to the surgery where Keith had his toe attended to. An important point here is that her boyfriend would also have seen Rolf Harris.

Sheila Clarke told the court that after they had finished at the doctor's surgery, she had taken Keith back to the apartment they were renting. Whilst he was resting, she went back to the bar on her own to thank Rolf Harris and the others for their assistance.

She said that she purchased a beer and then engaged in conversation with Rolf Harris and the two other men who were in the bar. As she was admiring a painting of two little boys with two wooden rocking horses that was on the wall in the bar, Rolf Harris invited her to see some more paintings. He had taken her into a small room just off the bar where there was a large red Chesterfield sofa in the middle of the room and some other paintings on the walls.

Sheila Clarke alleged that once they were inside the smaller room Rolf Harris pushed her against a wall, fondled her breasts and briefly put his hand inside her knickers. He then stopped, gave her a hug and apologised. They both went back to the bar and continued talking as if nothing had happened. The other two men were still there. One of them asked her if she wanted a photo taken with Rolf Harris, which she agreed to.

The photo was produced as an exhibit by the Crown Prosecution Service to prove that Sheila Clarke had indeed met Rolf Harris. She said that it had been taken outside the same bar at which she claimed he had assaulted her.

In the photo Rolf Harris is wearing sunglasses and a wide-brimmed Akubra or Akubra-style hat of a type that is very popular in, and synonymous with, Australia. Sheila Clarke has one arm around him and the other on her hip. She is wearing a cotton shift dress.

This is yet another example of someone who claimed to have been indecently assaulted by Rolf Harris keeping a photo of herself with her alleged assailant for many years – in this case 44 years, according to her testimony.

Sheila Clarke told the court that at the time she felt flattered that Rolf Harris had paid attention to her. She admitted that she had done nothing about the alleged assault at the time or in the years since until she had reported it to the police in the run-up to the first trial. She told the court that it had not had any lasting effect on her, and in the past 44 years it had been in the back of her mind rather than at the front. When she heard that Rolf Harris and other well-known people had been charged with sexual offences, she thought she should let the police know about what she alleged had happened to her.

When Sheila Clarke was giving her evidence in court, the Crown Prosecutor, Sasha Wass, asked her two specific questions. These appeared to be innocuous but in the context of my later investigations they proved to be anything but.

Q.  *And have you any financial incentive in making up this account against Rolf Harris?*

A. *Not at all. I'm not interested in anything like that.*

Q. *Do you enjoy coming to court to give evidence about....*

A. *I have never been – I have never been to court before apart from my divorce.*

Prosecutor Sasha Wass quoted Sheila Clarke as having described her alleged experience at the hands of Rolf Harris as 'surreal'. She went on to say, "Mr Harris behaved as if nothing had happened. You can see this is a pattern. It's just a lunge and then straight in there."

I consider 'surreal', which means 'resembling a dream' or 'like a fantasy' to be an interesting word for Sheila Clarke to have used under the circumstances. Additionally, there might well have been a reason why Rolf Harris would have behaved as if nothing had happened, this being that the 'surreal' experience hadn't happened at all. This is, of course, assuming that she had even met him on the holiday that she told the court had taken place in 1970.

Unfortunately, Rolf Harris's defence team at the first trial had not carried out any meaningful investigations into the allegations made by Sheila Clarke. This meant that his defence barrister, Sonia Woodley QC, was limited in what she could ask during cross-examination. In a nutshell, the jury was presented with bad character evidence that had gone largely unchallenged.

## CIVIL CLAIM

Contrary to what Sheila Clarke had told the jury, which was that she was not seeking compensation but had come forward to support other women, a few months after the conclusion of the first trial she made a civil claim against Rolf Harris. She was pursuing compensation on the basis of what he had allegedly done to her 44 years previously.

The 'no win, no fee' firm of solicitors Slater and Gordon lodged the claim on her behalf. It was handled by a solicitor who specialised in the field of sexual abuse.

When I came on board as an investigator, over a year had passed since Rolf Harris had been convicted and sent to prison. The law firm Kennedys had been instructed by Rolf Harris to handle the civil claims for compensation that were being lodged by the complainants, who were now being referred to as victims on the basis that Rolf Harris had been found guilty. Three of the five civil claims had been settled by the end of 2015.

As Sheila Clarke had allegedly been indecently assaulted in Malta, which is outside the jurisdiction of the UK courts, and Rolf Harris had not been convicted of any crimes against her, the civil claim she had lodged in October 2014 had been neither agreed nor settled.

Owing to the progress I was making on the investigation into Wendy Rosher, Kennedys was asked by the Harris family to instruct me on behalf of Rolf Harris to investigate fully the allegations and the claim for compensation made by Sheila Clarke.

It is worth noting that if the civil claim for compensation had been paid earlier, I would never have been instructed to carry out an investigation, and the evidence presented to the court by Sheila Clarke would have remained unchallenged.

## INVESTIGATIONS

The research that formed part of my investigations into Sheila Clarke's testimony went back 44 years and involved locating her ex-boyfriend Keith as well as her former husband. I also had to locate people who had been associated with Caesar's Nightclub and Restaurant in Bugibba,

St Pauls Bay, Malta, which had been part-owned by Rolf Harris in the 1970s.

Sadly, a number of the people who were involved with Caesar's are no longer living but I was able to interview two people who were closely associated with the nightclub. One of them had worked there, and the other had lived in a flat above Caesar's. Both knew Caesar's intimately.

Once I had all the information the witnesses could provide, I decided that I had to visit Malta to piece together what had turned into an intriguing jigsaw puzzle. I had been given the names of local businessmen who had been living in the area in the early 1970s, who knew the history of the town and who had knowledge of Caesar's. These men were still operating businesses in Malta, so I was hopeful that they would be able to assist me in my reconstruction of the events leading up to the alleged indecent assault on Sheila Clarke.

## CAESAR'S NIGHTCLUB AND DAY BAR

This venture had been initiated by Don Charles, who was an English entertainer and singer in the 1960s. Don had been managed by International Artistes Limited, the same company that had managed Rolf Harris, which was then owned and operated by theatrical agent Phyllis Rounce. Don Charles, Rolf Harris and Phyllis Rounce were business partners in Caesar's.

Don Charles was the live-in manager. He moved to Bugibba, St Pauls Bay, Malta with his wife and two daughters. They lived in a flat above Caesar's Nightclub and day bar and became full-time residents. Although Rolf Harris and Phyllis Rounce were involved financially, they remained based in London, which was unsurprising given their business commitments and heavy work schedules.

The plan was that Don Charles would be the resident host of the club. Rolf Harris, when he was available, would perform there along with other musical acts that would come to Malta for the summer season. As it turned out, other than spending a bit more time there during the opening of Caesar's, Rolf would visit Malta twice a year at most for about two to three weeks at a time and perform nightly.

Don Charles, his wife and Phyllis Rounce are deceased. Other than Rolf, the only witness available to give evidence at the trial was Don Charles's younger daughter, Joanne. She was aged between five and 11 when she lived with her parents at the flat above Caesar's. They had moved to Malta in 1969 and left in September 1976.

Caesar's was very much a new venture. Don Charles and his business partners had identified and bought the land, developed it from scratch and created a new bar, restaurant and entertainment venue in the centre of Bugibba. The intended customer base was tourists and British and NATO service personnel who were based in Malta.

The construction of the bar and nightclub commenced in 1970 and Caesar's opened for business on 5th June 1971. The opening was heavily promoted beforehand, including through advertisements in *The Times of Malta*.

On Monday, 31st May 1971 an advertisement in *The Times of Malta* announced that Caesar's Nightclub and Restaurant would be opening on 5th June. This was followed up on Friday, 4th June 1971 with an advertisement stating that it would open 'tomorrow'.

*The Times of Malta, 31st May 1971*

*The Times of Malta, 4th June 1971*

In 2001 Rolf Harris published his autobiography *Can You Tell What It Is Yet?*. On pages 262, 263 and 264 he describes the opening of Caesar's in June 1971, which was two weeks prior to the Malta election when the Labour leader Dom Mintoff took office. To be more specific, Dom Mintoff took office on 21st June 1971 as the eighth Prime Minister of Malta.

## SUZANNE BARRY

There was a very important witness who was never interviewed by either the prosecution or the defence. This witness was Suzanne Barry.

Suzanne Barry is retired and lives in the north of England. She worked at Caesar's from 5th June 1971 – the day it opened – until January 1973.

Suzanne had arrived in Malta from her then home in Liverpool on 23rd May 1971, which she was able to verify by the date stamp in her old passport. She had rented a flat in Mosta. Through a friend – a saxophone player who was working at Whispers, which was a nightclub and restaurant in Mosta – she had found out about the opening of Caesar's, the new nightclub and restaurant that was opening in Bugibba. Her friend had told her that he was going to leave Whispers to work at

Caesar's and might be able to get her a job there.

Suzanne did get a job at Caesar's, which she started on the opening night. She worked on reception, which also meant looking after the cloakroom. She did not last long because she had upset a customer by commenting on her fur coat, so she was moved to the office.

About two months later, one of the band members heard her singing. After an audition she became one of the resident singers and remained in this role until January 1973, when she returned to England because her mother was unwell and wanted her back home.

According to Suzanne, Rolf Harris came to Malta twice a year for perhaps two weeks at a time. She said he couldn't manage any more time because in the early 1970s he was world famous and was very busy travelling and performing.

I asked Suzanne if she knew of Rolf Harris having visited any other bars in Bugibba or in the wider St Paul's Bay area when he was there. She told me that Rolf was a non-smoker and if he drank alcohol then he was a very light drinker. There were not many bars around the area in the early 1970s and when Rolf came to Malta it was to perform at Caesar's. He was not there to promote any other club or bar in the area, or for that matter anywhere in Malta, because they were in competition with Caesar's.

Rolf Harris was very popular with tourists and the locals. He enjoyed nothing more than having a coffee and a chat. The Maltese people loved him and there were always people wanting his autograph or a photo with him. Suzanne said that she could remember queues of people lining up for his autograph and a photo. During the day he would pose for photos outside the front door of Caesar's day bar.

I showed Suzanne the photo of Sheila Clarke and Rolf Harris. She said that she did not recognise the woman, but it appeared to her that it was one of the many tourist photos that Rolf would have posed for outside the front of the day bar.

The information provided by Suzanne Barry was my first clue that Sheila Clarke's testimony may not have been accurate. If Rolf did not visit other bars in Bugibba or in the wider St Pauls Bay area, and he posed for photographs with tourists outside the front of Caesar's day bar, then the date of the alleged indecent assault was probably after May 1971, when Caesar's opened.

## KEITH, SHEILA CLARKE'S FORMER BOYFRIEND

By now I was starting to have some concerns about the validity of Sheila Clarke's evidence but what I discovered next came as quite a shock and was certainly unexpected. When she had given her bad character evidence in court, Sheila Clarke had testified that she had been on holiday with her then boyfriend, Keith, when the alleged indecent assault by Rolf Harris had occurred.

I asked my dedicated research team to try to find Keith. We had only his first name and surname, and an approximate age, to go by. They came up trumps and located him living in retirement in southern England, with his wife of over 40 years, Susan.

I headed south to speak with Keith. He was not at home, but fortunately Susan was. After I had told her the purpose of my visit, she invited me in to wait for Keith, who was due home at any time.

When I interviewed Keith and his wife it was March 2016. By that time Rolf Harris had spent 20 months in prison. Both Keith and Susan were very helpful, but it was what they told me that bothered me.

Keith had already been spoken to by a member of the Operation Yewtree team in January 2014 and had provided a statement. This was over three months prior to Rolf Harris's first trial. Keith could not immediately recall the name of the detective constable who had interviewed him, but he contacted me shortly after our meeting to give me this information.

I took a statement from Keith. He told me that basically he was repeating what he had told the police, but it soon became apparent that I was asking other questions that the detective constable who had interviewed him had failed to ask.

## KEITH'S STORY

Keith told me that he had met Sheila Clarke in a pub around 1972. He was three or four years older than she was. Sheila lived nearby and worked for a local company picking up and delivering goods to customers, for which she had a company car. Keith was able to describe the two company cars that she drove during the time that they were going out together.

Sheila and Keith were together for around three years and went on three overseas holidays. The first holiday was to Salou in Spain, which they visited with other members of Keith's family. They were part of a convoy of four cars on this trip.

The second holiday was in 1973 to Bugibba in Malta. Only the two of them went on this holiday. Keith told me that Sheila's father had owned an apartment there and that she used to visit Bugibba with her family regularly.

They flew out to Bugibba for their third holiday on 10th August 1974. Keith was precise about this date because it was of personal significance to him. This time they were accompanied by two other people – Paul, who was a workmate, and Paul's girlfriend, whose name Keith could not remember. Keith, Paul and Paul's girlfriend flew out together, and Sheila followed later that same day.

By this time Sheila was working in the travel industry and had managed to get a standby seat on a flight to Malta, which was probably linked to the privileges afforded to staff.

The day following their arrival was a Sunday. The four of them went to a bar called Angelo's in St Paul's Bay. Keith said that Sheila knew Angelo, the owner.

They were drinking at Angelo's, which overlooked a small cove, when Sheila, Paul and Paul's girlfriend decided to go for a swim. Keith stayed sitting outside the bar but as it was so close to the sea, he was still able to converse with them. They kept asking him to join them and eventually he did.

This does not reflect what Sheila Clarke told the court. She had testified that she had stayed sitting outside the bar while her boyfriend and the other couple went swimming.

It was when Keith was walking into the sea that he cut his toe quite badly. He was directed by someone to a doctor's surgery that was about 400 yards away from the bar. To his relief, he found that the surgery was open on a Sunday. The doctor put seven stitches into his big toe and gave him a tetanus injection.

Sheila Clarke had stated in her testimony that it was Rolf Harris who had directed them to the doctor's surgery. Had Rolf been at Angelo's bar and pointed them in the right direction of the doctor's surgery, it seems reasonable to assume that Keith would have remembered this.

The following day they all went to Valletta. It was very hot. Sheila, Paul and Paul's girlfriend were complaining about how hot it was, but Keith said he was enjoying it. When they returned to the apartment the other three did not want to go out again, so Keith decided to walk down to a local bar on his own. It was there that he met Rolf Harris and his wife, Alwen.

Keith soon realised that this bar, which was Caesar's day bar, was owned by Rolf Harris. (I should clarify here that it was part-owned by Rolf, but a tourist could not be expected to know this level of detail.) He told me that this was not the same bar as the one at which they had been drinking the day before, when he had cut his toe. That bar, which was called Angelo's, was further along the road.

I asked Keith if Sheila Clarke had ever mentioned meeting Rolf Harris on their holiday and if she had told him that Rolf Harris had kissed her. He said he did not recall Sheila ever having mentioned to him that she had met Rolf Harris during the holiday and, as far as he was concerned, she hadn't.

Shortly after they returned from this trip Keith broke up with Sheila Clarke. He met his wife, Susan, about four or five months later.

## SUSAN'S VERIFICATION

Susan told me that she met Keith in 1975. Keith told her about his previous girlfriend, Sheila Clarke, and Susan knew that they had broken up about five months previously. She recalled that at the time they started going out together he was still receiving telephone calls from her.

## RED FLAGS

It was fast becoming evident that Sheila Clarke had not told the truth about the holiday in Malta during which her boyfriend had cut his toe and Rolf Harris had allegedly indecently assaulted her in a bar. Some interesting background information had also come to light.

- The year of the alleged assault would have been 1974, not 1970 as Sheila Clarke had stated, and she would have been 22 years old, not 18.
- She knew Angelo, who was the owner of the bar known as Angelo's.
- Her father owned an apartment in Malta, and she went there regularly. She knew the St Paul's Bay area well.
- There were four people on the holiday in 1974, which she did not tell the court. She was swimming in the sea with the other couple. It was Keith who was sitting outside the bar watching them swimming.

- She did not say anything to Keith about having met Rolf Harris, so it follows that she did not tell him about anything that had allegedly taken place.

The police had all this information three months prior to the first trial but they allowed Sheila Clarke to provide testimony in court that was at best inaccurate and at worst untrue. Even if they did not believe Keith, and there was no reason not to, a quick check on the internet would have alerted them to the fact that Caesar's did not open until 1971. So why did police officers on Operation Yewtree allow a bad character witness to give to the court evidence that they must have known was inaccurate?

It is one of the many mysteries that surrounded this bad character evidence enquiry and the entire sorry saga of Operation Yewtree's pursuit of Rolf Harris, and indeed other celebrities, which, with some justification, has been likened by some to a witch hunt.

My concern about the reliability of Sheila Clarke's evidence was increasing with each enquiry I made. I decided to take a risk and get closer to her, which meant locating and interviewing members of her family. They were likely to know more about the history of her visits to Malta than anyone else.

My researchers had identified and located a possible address for her former husband. It was with some apprehension that I made the decision to call on him unannounced. I took with me a security guard, not for my protection but to have an independent witness with me in the event of any unfounded accusations. This is always a sensible precaution when visiting family members, as an historic sexual allegation can be quite a sensitive topic to discuss.

As it happened, I had nothing to worry about. Sheila Clarke's former husband, Richard, was at home. He greeted us with a bit of caution at first until I explained the purpose of my visit. He later told me that he had thought we were a couple of double-glazing salesmen. Richard welcomed us in, and we left over three hours later.

# FORMER HUSBAND RICHARD'S STORY

In the interests of openness and transparency I will point out at this juncture that what Richard told me was never tested in court. However, I do consider that what he told me is pertinent in terms of background information.

Richard told me that he had first met Sheila Clarke when he was a young man, and she was living in suburban Middlesex. He had worked with her father, Jim Clarke, in the travel industry for 30 years. Richard is 15 years older than Sheila and he is now retired.

Richard and Sheila started their relationship around 1976 and they soon married. The marriage was turbulent and lasted only six months. There followed protracted family court proceedings, during which time Sheila attended many hearings. At some of them she acted in person.

Richard said Sheila became extremely court-wise and would present herself to the court as a mousy, poor woman who would never do any harm to anyone. She was softly spoken, would wear cardigans with holes in the elbow and have unkempt hair. This was quite a contrast to the well-groomed image that was usual for Sheila owing to the requirements of her job in the travel industry.

Richard freely admits that he was no match for her because he is a big man with a deep authoritative voice. In the eyes of the male magistrates who sat in the Magistrates' Court, she was the poor downtrodden woman, and he was the big bully.

Sheila was still working in the travel industry but as far as Richard was aware she was never asked to provide details of her income. She would tell the court that she had no money. She outclassed Richard's lawyer and always won her case, and Richard was ordered to pay more.

It was not until 2000 that Richard's financial nightmare finally ended. During a Crown Court hearing his barrister informed the court that Sheila was earning good money working in the travel industry. After the judge had considered all the evidence, including details of Sheila's income, she made a court order that Richard did not have to make any further payments. The court had also refused Sheila's application for a share of Richard's pension. Finally, after 21 years involving 19 court appearances, Richard's nightmare ended.

Pausing briefly on Richard's story, I will draw attention to what Sheila Clarke told Southwark Crown Court, under oath, when giving bad character evidence against Rolf Harris in his first trial.

*Q. Do you enjoy coming to court to give evidence about....*

*A. I have never been – I have never been to court before apart from my divorce.*

It is little wonder that she hesitated when answering the question put to her in court. She may well have attended court only in relation to her divorce but what she omitted to tell the court was that she had been to court 19 times in 21 years. She had not only given witness testimony during those 19 court hearings; she had also become very adept at representing herself. Her 19 court appearances were always for the purpose of obtaining money from her former husband. This was not because he didn't pay the maintenance that the court had ordered him to pay – it was to get more money each time.

Sheila Clarke was not quite the novice witness that she had tried to portray herself as during Rolf Harris's first trial. She was a very experienced litigant who knew her way around the court system.

Returning to Richard's story, he was aware of the allegations that Sheila had made against Rolf Harris. He described them as 'total garbage' and said that, if what Sheila alleged Rolf Harris did to her had actually occurred, she would have been very open about it with everyone and would definitely have told him and her father.

Sheila had never said a word to Richard about Rolf Harris. Richard went to Caesar's often when he holidayed in Malta, and sometimes

Sheila accompanied him to the nightclub. Bugibba was like a second home to Sheila and her family.

Sheila's father, Jim Clarke, had introduced Richard to Angelo. Richard told me that he had stayed at Angelo's hotel, Sea View, which is now owned and operated by Angelo's son Isaac. Richard went on holiday to Bugibba with Sheila, and he has been back about 20 times since.

I showed Richard the photo of Sheila Clarke with Rolf Harris outside a building. He told me that he had never seen this photo before, and he believed that he would have seen it if Sheila had had it when they were together. He said that Sheila was never interested in photography, and he never saw her with a camera. She did not have photo albums and there were never any loose photos lying around the house. He said it was more than likely that the photo had been in an album owned by another member of the family, probably her mother. As Sheila Clarke's family had spent so much time in Malta, it was not inconceivable that the photo had been taken by a family member.

## MALTA INVESTIGATIONS

By this time, I had gathered enough information from my enquiries in the UK to go to Malta, where hopefully I could complete the jigsaw puzzle. I took my wife Maggi with me, which turned out to be a good move. Her PR background in the entertainment industry greatly helped with breaking the ice with the people we met along the way.

My first task was to establish where the photo of Sheila Clarke with Rolf Harris had been taken. This turned out to be more difficult than I imagined. The buildings around Bugibba Square in St Paul's Bay had undergone many changes, and I could not find any building that looked like the one in the photo.

I moved on to the next task and that was to locate Angelo's, near to where Keith had told me he had cut his big toe. This enquiry proved to be far easier. I was soon directed to the Seaview Hotel, which Sheila Clarke's former husband Richard had told me about. This is now owned and operated by Isaac Vella. I arranged a meeting with Isaac, who as it turned out was a mine of information on the history of Angelo's.

## ISAAC VELLA

Isaac Vella is the son of the late Angelo Vella. Angelo had purchased the Bognor Snack Bar on 15th January 1969, which was his first business venture in the area. The snack bar, which was situated in St Paul's Bay, was known to all in the area as Angelo's. It now operates as the Paulus fish restaurant and has no connection to the Vella family.

*The site of Angelo's snack bar in St Paul's Bay. The outlet has since changed hands and is now the Paulus fish restaurant.*

Isaac recalls working in the bar with his father. In the early 1970s it was frequented by servicemen owing to the cheap price of the drinks. The bar was small, with only two tables and a few chairs outside.

Customers also sat on wooden beer crates outside the bar.

The building in which Angelo's was situated is close to a bend on the main road, Dawret Il-Gzejjer, opposite where the breakwater is now located. Isaac informed me that in the 1970s the road was much narrower. These days there are two roads, a high road and a low road, which are divided by a traffic island.

*The solid white line that forms the left-hand border of the area with the diagonal lines was the edge of the road in the 1970s. This is where the old jetty was. The traffic island was constructed more recently along with everything else to the right of it.*

Back in the early 1970s only the higher part of the road existed. The sea was a lot closer. When the wind was blowing in, sea spray would come over the road and into the front of the bar.

To the right of the jetty was a cove with clear water. It was a popular place for swimming. Unfortunately, the rocks were very sharp, so it was easy for swimmers to cut their feet. The sea was so close that anyone sitting outside the bar could talk to people who were swimming. I told Isaac about Keith cutting his toe in 1974. He told me that the only place where he could have been talking to people who were swimming, then cutting his foot on sharp rocks, would have been at the cove opposite Angelo's.

I asked Isaac if there was a room off Angelo's bar and he replied that there wasn't. I asked him if there had ever been anything like a red Chesterfield sofa anywhere in the bar, or whether he remembered one, and he said no.

I also asked Isaac if he could recall Rolf Harris and Don Charles. He replied that he did recall them and knew that they had owned the Caesar's Nightclub and Restaurant in Bugibba Square, which was next to a doctor's surgery. The doctor's name was Dr Sansone.

Isaac told me that he had never seen or heard of Rolf Harris going to Angelo's.

## THE DOCTOR

My next assignment was to identify the doctor who would have attended to Keith after he cut his big toe. I was pointed in the direction of Dr Frendo.

## DOCTOR FRENDO

I turned up at Dr Patrick Frendo's surgery, which is situated at the rear of the St Simon's pharmacy in Bugibba. Dr Frendo told me that he had started his practice in either 1975 or 1976. The surgery was purpose built, along with the pharmacy, so there was no doctor or pharmacy there prior to 1975.

He told me that there had been only one doctor in the St Paul's Bay area prior to him setting up his practice, and that was Dr Sansone. Dr Sansone, who had died some years ago, had had his surgery in Bugibba Square.

I measured the distance from the jetty where in the 1970's Angelos was situated (now Paulus) to Bugibba Square where Dr. Sansone's surgery was, and the distance was about 600 yards.

*St Simon's Pharmacy. The Paulus fish restaurant is just around the left-hand bend.*

My investigations revealed that the son of the previous owners of the pharmacy, Simon Sammut, still lived in Malta and was residing in Mosta. I arranged a meeting with Simon, who is an electrician. He confirmed that his parents had opened the pharmacy around 1975 or 1976 and prior to that there was no pharmacy or doctor's surgery there. He further advised me that his mother, Josephine, was now living in England.

Simon kindly agreed to telephone his mother. She agreed to talk with me but first she had to locate the pharmacy's old prescription books, which she still had in storage.

I arranged to call Josephine when I returned to the UK to allow her the time she required. When I did call her, she had everything to hand and was able to tell me that the first prescription had been written out in January 1976, so this is when they opened the pharmacy. They had owned the building prior to the opening of the pharmacy and had used it as a holiday home when they were living in Mosta. They decided to turn it into a pharmacy because there were no other pharmacies in the area at the time.

Josephine told me that the only doctor in the Bugibba and St Paul's Bay area in the early 1970s was Dr Sansone, whose surgery was located in Bugibba Square. She reiterated what other locals had told me – that in the early 1970s there were only a few businesses operating in the area, and there were very few residents. Most of the buildings were holiday homes and that is why there was no requirement for more than one doctor. By the mid-1970s the area was starting to expand and there was an opening for a pharmacy and another doctor. This is what prompted her to invite Dr Frendo to join their pharmacy. He joined them in early 1976.

My enquiries confirmed that the only doctor who could have attended to Keith would have been the late Dr Sansone.

## DR SANSONE – VALLETTA ENQUIRIES

I travelled to Valletta to find two brothers, Raymond and Alex, who had a shoe shop in Bugibba Square in the early 1970s. Suzanne Barry had told me to contact them because she knew both of them when she was working at Caesar's and had kept in touch. I found both and asked them about Bugibba Square in the 1970s.

They told me that they had owned and operated a shoe shop in Bugibba Square and that they lived over the premises. The shoe shop was opposite Caesar's. They were resident there from 1963 until about 2001, when they moved the shoe shop to Valletta. They no longer had any ties to Bugibba Square and the shoe shop they once owned is now a restaurant. I can confirm this as my wife and I had dinner there one evening.

Both brothers told me that they remembered Caesar's, which was unsurprising given the location of their shoe shop. They also remembered Dr Sansone, who lived above his surgery, which was next door to Caesar's. They knew that he had died some years ago and that prior to the arrival of Dr Frendo he was the only doctor in the area. They also made reference to a jeweller's shop called Osaka, which was next door to Caesar's on the other side.

I asked Raymond and Alex if they were aware of Angelo's. They told me that there were three Angelo's bars. The oldest one had been situated on the corner opposite the jetty on Dawret Il-Gzejjer, the main road running alongside the waterfront.

## PAUL BUGEJA

I was told on my first day in Bugibba that the man I needed to speak with was Paul Bugeja, the owner of the building that was once Caesar's and which is now a nightclub called Club Black & White. Paul Bugeja is a former mayor of St Paul's Bay.

Maggi and I spent the three days we were in Malta trying to track Paul down. I had left messages at the restaurant for him and had been told that he would be there at a certain time. He wasn't, so I continued with the remainder of my enquiries. This happened three times and I started to think that I would never catch up with him, and a golden opportunity to speak to a man with so much knowledge of the area would be lost. However, on our last night we dropped by the restaurant, and I spoke with Paul's son, to whom I had spoken earlier.

He pointed cheerfully to a gentleman who was sitting at one of the tables and said, "There he is!" I turned and there was Paul looking at us with a big smile on his face. I later found out that he was not avoiding us – he just did things in his own time. A bit like in Spain – *mañana*.

Paul was more than happy to talk about St Paul's Bay. He confirmed that he had been the mayor of St Paul's Bay and had lived there since 1964.

In 1979 Paul had purchased the building in which Caesar's Nightclub & Restaurant and the day bar were situated. He knew the building well as he was a customer when Caesar's was being run by Don Charles. He also knew that Rolf Harris had been a partner in the club, and he had seen him performing there. When he purchased the building there had been no alterations made to it and it was the same as it had been when it was being operated by Don Charles.

Over the years he had made several additions and alterations, particularly to the front where the day bar was. He had built a much larger day restaurant, which until recently was called the Victoria Pub. It had since been upgraded again and is now known as the Victoria Gastropub. When he showed me around the inside of the building, I noticed that the old day bar was no longer being used as a bar. It is now part of the main kitchen that services the Victoria Gastropub. The front entrance to the day bar is still in situ, although it is not being used. A white metal shutter door has closed this off. The entrance to the nightclub is still the same and it is now the front entrance to Club Black & White.

I showed Paul Bugeja the photo of Rolf Harris and Sheila Clarke and asked him if he was aware of where this had been taken. Without a moment of hesitation, he pointed to the far end of the building where the restaurant kitchen is now and said, "There."

*The photo provided by Sheila Clarke of her with Rolf Harris*

supporting pillar

The photo had been taken outside and to the right of where the day bar had been in the 1970s. The frontage of the building shown in the photo has since been altered and modernised but before the alterations it was a jeweller's shop called Osaka. Part of this name plate can be seen above Sheila Clarke's head.

supporting pillar

*This photo shows how the walkway in front of the day bar looks today. It has been covered in and is now an extension of the Victoria Gastropub. The man standing in the photo is Paul Bugeja, the current owner of the building and former mayor.*

The entrance to the Victoria Gastropub is to the left of the above photo. The original entrance to the day bar is now covered by a white roller door, which is visible in the centre of the photo behind the trolley.

I made a closer inspection and sure enough I found the supporting pillar that can be seen behind Rolf Harris and Sheila Clarke in the photo that she supplied. When the alterations were done the pillar had been boxed in with cedar-coloured marine ply. However, it is still in situ and so is the door, which is on Rolf Harris and Sheila Clarke's left, with the window to their right. The door has been widened and modernised and the window has been upgraded.

With Paul Bugeja's assistance I had found the last piece of the jigsaw, which confirmed what I had been told by Suzanne Barry, the former singer at Caesar's. When Rolf Harris made his twice-yearly visits to perform at Caesar's he posed for photos with locals and tourists outside the Caesar's day bar. Paul also confirmed that this was where Rolf Harris normally had photos taken with tourists. The photo of Rolf Harris and Sheila Clarke had been taken outside Osaka, which was next door to Caesar's day bar.

I asked Paul if he could recall how many doctors were in the Bugibba and St Paul's Bay area in the 1970s. He had no hesitation in advising me that the only doctor was Dr Sansone, whose surgery was located next door to Caesar's. He said that Dr Sansone worked long hours and confirmed that he did work on Sundays. Another doctor, Dr Frendo, had set up a practice at St Simon's Pharmacy in the mid-1970s and he was still running his practice from this pharmacy.

As I had already spoken with Dr Frendo, I know this to be correct.

What I ascertained from Paul was that Caesar's day bar and the entrance to the nightclub were flanked by the doctor's surgery occupied by Dr Sansone on one side and by the jeweller's shop Osaka on the other. This was the shop outside of which the photo of Rolf Harris and Sheila Clarke had been taken. Paul, whose memory on these matters was excellent, told me that Osaka had been operated by a Thomas Cuschieri.

## PLAN OF CLUB

At the trial a sketch plan of Caesar's as it was in the 1970s was drawn and supplied to the court by Don Charles's daughter Joanne. Using this plan as a guide, and with feedback from the three people who knew Caesar's better than anyone – Suzanne Barry, Joanne Charles and Paul Bugeja – and based on my own inspection, I arranged for the construction of a computerised plan.

# COMPUTERISED PLAN OF CAESAR'S

I am confident that this plan, which is not to scale, depicts an accurate overview of how Caesar's Nightclub & Restaurant and the day bar were set up from the first day of opening, which was 5th June 1971.

Floor Plan of Caesar's Night Club Malta

When Caesar's was under the management and control of Don Charles, which was from 1971 until 1976, the entrance to the day bar was from Bugibba Square. The day bar and nightclub were not open on Sundays because that was the day that Don Charles took off to enable him to enjoy some time with his young family. This is significant because Keith had injured his toe on a Sunday, and Sheila Clarke had alleged that Rolf Harris had indecently assaulted her on the same day.

The day bar had two doors. One was at the main entrance in Bugibba Square and the other was an interconnecting door that led directly into the nightclub. There was no natural lighting in the nightclub, so when the front entrance doors to the nightclub were closed it was in darkness until the lights were switched on.

Notwithstanding the fact that the day bar wasn't open on a Sunday, if – as Sheila Clarke said in her evidence – Rolf Harris had taken her into another room off the day bar, she would have found herself in the nightclub, which would have been in total darkness. Lights would have had to be switched on. There was no other room as she had described. Neither was there a red Chesterfield sofa because the nightclub had wicker furniture.

In the nightclub there were two large murals on the walls. All witnesses spoken to told me that there was no painting of two little boys anywhere in the day bar or in the nightclub.

The bar in which Sheila Clarke alleged that she had been indecently assaulted could not have been Caesar's day bar or Angelo's. However, the photo of her standing next to Rolf Harris – which she claimed had been taken on the same day as the alleged assault – had been taken outside Osaka, the jeweller's shop next door to the day bar. Rolf would have had many photos taken with locals and tourists in the immediate vicinity of Caesar's. Her photo could have been taken at any time between 1971, when Caesar's opened, and 1976, when Rolf Harris and his business partners closed it.

## ST PAUL'S BAY AND BUGIBBA – RECONSTRUCTION

I find that picking up a tourist map is always a good start when I am new to an area because it helps to build up an overall picture of where everything is. So, the first item I collected before I commenced my reconstruction of the happenings on that eventful day – Sunday, 11th August 1974 – was a tourist map of St Paul's Bay, Bugibba and the adjacent area of Qawra.

The two points of interest that pertain to my investigation and reconstruction have been identified on this map. The dotted line along the sea front is listed in the index of the map as Sea Front Walk, although the actual name of the road is Dawret Il-Gzejjer.

On the tourist map I have added a black arrow and the name Angelo's Bar to show where Angelo's was situated in the 1970s. The thin white tail-like object opposite Angelo's is a breakwater, which one can walk along to get to the boats that are now moored in the harbour. This breakwater is a more recent construction. It was not there in the 1970s.

I have added a black arrow and the name Caesar's Bar to show where Caesar's and Dr Sansone's surgery were located in the 1970s.

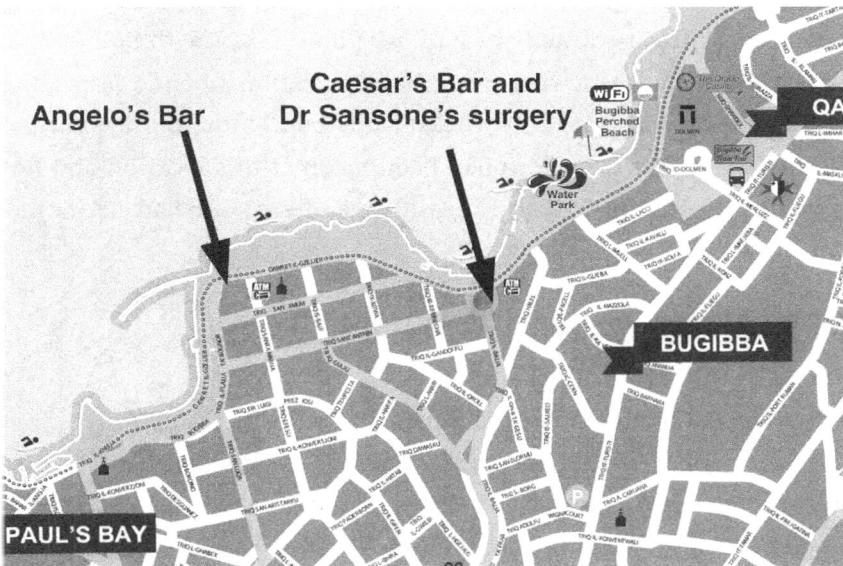

## ROUTE FOLLOWED FROM ANGELO'S BAR TO THE DOCTOR'S SURGERY

Sheila Clarke and her former boyfriend Keith both described how they were directed to a doctor's surgery in order for Keith to have his badly cut toe seen to. Keith said they walked about 400 yards to the surgery and were pleased to find that it was open on a Sunday.

As mentioned previously, the only doctor in the area in 1974 was Dr Sansone. His surgery was in Bugibba Square, which was in the direction in which they said they had walked. They would have followed the dots along the sea front on the tourist map from Angelo's to Bugibba Square. I measured the distance from Angelo's to Bugibba Square, which is about 600 yards. Given that this was over 40 years ago, and Keith was in pain from his injured toe, 400 yards is not a bad estimate on his part.

Sheila Clarke had told the court that she had gone back to the bar on her own later that same day to thank the people in there who had helped them. This is when Rolf Harris indecently assaulted her, according to her testimony. We are supposed to believe that immediately after having been indecently assaulted she had her photo taken with Rolf Harris, which shows her somewhat intertwined with him, outside Osaka, the jeweller's shop next door to Caesar's day bar. As mentioned earlier, I established that the photo had been taken at this location and not outside Angelo's, the bar opposite the cove where Keith had cut his toe.

## SHEILA CLARKE: OMISSIONS AND INCONSISTENCIES

What Sheila Clarke did not tell either the police or the court was that she knew Angelo, and so did her father. St Paul's Bay was like a second home to her and her family because her father owned an apartment in Bugibba, and they would have qualified for free or heavily discounted flights through working in the travel industry. She had led everyone to believe that she was not familiar with the bar where Keith had cut his toe.

Sheila Clarke omitted to tell the court that there were four people on the holiday. She mentioned only that she was there with her boyfriend. The court could be excused for thinking that there were only the two of them.

Sheila Clarke ought to have known full well where the photo of her and Rolf Harris was taken. It was not taken outside the bar where Keith cut his toe. It was taken at some other time outside Osaka, the jeweller's shop next to Caesar's day bar.

The room described by Sheila Clarke in which the alleged indecent assault had occurred was not at Caesar's, and according to Isaac Vella there was no such room at Angelo's. Either it did not exist, or it was a room somewhere else that had no connection to either bar.

Until she contacted the police in the run-up to the first trial, Sheila Clarke had not told anyone that she had met Rolf Harris on the holiday in 1974. This included Keith, who she said in evidence that she had told. According to her former husband, Richard, she would have told everyone if she had met Rolf Harris, especially if he had kissed her or indecently assaulted her.

Sheila Clarke told the Crown Prosecutor under oath that she had been to court only in connection with her divorce. While it appears that there was some truth in this, the frequency of her court attendances was not mentioned. According to Richard, she had been to court 19 times over 21 years, each time seeking more financial support from him. She had become so experienced in the workings of the court that she had dispensed with both her solicitor and her barrister and represented herself.

Sheila Clarke told the court at the first trial that she was not providing bad character evidence to obtain money from Rolf Harris. She was doing it to help others. After the court case she commenced a civil action against Rolf Harris for financial compensation in relation to the alleged indecent assault.

## SEQUEL

Often complainants are quite indignant when their complaints are investigated and challenged.

They do not accept that the accused has the right to investigate the validity of the allegations made against them.

Following my investigations into Sheila Clarke's civil action in claiming compensation, she became aware of investigators uncovering evidence that refuted her allegations. She then tried to withdraw her civil action against Rolf Harris, but she had not read the small print in the contract. If she withdrew, she was liable to pay her solicitor's costs. This was something that she had not anticipated.

Faced with my evidence, and a reluctant client, her solicitors had to consider the possibility that they would not win a civil court case. They decided to invoke what is called a Part 36, which is a provision in the Civil Procedure Rules that is designed to encourage parties to settle disputes without going to trial. Both claimants and defendants can inform the other side, via their respective solicitors, what they will accept in terms of an offer to resolve a dispute.

I do not know how this worked in practice, but my understanding is that when the civil claim was notified to Rolf Harris, his legal firm made a Part 36 offer to avoid unnecessary court costs. This offer was still on the table and could not be withdrawn, so Sheila Clarke's solicitors accepted it and her claim for compensation was closed.

My investigations ceased at this point.


## THE UNFAIRNESS OF BAD CHARACTER EVIDENCE

I fully investigated only one of the bad character witnesses used against Rolf Harris in the first trial. As I mentioned at the beginning of this chapter, bad character witnesses were used to bolster the evidence of the complainants because the evidence provided by the complainants was too weak to stand on its own.

The unfairness of using bad character witnesses is that anyone can say what they like about an accused and, as I have shown in this case, often the police will not carry out even the most basic checks to ensure that the evidence being provided by a bad character witness is genuine.

As part of their training, police detectives are taught to check out complaints. This will include bad character witness complaints. The problem with Operation Yewtree is that they ignored these principles and chose to accept almost anyone who was prepared to slate Rolf Harris.

Once again, we see the same old problem arising when it is advertised that complainants can receive large compensation payouts and to come forward. To come forward, no matter how unlikely the story, means that "**You will be believed.**"

*The construction of Caesar's in 1970/1971*

*Rolf Harris performing in Caesar's Nightclub during one of his twice-yearly visits to the club. Behind him is one of the two large murals that he painted on the walls of the nightclub.*

*Don Charles with his wife and daughters at Caesar's. Left to right, Anne Charles, Jo Charles (on stool), Julie Charles and Don Charles.*

# CHAPTER 12
# BALANCING THE
# SCALES OF JUSTICE

## THE FIRST TRIAL

Rolf Harris stood trial for the first time in May 2014. The trial took place at Southwark Crown Court, which is situated at 1 English Grounds on London's South Bank. In close proximity is London Bridge station, part of which exits on to Tooley Street, the main road leading to the court.

Opposite, moored on the Thames, is the retired Royal Navy warship HMS Belfast. A few years ago, in a curious juxtaposing of ancient and modern justice, or what once passed for justice, the London Dungeon tourist attraction was a neighbour.

Southwark Crown Court, which opened in 1983, is one of the country's largest court centres. This drab, inhospitable place was the venue for the London-based trials of celebrities who had been charged with historic crimes of a sexual nature.

Rolf Harris's first trial involved four accusers and a total of 12 charges. Seven related to one woman, whose friendship with Rolf Harris's daughter went back many years, three to another woman, and one each to the remaining two women. All involved allegations of indecent assault.

The trial commenced on 6th May 2014 and lasted eight weeks. On 19th June, the jury retired. Finally, on 30th June, the verdict was delivered: Rolf Harris had been found guilty. The jury had reached unanimous verdicts on all 12 counts.

## THE JURY

Most people will be unfamiliar with the practical aspects of a Crown Court trial. Inside Court 2 at Southwark Crown Court, Rolf Harris, being the accused, had to surrender himself to the court when he first arrived, following which he was taken into custody.

Throughout the trial Rolf Harris was seated next to a security guard in what I can only describe as a closed glass cage. To the right of this cage was seating for family and the press, and immediately behind was seating for the public. Owing to the intense media interest, journalists from the UK, Australia and New Zealand were also seated in the body of the court directly opposite the jury bench. In front of Rolf Harris were the prosecution and defence teams, which were overseen by the judge. Those seated in the area behind the glass cage struggled to hear the proceedings. On one occasion, a disgruntled member of the public shouted out to the judge, "Justice should be seen AND heard."

At the commencement of the trial the jury entered from the left of where Rolf Harris was seated in the glass cage. On the basis that most jurors will not have set foot in a Crown Court before, it must have come as quite a shock to some of them that the first thing they saw when entering the courtroom was a caged man with a security guard next to him.

Many will argue that it is the same for everyone charged with criminal offences. They are correct, but does that make it right? If the accused in these very historic sexual offence cases were a danger to the public, I would agree – but they are not. I was told that the biggest complaint Rolf Harris had throughout his trial was that he did not have free access to his legal team. From time to time, he would tap urgently on the glass with a pen; his legal team rarely ever heard or responded.

In England and Wales, when a criminal case has been sent to a Crown Court for trial a jury made up of 12 members of the public hears the case and decides whether the accused is guilty or not guilty. A judge presides over the hearing and directs the jury on matters of law.

The jury system consisting of twelve free men was first introduced by Henry II in the twelfth century to resolve land disputes. The present-day jury system developed from there and the criminal courts in the UK still operate in this way today. Twelve men and women are selected randomly from electoral rolls in the vicinity of the court, except for in Scotland, where there are 15 people on a jury in a criminal case.

The jury system has always been seen as a fair way of being judged by one's peers, and I agree with this concept. However, one must question whether some younger jurors of today are in a position to sit in judgement when the accused is elderly and the offences for which he or she is being charged date back over forty or fifty years.

What was considered to be normal conduct forty or fifty years ago is viewed in a completely different way now. We even have programmes showing celebrities watching clips from that time and being horrified as to what 'everyone' considered light-hearted fun, and 'the norm' – sexism, ageism and racism to name a few. I am not condoning this or saying it was right, but it was commonplace and, in most quarters, acceptable behaviour at that time.

In my view, a true jury of Rolf Harris's peers would have been made up of people who were teenagers or adults during the time when the offences were allegedly committed, and who were familiar with the social conventions that applied at the time. This would not have been as difficult as it sounds, as the jurors' ages would have ranged from, say, 60 upwards. My opinion is shared by others with whom I have discussed this thorny issue.

Back to the jury and what they faced coming into this trial. From the outset there was a media frenzy, with the tabloid press branding Rolf Harris and other celebrities who were charged with historic sexual offences 'paedophiles', 'shamed stars' and various other pejorative terms that were guaranteed to sell newspapers. Unflattering photographs of them were splashed over the front pages. By the time Rolf Harris's trial commenced the gutter press had effectively convicted him several times over and would continue to report in this manner throughout his trial.

At the end of each day the jurors returned to their homes and mixed with family and friends. As with any jurors, they would have been subjected to the opinions of various people outside the court, many of whom would have made up their minds about the accused's guilt or innocence from what they had read in the press. Anyone who thinks the average juror will not discuss the case with friends and relatives, or read about it online or in the papers, is living on another planet.

Now, having had to deal with all of the above, these average everyday people had to walk into a courtroom every day and see the accused caged up with a security guard beside him.

Most people's experience of court cases comes from seeing programmes on television, or from American films of courtroom dramas. The accused normally sits next to their defence counsel as a free, innocent person accused of a crime. The defence counsel then argues the case on behalf of their client and evidence is produced by the prosecution and defence. The viewer is left with the impression that the accused received a fair trial. The guilty are sent to prison, the innocent are freed.

Am I being too harsh on the English court system? I am sure there are some out there who will think that, but I believe in a justice system where everyone is given a fair hearing. As the saying goes, a picture is worth a thousand words.

The jury was made up of 12 members of the public who would initially have been part of a larger group selected randomly from the electoral register. It would be unusual for any of the jurors to have served on a jury before, so it would be safe to say that they would have had very little or no experience of the workings of the criminal justice system. It is for the judge to explain to them how the system works, and at the end of the trial they have to make decisions based on what they have heard and seen in the courtroom. When a trial lasts for several weeks, they need to balance their home and personal lives around the court case.

I will now refer to a matter that received only limited press coverage at the time and which will undoubtedly be a cause for concern for many people. It certainly rocked the Harris family and Rolf's supporters. There was one juror whose understanding of the criminal justice system could have influenced other members of the jury during deliberations, in theory at least.

In the first trial one of the jurors was a serving Metropolitan Police officer: a police officer who was serving in the same police force that was controlling the Operation Yewtree team. We are not talking here about a serving police officer who was working in another police force within the UK. Even that could be argued as being a conflict of interest, but surely a policeman working in the same police force is a clear conflict of interest. In my opinion this should never have been allowed.

How could this have been permitted? Quite easily, it seems, because in England serving police officers can serve on a jury. The officers are supposed to act as civilians but there is nothing to preclude them from advising their fellow jurors of their occupation. Not that they would not pick up on the fact that this juror had a lot of knowledge about how the criminal justice system operates.

I am sure most people in England will be quite amazed, if not a bit shocked, to hear that a police force can permit one of their own to be on a jury, hearing charges that the same force has been tasked with investigating. It is not permitted in countries like New Zealand, Australia and Canada. In fact, it is not allowed in Scotland and Northern Ireland, so why in England?

The Jury

Hello
Hello
Hello

The jury in the first trial differed greatly from the juries in the second and third trials. As well as having a serving Metropolitan Police officer on the jury at the first trial, there were three, possibly four jurors who appeared to have difficulties with literacy and numeracy and who had difficulty in finding documents in the jury binders. One older man kept falling asleep and was elbowed in the ribs from time to time by the woman beside him to keep him awake. She was subsequently revealed to be the foreperson of the jury.

One woman who was present at all three trials remarked to me following the third trial that the contrast between the jury at the first trial and the juries at the two subsequent trials was such that "It was awful to watch."

# THE TRIAL

The initial allegation of indecent assault that led to Rolf Harris's arrest and subsequent trials at Southwark Crown Court was made by a former friend of Rolf's daughter. The woman has anonymity so I will refer to her as Pamela Broadhurst.

When the news broke that Rolf Harris had been arrested and interviewed, three other women came forward with complaints of indecent assault. All three had a legal right to anonymity. Two of the women, Wendy Rosher and Theresa Malcolm, waived their right to lifelong anonymity and sold their accounts to the media. As the rules surrounding anonymity are somewhat complex, Theresa Malcolm is a pseudonym. Wendy Rosher died a few years after the trial ended, so no longer has anonymity. The third woman, who I will refer to as Deidre Connor, retained her right to it.

The trial judge, Justice Sweeney, rearranged the charges in the first trial to be heard in date order. This meant that the charge relating to the alleged assault on Wendy Rosher would be heard first. The downside, as far as the defence was concerned, was that this would cement in the jury's minds at an early stage the message that Rolf Harris had been assaulting women and girls from 1969, when he was aged 39. Of course, we now know that Rolf had never met Wendy Rosher and had never set foot in the community centre where she claimed that he had assaulted her.

In her opening address, the Crown Prosecutor, Sasha Wass QC, provided the jury with a summary of the evidence that the Crown intended to produce in support of the charges that had been laid against Rolf Harris, which included the bad character evidence. The Crown Prosecutor had this to say:

*The evidence of the four complainants combined with the evidence of bad character (much of which occurred within the same time frame) demonstrates a persistent pattern of sexual offending by the defendant over a thirty-year period.*

1.  *The evidence demonstrates that the defendant had:*

    a.  *A sexual interest in underage girls.*

    b.  *A tendency to use his celebrity status to sexually touch females with impunity.*

    c.  *A tendency to touch females of all ages in a sexual manner in public circumstances.*

2.  *All of this evidence taken together makes it less likely that each or any of the complainants have fabricated their allegation.*

## COMPLAINANT ONE

First to give evidence was 53-year-old Wendy Rosher. She was a compelling witness. Her presentation of a fabricated story was so well executed that she convinced not only the jury but also the trial judge that she was telling the truth when she alleged that she had been indecently assaulted by Rolf Harris when she had just turned eight years of age. I think it is fair to say that her testimony set the scene for the remainder of the trial.

With the scene set it was time for Sasha Wass QC, to launch a scathing attack on Rolf Harris's character – and attack she did. At the commencement of her cross-examination, she made her intentions very clear when she told Rolf Harris that the jury had "to decide whether underneath your friendly and lovable exterior, there is a darker side lurking."

Her attack on the character of the then 84-year-old Rolf Harris continued unabated throughout the two days he was on the witness stand. She belittled him, in my view, and seemed to delight in enlightening the jury about how he had betrayed his wife's trust by having two extra-marital affairs, which she described as 'secret sexual episodes'. She continued with her Star Wars 'dark side' theme by telling Rolf Harris "You are pretty good at disguising that dark side of your character, are you not, Mr Harris?" And again, "The issue that we really have to fathom in this court is how dark that dark side actually is."

Sasha Wass QC's cross-examination of Rolf Harris was truly like something out of Star Wars. Her tactics were to take Rolf Harris completely out of his comfort zone by targeting his deep sense of guilt in betraying the trust of his wife and daughter. She could then present to the jury a beloved entertainer who had a dark side that turned him into a sexual predator. If successful, which it was, this would divert the judge and jury's thought processes away from the fact that the evidence on all the counts was weak and would not stand alone.

Am I being too harsh? I think not because Justice Sweeney wrote the following in his published sentencing remarks dated 4th July 2014:

*On Count 1 you indecently assaulted 'A' in 1969 (when she was aged 8 and you were aged 39). You did so when you made an appearance at the Leigh Park Community Centre in Havant, and she approached you for your autograph. Others were present. Taking advantage of your celebrity status, you twice put your hand up her skirt between her legs and touched her vagina over her clothing. In her Victim Impact Statement 'A' states, which I am sure is true, that you took her childhood innocence – for which she blamed herself and became an angry child and teenager, unable to express herself and unable to trust men. She continued, "I have carried what Rolf Harris did to me for most of my life; it took away my childhood, it affected every aspect of my life from the point he assaulted me. Something that he did to me for fun that caused me physical and mental pain for his own pleasure and then probably forgot about as quickly as he did it, has had a catastrophic effect on me..."*

As far as I am aware, 11 of the 12 jurors in the first trial had little or no experience of the law and were unfamiliar with court procedure. I think it would be fair to say that some of them would have felt somewhat daunted by the huge wave of media interest.

However, no matter how daunted or otherwise the jury felt, their job was to examine the evidence and return the right verdict. Judge Nigel Sweeney was an experienced campaigner who I would have thought had learnt enough in his years on the bench to see through Oscar-winning performances. He should have ensured that the jurors were brought back down to earth and instructed to examine the evidence, which in the case of Wendy Rosher was non-existent apart from her own testimony and the rambling account of the witness David James.

Three years later, three Court of Appeal judges were able to do this. Had a different approach been taken at the first trial, Wendy Rosher's allegation would have been shown up for what it was – a fabrication.

It follows, therefore, that if the scanty and unreliable evidence of Wendy Rosher had been discounted, as it should have been, a completely different scenario would have been presented to the jury from the outset, given that the charge involving Wendy Rosher was the first to be heard. In view of her age at the time of the alleged assault, and the shock factor associated with this, I think it is likely that her evidence became the benchmark by which the remaining cases were judged. Had her evidence been discounted, it is likely that the evidence of the other complainants and bad character witnesses would have been viewed in a different light.

As it stood, Wendy Rosher's testimony was taken at face value and believed. And as the trial progressed, the prosecution interpreted anything that stretched the bounds of credibility as being down to Rolf Harris's love of taking risks and his 'dark side'.

## COMPLAINANT TWO

As mentioned earlier, I have given the second complainant the pseudonym Deidre Connor as she has anonymity.

The oft-used idiom 'You can't make this stuff up' must surely apply to Count 2 of the first trial. The situation was nothing short of extraordinary, and it still defies belief that Rolf Harris was found guilty on this charge.

Deidre Connor claimed that Rolf Harris had indecently assaulted her by rubbing her buttocks, over her clothing, when she was 13 years old and working as a waitress to earn pocket money at the BBC's televised game show It's a Knockout. She testified that the event had taken place at Parker's Piece, a green in the centre of Cambridge. Notwithstanding the fact that she had the location wrong – this event had been held at Cambridge City FC's ground, and not at Parker's Piece – her account was accepted by the prosecution.

The court was told that this large-scale event had been held in 1975 and televised for BBC1. All the evidence produced by the prosecution centred around 1975 and It's a Knockout. Deidre Connor gave her evidence, and the prosecution closed their case. It was then time for Rolf Harris's defence team to present their case.

The defence team provided irrefutable evidence that Rolf Harris had never appeared at this event because at the time he was performing in a concert in Toronto, Canada. However, when providing his testimony in court he made a mistake that was to cost him dearly. He said he had never been to Cambridge prior to 2010.

As the media were reporting constantly on the trial, the evidence that Rolf had not been at It's a Knockout in 1975 attracted widespread publicity. This prompted Jackie Daniels, whose subsequent allegations are covered in Chapter 9, to contact the police and tell them that Rolf Harris had been in Cambridge prior to 2010 because she remembered him participating in ITV's Star Games in 1978. This event had been held at Jesus Green, which is situated to the north of the city centre. The police checked this information and located evidence that Rolf Harris had indeed participated in Star Games, and they obtained the televised footage of the event.

The prosecution made an application to adduce further evidence whilst Rolf Harris was still giving his testimony. Halfway through the trial they revealed that they had a new witness who had come forward. The amendment of Count 2 to change the date range of the allegation from between 1st January 1975 and 1st January 1976 to between 1st January 1975 and 1st January 1979, after the close of the prosecution case, caused unfair prejudice and injustice to Rolf Harris. The prosecution application was made, in part, to rebut evidence given by Rolf Harris during the course of his evidence in chief that the first time he had visited Cambridge was in 2010.

The defence had at all times been prepared to meet the prosecution case as it was understood to be, which was that the alleged assault had taken place at the recording of It's a Knockout in 1975 when the complainant was aged 13.

Once the application had been accepted by the judge, Rolf Harris and his defence team found themselves in the unenviable position of being required to answer a very different case, one for which they had not prepared.

It wasn't only the date that had changed. Deidre Connor's age had changed, her employer at the event had changed, the venue had changed, and the programme and broadcaster had changed. The judge allowed this, giving no adjournment to allow Rolf's defence team the opportunity to investigate these changes.

As an investigator I need to ask the question, how was this allowed to happen? In this case one cannot blame the defence lawyers, as they had prepared the defence case to answer the charge. Their investigations revealed that Rolf Harris had not participated in It's a Knockout in Cambridge in 1975, so Deidre Connor was either lying or she had mistaken Rolf for someone else. Neither Rolf Harris, nor his defence lawyers, would have had any inkling that mid-trial the charge would be changed to reflect a different venue, and a different event, held three years later.

In her evidence Deidre Connor told the court that she was a mature 13-year-old when she was working at It's a Knockout when the event was taking place at Parker's Piece, Cambridge. I will add at this point that she lived in the area and attended a local school, so she should have known the difference between Parker's Piece and Jesus Green.

Whilst Parker's Piece and Jesus Green are both in Cambridge, they are over a mile apart and look quite different. Parker's Piece is close to the city centre and is surrounded by steeples and university buildings, whereas Jesus Green is to the north of the city centre and borders the River Cam. Moreover, Jesus Green has a lido – a large and unmistakable outdoor swimming pool.

It's a Knockout held in Cambridge in 1975 – which took place at Cambridge City FC's ground, and not at Parker's Piece – was a huge event. There are reports that over 25,000 people attended, with many being turned away because of overcrowding.

On Saturday, 24th May 1975 the Cambridge Evening News reported on its front page:

*Champagne corks popped last night as the Cambridge "It's a Knockout" team took time off from limbering up for tomorrow's three-cornered battle to toast themselves in bubbly.*

*The team meets teams from Oxford and Peterborough for the marathon tussle at the Cambridge City football ground – a full day of practice, full rehearsal and the final game recorded for BBC television.*

In contrast, Star Games in 1978 was a more modest affair, with only a few thousand people attending. It is hard to see how Deidre Connor could have mistaken one event for the other, particularly if she was by then 16, as she would have been once the venue and date were changed by the court.

If what I have written so far sounds a bit confusing, or maybe even fanciful, imagine how Rolf Harris and his family felt when the court allowed the change of venue and date. He found he was no longer facing a charge of indecently assaulting a 13-year-old; he was now facing a charge of indecently assaulting a 16-year-old, at a different venue, three years later.

So, why wasn't this charge dropped when Rolf Harris was able to show that he was not in the country when It's a Knockout took place, and that he did not participate in it? At the very least the complainant Deidre Connor should have been recalled to the witness stand to change her evidence to fit in with the new date and place, three years later. She was not.

The ruling of Mr Justice Sweeney in allowing the change of date is hard to follow. Initially he stated that the change of date would be prejudicial to Rolf Harris, but then he did a complete about-turn and argued that it wasn't prejudicial. He then repeated what the prosecution had argued, "There was no realistic possibility that the television crew, other celebrities or unbroadcast footage could provide any evidence of value, and the relevant catering company had gone into liquidation and none of its records had survived (thereby depriving both sides of those records)."

The views of the judge on the submissions of the prosecution show just how out of touch judges can be with what a professional investigation can uncover. Had I adopted this attitude when investigating the second complaint in relation to Star Games, which I have covered in Chapter 9, I am quite convinced that Rolf would have been found guilty on this charge also. Of course, the television crew, other celebrities and television footage could have provided evidence of value, as I have illustrated in Chapter 9.

When I received my instructions to investigate the convictions a year after the first trial had ended, I was told that the priority was the conviction relating to Wendy Rosher. This was because Rolf was adamant that he had never set foot in the community centre where she alleged that the incident had occurred. It was also a matter of concern that she claimed to have been only eight years old at the time of the alleged offence. It goes without saying that it was this charge in particular that led to the media branding Rolf Harris a 'paedophile'.

I did start to make some enquiries into the convictions that involved the other three complainants at the first trial but, as previously mentioned, these enquiries were curtailed when further charges were laid. I had to prioritise all my future investigations owing to time restraints and finances.

As part of my enquiries, I needed to establish whether Deidre Connor was living in Cambridge in 1978. The Crown Prosecution Service and the police had been so delighted at finding that Rolf Harris had been at Star Games in 1978 that they overlooked the not entirely insignificant matter of whether Deidre Connor was there.

My research team did establish that Deidre Connor's parents were listed on the electoral roll as living in Cambridge in 1975. They next showed up on the electoral roll in Oxford in 1979.

The line of enquiry I was intending to follow was to establish whether Deidre Connor was living in Cambridge when Star Games was taking place.

It appears that no-one pursued the line of enquiry as to where Deirdre Connor was living at the time. Their interest was concentrated solely on where Rolf Harris was.

One of the enquiries a member of my team made was with the sister of Deidre Connor. She was not prepared to assist. Shortly after, I received a telephone call from Diedre demanding to know why I was making enquiries when Rolf Harris was convicted and in jail. I advised her that we had been instructed to complete investigations to establish whether there were grounds for an appeal. She became quite aggressive and told me not to interview her teenaged daughter. I told her that I had no interest in interviewing her daughter as she had not been born at the time of the alleged incident.

The telephone call continued in the same vein for a while longer, with Deidre Connor telling me not to contact her daughter and me in turn advising her that I had no intention of doing this. She then asked me what I wanted to know so I told her that my enquiries had led me to suspect that she was not living in Cambridge in 1978, and that she was living in Oxford. I then asked her outright and her reply was, "That's for you to find out." She then terminated the call.

I am sure there were doubts about the authenticity of this complaint and I am equally sure that the Crown Prosecution Service knew this. But what did come out of this complaint was Rolf Harris stating in his evidence that he had not been to Cambridge prior to 2010. This point was seized on by the Crown prosecutor Sasha Wass QC and she made a real meal out of it. Clearly, she was aiming to convince the jury that Rolf Harris had lied deliberately to cover up the fact that he had taken part in Star Games in Cambridge in 1978.

The question is, did Rolf Harris lie? The answer is simple. He did not.

Rolf Harris would have attended thousands of events during his career as an artist and entertainer. Other celebrities who attended Star Games told me that they would have difficulty in recalling where they had been on a specific date or where certain events had been held years ago – and in some cases even during the previous year – unless something significant had occurred. The length of their careers did not match that of Rolf's, yet he had been expected to remember an event that had taken place 35 years previously. It also needs to be said that, at 84, Rolf's memory might not have been quite as sharp as it would have been in his earlier years.

In the course of my investigations, I learned that it was common practice to put celebrities and the film crew on a coach for big events and transport them back again afterwards. They might end up in lookalike towns or featureless parks. As I have already pointed out, Jesus Green is not in the centre of Cambridge and there is nothing to remind any visitor that this is the famous university town. I have addressed this point in more detail in Chapter 9.

So why did Rolf Harris tell the court that he had not visited Cambridge prior to 2010?

Two reasons.

Firstly, he could not remember going there. It was not until he was shown the archived TV footage of the event that he recognised himself and remembered competing at Star Games. He had been asked to recall one of the many locations that he had visited in a career spanning over 60 years and simply had no recollection of it.

Secondly, and even more importantly, was that Rolf Harris had been told by his legal advisors that his first recorded visit to Cambridge was in 2010, when he visited the city to promote some of his paintings.

## COMPLAINANT THREE

By the time the third complainant was called to give evidence, Rolf Harris had been branded a liar and an adulterer who had a 'dark side' that he had kept hidden. The complainant, who has anonymity and who I will refer to as Pamela Broadhurst, had been a friend of Rolf Harris's daughter, Bindi, for many years. They had been neighbours and had grown up together. Pamela and Bindi had been inseparable until they were in their mid-teens, when the Harrises moved away from the area.

Pamela Broadhurst's complaint accounted for seven of the charges against Rolf Harris. She was the person who had first contacted the police, following which an investigation had been launched and proceedings brought against Rolf Harris by the Crown Prosecution Service. He was accused of grooming Pamela Broadhurst when she was in her early teens, which he denied. He had no interest in Pamela Broadhurst and was so busy touring and performing that he hardly ever saw her, let alone groomed her. He did admit to having met with her occasionally after she had turned 18, and that sexual activity had taken place, but he was adamant that she had instigated it.

The evidence revealed that contact between them, either written, by telephone or in person, was infrequent. Often there was a year to 18 months without any contact. This could hardly be described as a relationship, and certainly not as grooming. It is also worth noting that these infrequent liaisons lasted until she was 29, which makes a mockery of the 'paedophile' label that the press attached to Rolf Harris.

There were accusations and counter-accusations about when the sexual relationship started but what was not in doubt was that they did have a sexual relationship that at best was made up of casual encounters. Pamela Broadhurst claimed that Rolf Harris had first indecently assaulted her in 1978, when she was 13 years of age, during a trip that she had been on at the invitation of the Harrises to Canada, Hawaii and Australia. Rolf Harris claimed that nothing of the sort had happened. He said that the affair-of-sorts had started when Pamela was 18 or 19 years of age, and that she had instigated it. There was no evidence to corroborate either version, so it was her word against his.

Rolf Harris's occasional extra-marital dalliances with Pamela Broadhurst were exposed around 1996 or 1997 when she contacted him by telephone asking for money, specifically £25,000, to enable her then partner to finance a bird sanctuary in which he had an interest. Rolf told her that he did not have that sort of money. The phone call ended acrimoniously. Soon after this telephone conversation a heavily intoxicated Pamela Broadhurst called Rolf Harris again and advised him that she had told her parents about what she described as 'the affair'.

What followed were verbal exchanges, a meeting ordered by Pamela Broadhurst and threats to go to the newspapers if Rolf did not give her the money. Pamela Broadhurst's father wrote to Rolf and told him that he was disgusted with his behaviour and did not want to see him or hear from him ever again.

Rolf Harris's reaction was to burn the letter, which he did, but it kept troubling him and eventually he decided to write to Peter Broadhurst. In this letter he asked Peter Broadhurst to forgive him and made it clear that the infrequent sexual activity that had taken place had been consensual.

This letter was kept by the Broadhursts and handed over to the police when Pamela Broadhurst decided to lodge a complaint 15 years later. It was used extensively by the Crown Prosecution Service. Rather than accept it as a letter of conscience, it was distorted to make it sound like a confession. An analysis of the letter does not reveal an admission of criminality by Rolf Harris.

The Broadhursts did not go to the police on receipt of this letter. Had they been of the view that Rolf Harris had committed a criminal act against their daughter, surely this would have been the expected course of action? One can only conclude that while they were not exactly happy about what had gone on between Rolf and their daughter, who was by now well into adulthood, they didn't consider it to be a criminal matter. Nowhere in the letter did Rolf Harris confess to the crimes with which he had been charged, but there is a clue as to Pamela Broadhurst's claim that he assaulted her from the age of 13.

In the letter to Pamela's father, Rolf explained that he had told Pamela that she looked lovely in her bathing suit. This, of course, is one of those comments that would have been taken at face value some years ago, but which now would be best avoided. I have bolded the relevant part of the letter.

*'[Pamela] keeps saying that all this has been going on since she was thirteen. She's told you that, and you were justly horrified, and she keeps reiterating that to me, no matter what I say to the contrary.* **She says admiring her and telling her she looked lovely in her bathing suit was just the same as physically molesting her.** *I didn't know'.*

Of course, telling someone that they look lovely in their bathing suit is not the same as physically molesting them, but Pamela's assertion that it is the same does shed some light on her belief that Rolf Harris assaulted her from the age of 13.

To his detriment, this letter, which had been written in good faith by a man who was rightly ashamed of himself for not rejecting the interest shown in him by his daughter's friend once she had become an adult, was used against him at his trial.

Furthermore, the police preparation in compiling Pamela Broadhurst's evidence was extraordinary. This caused Sonia Woodley QC, Rolf's defence barrister at the first trial, to call it 'a rehearsal'.

It was not until November 2012 that Pamela Broadhurst went to the police and made the complaint against Rolf Harris.

On 20th November 2012 she gave an account to the police that was captured on video and which lasted two hours.

She returned on 8th February 2013 to go over some of the matters she had already spoken about in the video interview, and to deal with one or two additional matters.

On 17th February 2013 she went back to the police again. There were two interviews on that day, lasting a total of 82 minutes.

She went back again on 27th February 2014. Again, there were two interviews, the first lasting 45 minutes and the second lasting 35 minutes.

On 15th March 2014 she made two witness statements to the police, all about what she claimed had happened between her and Rolf Harris.

On 28th April 2014, shortly before the start of the first trial, and on 7th May 2014, the day after it started, she sat with the police and watched the recorded video interviews she had provided on 20th November 2012 and 8th February 2013. During the review of the video interviews, Pamela Broadhurst changed parts of her initial statement.

If one considers the actions of the Operation Yewtree officers in a cynical way, the amount of preparation and rehearsals involved in compiling the testimony of Pamela Broadhurst could surely be interpreted as 'grooming a witness'.

## COMPLAINANT FOUR

I have given complainant four the pseudonym Theresa Malcolm. She was a child actress from New South Wales, Australia. In 1986, at the age of 15, she was a member of a theatre youth group that was on a five-week tour of England. Her allegations accounted for three of the charges against Rolf Harris, which were Counts 10, 11 and 12.

Theresa Malcolm alleged that when the group arrived at Heathrow Airport on a flight from Sydney they were met by Rolf Harris and his wife Alwen, who were friends of the artistic director who had arranged the tour.

According to Theresa Malcolm, later that evening they had dinner at the Queens Arms pub in Woolwich, London. It was during this informal dinner that Rolf Harris sat her on his lap and indecently assaulted her. Following this he then waited for her outside the ladies' toilets, and when she came out, he indecently assaulted her again.

No other person in this crowded pub saw or heard anything, and Theresa Malcolm told no-one about what she alleged had happened to her. When questioned over this incident Rolf Harris said that he did recall the dinner at the Queens Arms, but he did not accept that the allegations were true. He had no recollection of Theresa Malcolm or of her sitting on his lap at any time, and he pointed out inconsistencies in her evidence about the timing of when these alleged assaults occurred.

At the point when Theresa Malcolm first contacted the British police, the allegations against Rolf Harris were being covered extensively by the British and Australian media. However, instead of going to the police in the first instance, Theresa Malcolm spoke to a well-known publicist, Max Markson, who was based in Sydney. Markson used his contacts in the media to sell her story. One of the interested parties was an Australian publishing company. However, they would not run a story without Theresa Malcolm first reporting her allegations to the police, which she did. Operation Yewtree detectives arrived in Sydney and took a statement from her.

Max Markson negotiated with two media groups for Theresa Malcolm to relate her story to a magazine and to broadcast a television exclusive. News reports at the time of the first trial state that the fee paid in total for these interviews was A$60,000. Although Theresa Malcolm claimed that she had not received the full amount owing to her after Max Markson had deducted his fee, she still benefited financially.

Whilst the UK police did not seem the slightest bit concerned about Theresa Malcolm attempting to sell her story to the media before reporting the alleged assaults to the police, and then selling her story via her publicist prior to the trial, the same view was not shared in Australia.

An Australian newspaper raised the issue of the possible wider consequences of Theresa Malcolm's decision to give paid interviews to a magazine and in a television broadcast. I quote:

*Any potential criminal trial involving Rolf Harris could be prejudiced by a [redacted] woman's decision to go public in paid interviews about how she was allegedly sexually assaulted by the entertainer.*

Max Markson asserted in the same article that Theresa Malcolm had given her interviews after she had gone to the police. What he did not explain was that he had brokered a deal with the two media groups before she had reported the allegations to the police, and that it had been agreed between the parties that the interviews would go ahead only after she had spoken to the police.

At the trial Theresa Malcolm presented herself as a woman whose life had been badly affected by what Rolf Harris had done to her as a 15-year-old. She said that at the time she had been a budding young actress and that this incident had virtually put paid to her acting and singing career.

There was a glaring inconsistency in her evidence that fell well short of credibility. Theresa Malcolm claimed that the alleged incident with Rolf Harris, which had happened at an informal dinner on the first night of the tour, had affected her so much that she had lost over six kilograms – about a stone – in weight, and that by the time she returned home five weeks later her mother said she hardly recognised her.

Research carried out by Rolf Harris's then defence team uncovered an important fact, which was that the informal celebration held at the Queens Arms pub in Woolwich had taken place shortly before the end of the five-week tour, and not on the first night.

When questioned about this, Theresa Malcolm simply replied that it was a long time ago and she could not be expected to remember everything.

Let's look at this evidence more closely. Theresa Malcolm claimed that she had lost over six kilograms over the five weeks of the tour as a result of what Rolf Harris had done to her when they had met at the start of it. But – and this is a significant but – the event at which she alleged that Rolf had assaulted her, and which had apparently caused her to lose such a large amount of weight, had taken place near the end of the tour. It defies belief that she could have lost six kilograms in such a short time.

Theresa Malcolm was permitted to brush aside this glaring inconsistency, which no-one really picked up on. Perhaps by then the jury had already made up their minds that Rolf Harris was guilty, and they were in no mood to consider any evidence that contradicted this.

## WITNESS: CRAIG MORTON

At the time Theresa Malcolm alleged that Rolf Harris had indecently assaulted her, she was in a long-term relationship with a man who I will refer to as Craig Morton. They had been together for about seven years and during that time they had three children.

According to Theresa Malcolm, Rolf Harris's name had come up in conversation with Craig Morton around 2008. They had been watching a television programme in which Rolf had been demonstrating to the audience how to use a wobble board. Craig Morton had commented that he didn't like him, to which Theresa Malcolm replied that she thought he was a dirty old man.

Theresa Malcolm went on to explain to Craig Morton that she had met Rolf Harris in a pub in London when she was aged 15 and on a tour. She told him, and later repeated this in court when giving evidence, that she had sat on his lap and had felt something that she thought might have been an erection.

Craig Morton maintained that nothing further had been said about it until 2013, when they were reading a newspaper article about British police being in Sydney to make enquiries about Rolf Harris following the allegations of indecent assault that had been made against him in Britain.

When Theresa Malcolm later gave her evidence in court, she said that Rolf Harris had asked her to sit on his lap, but the way in which she described how she had sat on his lap made the allegation implausible. She said that when she sat on his lap, she was straddling him with her back to him. In 1986 the Queens Arms pub in Woolwich had long wooden bench seating along the wall with large heavy wooden tables in front of the bench seating. The table would have prevented anyone from sitting on another person's lap. Another potential difficulty is that Rolf's wife, Alwen, and the tour organisers were sitting with him.

As I pointed out earlier, Max Markson negotiated with the two media groups for interviews with Theresa Malcolm. According to what Craig Morton told Rolf Harris's solicitors, the payment for these interviews was between A$60,000 and A$70,000, which is higher than the figure of A$60,000 quoted by various newspapers.

According to Craig Morton, Max Markson had asked him to confirm that in 2008 Theresa Malcolm had told him about meeting Rolf Harris. Craig Morton agreed that Theresa Malcolm had told him that she had sat on Rolf's lap, but that is all she had told him. He later told Rolf's solicitors that just prior to the police interview she added the part about Rolf indecently assaulting her. Craig Morton said that he was not prepared to lie and say she had told him this in 2008.

Craig Morton said that after Theresa Malcolm had concluded her interview with a magazine publisher, she had filled him in on the details. He alleged that she said that she had added the part about Rolf following her to the lavatory and assaulting her twice more. When Craig Morton asked her why she had told these lies he further alleged that she had replied, "He's just a fucking paedophile anyway, so why not?"

Theresa Malcolm appeared on a television programme in 2013, a year before the trial. The reporter who interviewed her was Ben McCormack. During her preparation for this interview, Craig Morton alleged that she had told him what the interviewer had said to her:

*"Look, [Theresa], focus on something that upsets you and puts you in a position where you are very emotional, and keep focusing on this whilst I am talking to you about what happened between you and Rolf Harris."*

According to Craig Morton, Theresa Malcolm told him that she had focused on a distressing series of events that had taken place when she was a child. Craig Morton subsequently relayed details of these events to defence solicitors and Operation Yewtree officers. These events did not involve Rolf Harris.

Both the police and solicitors from Rolf's defence team interviewed Craig Morton. However, he was not called to testify at the first trial.

The reason given by the police and defence for not calling Craig Morton as a witness was that, in their opinion, his evidence was tarnished, as there had been a big fall-out between Theresa Malcolm and Craig Morton. He was charged and convicted of assault, for which he served three months in prison. As a result, it was thought that his credibility as a witness would suffer, as the Crown Prosecution Service could allege that his evidence was intended to exact revenge against Theresa Malcolm.

There is no doubt that Craig Morton's evidence would have muddied the waters but if the same stance were taken by the police in the investigation of other crimes, we would see many crimes go unsolved. Witnesses with criminal records, and those who have axes to grind against the accused, a complainant, or other witnesses, are called to testify in major criminal cases along with paid informers.

There are some areas in large cities which are 'no go' areas. If witnesses who had criminal convictions or ulterior motives were excluded from giving evidence, there would be no credible witnesses. No-one committing crimes in these areas would be brought to justice.

Handling a witness such as Craig Morton is not difficult for an experienced investigator. All that is required is to use the information provided by the witness and either verify it or discount it. In this case Craig Morton's witness statement had identified numerous leads that could have been pursued to confirm if he was telling the truth.

Craig Morton gained financially out of Theresa Malcolm's interviews. By exposing any embellishment of her evidence, he was putting this in jeopardy. He did say that his main reason for not backing what he described as the fictitious part of Theresa Malcolm's account was that he believed he would be implicated if the courts found out that she was not telling the truth and he would then be charged as an accomplice.

Theresa Malcolm admitted during cross-examination that she had lied to the police by giving them the impression that she had not approached the media, albeit via a publicist, to sell what she claimed to be her story.

On 21st May 2014 the *Sydney Morning Herald* reported an exchange between Rolf Harris's defence barrister and Theresa Malcolm.

"You looked that officer in the eye and told a bare-faced lie," defence barrister Sonia Woodley said.

"Yes," Ms [Malcolm] replied. She blamed her partner for 'aggressively' chasing the media deal. "I felt like I was trapped," she said. "It was a huge whirlwind."

On being questioned further by Sonia Woodley QC, Theresa Malcolm denied having 'spiced up' her story for the magazine, despite a draft version of the article having been produced in court along with the final version. Theresa Malcolm said that she had just been asked to add detail, whereas notes on the story showed that the magazine had asked for 'emotional quotes' and the 'smells and songs' that had featured at the dinner with Rolf Harris.

Theresa Malcolm's evidence was believed by the jury. Rolf Harris was convicted on the three charges laid by the Crown Prosecution Service in relation to her allegations. Following the trial, she instructed 'no win, no fee' solicitors Slater and Gordon to lodge a claim for compensation, which, when added to the amount of money she had already received from her media interviews, made for a very tidy sum.

## BEN MCCORMACK

There was a bizarre twist in relation to the televised interview of Theresa Malcolm, for which the reporter and interviewer was Ben McCormack.

Four years after having interviewed Theresa Malcolm, Ben McCormack was convicted on child pornography charges. It was confirmed that McCormack had paedophilic tendencies years before he was arrested. This meant that at the time he interviewed Theresa Malcolm, and when she was allegedly being given instructions on how to present herself as a victim, the man preparing and interviewing her for the television programme was not thinking as an unbiased reporter.

## ANOTHER SETBACK

There was a major setback for the defence towards the end of the first trial, which unfortunately came at a particularly critical point. On the day after the prosecution had summed up, and when Sonia Woodley QC had been scheduled to sum up for the defence, she was taken ill and was unable to attend court. This of course was unavoidable, but it was very unfortunate.

Initially there was no indication of when Sonia Woodley QC might be able to return. As the prosecution had already summed up their case, the jury had been subjected to only one side of the closing address, which favoured the complainants. This created a problem because several days went by without anything happening. The jury had had all of this time to consider what the prosecution had told them without hearing anything from the defence to balance it.

When it became clear that Sonia Woodley QC would not be returning to the court in the short term, the decision was made for a junior barrister, Simon Ray, to present the defence's closing address to the jury.

Sonia Woodley QC returned to the court a week after her junior had completed the closing address and when the jury was into its eighth day of deliberations.

## INVESTIGATORS

Having professional investigators as part of the defence team is commonplace in some countries, for example in the USA. However, the practice is not widespread in the UK. I can remember one barrister telling me that he was being questioned by his colleagues as to why he was using a private investigator. It was as if he were somehow degrading the legal profession by doing this. The criminal justice system has worked well for centuries without having to resort to employing private investigators, so why change? If the barrister could not produce evidence to prove an accused person's innocence, then the accused must be guilty.

Well, as it worked out, the barrister who was questioned by his colleagues went on to win the difficult and protracted case at hand and proved his point. Now other lawyers and barristers are starting to see the merits of using a professional investigator. It is worth noting that during the Operation Yewtree enquiries, the Metropolitan Police used civilian investigators who were neither serving nor sworn police officers.

The media are very quick to use the term 'digging up the dirt on victims.' I prefer to use the correct term for 'victims' prior to an alleged perpetrator having been convicted, which is complainants. The role of a professional investigator is to gather information that might previously have been unknown to the defence, or even to the prosecution, or which has accidentally or deliberately been omitted from reports detailing the police investigation.

Hence with the additional information uncovered by a professional investigator, there is more scope for questioning and unearthing things that the complainant might have wished had not come to light. It is not in anyone's interest to have an innocent person jailed because a complainant has been either economical with the truth or has lied.

## SEXUAL HISTORY

Referring to a complainant's sexual history is not permitted during a trial that involves rape, indecent assault or any other type of sexual crime. I can understand the reasoning behind this. A sex worker, for example, who has been subjected to a crime of a sexual nature should be able to make a complaint to the police without their sexual history being used against them. However, the same should apply for the accused, but that is not the situation. Accused people are interrogated on their sexual history, including affairs and acts of adultery.

At the commencement of the first trial, Rolf was 84 years of age. He had no previous criminal convictions and there was nothing untoward in his history. Despite this the Crown Prosecution Service went to great lengths to convince the jury that there was a 'dark side' to Rolf Harris in that he was a sexual predator, experienced in grooming young girls. The inference was that Rolf Harris had gone off the rails at the age of 39 when he had pounced on eight-year-old Wendy Rosher – something that we now know did not happen.

In contrast, nothing was permitted to be produced in evidence about the sexual behaviour and experiences of the complainants. All the jury was allowed to hear on this theme was how the accused had engaged in extra-marital relations with two women at different times in his life. So much emphasis was placed on this that one might have been forgiven for thinking that marital infidelity was a crime rather than what most would consider a moral transgression.

The image presented to the jurors was one of innocent young women who had been abused by a sexually rabid older man, the outcome being that they had been left with psychological problems. Conversely, far less emphasis was placed on the fact that Rolf Harris, at the age of 84, had never faced criminal charges before.

In my view the rules should apply equally to both parties, complainant and accused.

# CONCLUSION

There were eleven complainants in total over the course of the three trials. The allegations made by seven of the complainants were fully investigated by professional investigators. Rolf Harris was acquitted on all of the charges that related to these seven complainants, which were heard at the second and third trials.

The allegations that were not investigated prior to going to trial were those made by the four complainants involved in the first trial. However, one of the convictions arising from the charges levelled against Rolf Harris at the first trial was fully investigated by my team. This conviction, which related to Wendy Rosher, was referred to the Court of Appeal. The conviction was quashed unanimously by three Court of Appeal judges in November 2017.

In contrast, the complaints lodged by the three complainants in the first trial that were not fully investigated by professional investigators resulted in Rolf Harris being convicted, and they remain as convictions. Surely this is no coincidence?

In an ideal world the police would complete a full and unbiased investigation. Their findings would be presented to the Crown Prosecution Service, who would review the evidence and decide whether the suspect should be charged. If the suspect is to be charged, then prior to the trial they would be required to disclose their evidence to the defence team. It goes without saying that the Crown Prosecution Service and the defence are reliant on the accuracy of the police investigation.

The evidence we uncovered during our investigation of the Rolf Harris trials revealed that the Operation Yewtree police officers, and their civilian investigators, did not conduct a full and unbiased investigation. This dismissive approach by the police towards gathering evidence to secure a conviction indicates that the defence team need to do everything in their power to balance the scales of justice to ensure a fair trial for the accused. Employing a professional investigator goes a long way towards achieving this.

Not one of the complaints contained sufficient evidence to stand on its own. They relied heavily on the support of the other complaints and the bad character evidence. Sonia Woodley QC in her submissions to the court stated the following:

> 'The emphasis placed by the Prosecution and reflected in the Judge's summing up of the accumulative effect of all the allegations was disproportionate to the strength of any individual Count on the Indictment.'

If prior to the first trial the Operation Yewtree detectives had conducted professional and balanced investigations into the allegations made by the casual encounter complainants – Wendy Rosher, Deidre Connor and Theresa Malcolm – more evidence would have surfaced that in all likelihood would have cast doubt on the complainants' accounts. That Rolf Harris was found guilty on flimsy evidence – and had a conviction overturned three years after having been found guilty – is a serious indictment of the justice system.

There have been calls for Rolf Harris to be given a retrial in relation to his remaining convictions from the first trial. This would involve the second, third and fourth complainants discussed in Chapter 12.

The calls for a retrial have come not just from Rolf Harris supporters but also from leading barristers who have read the judgments and studied the evidence that led to the convictions.

Should there be a retrial? The answer to that is a resounding YES.

Will there be a retrial? The answer to that is no.

The chance of the Appeal Court allowing a retrial is very slim. Even if a retrial were granted, there is no way that the Harris family would want Rolf to go through this again. He is now in his nineties and, contrary to speculation in the media, his resources are limited.

Rolf was 83 when he was first charged. He was forced to endure three trials, an appeal, and just under three years in prison for crimes that he emphatically denies ever took place. The evidence produced in court after the first trial supported his denials. There is a limit to what one person can be expected to endure.

So, what should happen?

If the UK justice system is as fair as it claims to be, a Royal Commission of Inquiry should be set up to examine all the evidence in respect of the first trial. A Queen's Counsel or judge, backed up by a small team of investigators, should be appointed to explore any new evidence and research fully the allegations made by the three women whose complaints were never properly investigated.

There would be no need for a further trial at which the complainants would be required to attend court to give evidence. The Queen's Counsel or judge would consider all the evidence without the theatrics that surrounded the first trial and reach a decision based solely on fact.

Will this ever happen? Probably not, but in my opinion this is the only way that Rolf Harris would get a fair hearing.

During the 1970s there was an infamous double murder trial in New Zealand that resulted in a man named Arthur Allan Thomas being convicted of murdering David Harvey Crewe and Jeannette Lenore Crewe in a shooting on a farm in Pukekawa, south of Auckland. He was sentenced to life imprisonment. It took 10 years of campaigning before a Royal Commission of Inquiry pardoned him for the crimes. Arthur Allan Thomas spent nine years in prison. When he was released, he was compensated to the tune of NZ$950,000.

The police investigation was labelled by the appointed Queen's Counsel, who oversaw the Royal Commission of Inquiry in 1980, as being both inept and corrupt. It was established that a cartridge from a firearm owned by Mr Thomas had been planted by the police officer in charge, Bruce Hutton, and his assistant, Len Johnston. Both are now deceased.

As an aside, I knew Bruce Hutton and I went to primary school with his children. They were a good family and I always had respect for Bruce Hutton, as did many of his ex-colleagues. The planting of the cartridge and the resulting fallout was a sad legacy for a man who was recognised for being a dedicated police officer.

It was public pressure that finally convinced the New Zealand government to appoint a Royal Commission of Inquiry when the Court of Appeal refused to hear an appeal in respect of Mr Thomas's case. The British investigative author, David Yallop, became involved and wrote a book about the double murders, *Beyond Reasonable Doubt*. This was later turned into a film of the same name.

Rolf Harris is an Australian icon who brought happiness and laughter to millions of people around the world with his brand of entertaining – painting, acting, comedy and singing. He was a shining light in the entertainment industry for over sixty years.

Sadly, it was his success that saw him included in the group of celebrities who became caught up in the wake of the Jimmy Savile furore. The conduct of the Operation Yewtree detectives and the civil investigators employed by them, in overlooking and ignoring evidence that supported Rolf Harris's innocence, cost him both his freedom and his good reputation.

I will finish this book by leaving the reader with a thought. When I was a young police officer in New Zealand, I attended a qualifying course to become a Detective Constable. There was a question in the final examination paper that has always stayed in my mind, and which has hopefully stood me in good stead for the last 50 years.

**New Zealand Police Detective Course 1975 - Examination Question**

*Q What is the purpose of an interview?*

*A. To obtain the truth.*

# POSTSCRIPT

Rolf Harris was released from HMP Stafford on 19th May 2017.

Now aged 92, he is retired and lives with his wife, Alwen, at their home in Berkshire.

# ACKNOWLEDGEMENTS

I would like to acknowledge and thank all those people who have offered advice and support to me whilst writing this book. Thank you also to my dedicated team of investigators and the volunteers who worked assiduously throughout.

- Paul Gambaccini – American-British radio and television presenter and author.
- Stewart Robbins – Author.
- The late retired Detective Superintendent Douglas Quade, who served in the Hampshire Constabulary until his retirement. Comment from the legal team: He was an enormous help to us and a witness who even the Court of Appeal could not view as anything other than totally credible. R.I.P. Doug.
- Professional investigators Douglas Bainbridge and Mike Kelly. Hard working, honest and reliable, with only one goal, and that was to uncover the truth.

- To the dedicated team of volunteer researchers, and supporters, whose combined efforts exposed the injustices that surrounded the Rolf Harris Trials.
- My wife Maggi who stood by me during the turbulent years of relentless pressure that came with the investigation of historic indecent and sexual assault cases. Maggi's knowledge of the entertainment industry, along with her many contacts, assisted me in the preparation and writing of this book.

*"William, a most brilliant investigator, finding extraordinary skeletons in numerous false accusers' cupboards."*

Comment from Jonathan King, pop music impresario who was prosecuted in 2018 on 26 counts of historic indecent and sexual assault going back 48 years. All charges were dismissed following a trial at Southwark Crown Court.

# THE TRIALS

All three trials took place at Southwark Crown Court in London. The complainants' names, with the exception of Wendy Rosher, are pseudonyms.

# FIRST TRIAL

| | |
|---|---|
| *Judge:* | The Hon. Mr Justice Sweeney |
| *Commenced:* | 6th May 2014 |
| *Concluded:* | 30th June 2014 |

There were twelve counts relating to four complainants.

| | |
|---|---|
| *Count 1* | Wendy Rosher |
| *Count 2* | Deidre Connor |
| *Counts 3 to 9* | Pamela Broadhurst |
| *Counts 10 to 12* | Theresa Malcolm |

| | |
|---|---|
| *Verdict:* | Guilty on all counts. The guilty verdict in relation to Count 1 was overturned on appeal in November 2017. |

# SECOND TRIAL

| | |
|---|---|
| *Judge:* | Judge Alistair McCreath |
| *Commenced:* | 9th January 2017 |
| *Concluded:* | 8th February 2017 |

There were eight counts relating to seven complainants.

| | |
|---|---|
| *Count 1* | Victoria Pringle |
| *Count 2* | Christina Newton |
| *Count 3* | Jane Hatfield |
| *Count 4* | Jackie Daniels |
| *Count 5* | Naomi Smith |
| *Count 6* | Monica Jackson |
| *Counts 7 and 8* | Patricia Morgan |

| | |
|---|---|
| *Verdict:* | Not guilty on Counts 2, 3, 7 and 8. The jury was unable to reach verdicts on Counts 1, 4, 5 and 6. |

# THIRD TRIAL

This was a retrial covering three of the four counts on which the jury had been unable to reach verdicts in the second trial, with an additional count for Jackie Daniels. The complainant Monica Jackson had decided not to proceed, which left three complainants from the second trial.

| | |
|---|---|
| *Judge:* | Her Honour Judge Deborah Taylor |
| *Commenced:* | 15th May 2017 |
| *Concluded:* | 30th May 2017 |

There were four counts relating to three complainants:

| | |
|---|---|
| *Count 1* | Victoria Pringle |
| *Count 2* | Jackie Daniels |
| *Count 3* | Jackie Daniels |
| *Count 4* | Naomi Smith |

| | |
|---|---|
| *Verdict:* | After the jury failed to reach verdicts the prosecution announced that they would not pursue a further retrial. Rolf Harris was formally declared Not Guilty on all counts. |

# OVERTURNING OF CONVICTION
# FOR INDECENTLY ASSAULTING WENDY ROSHER

## FIRST TRIAL, COUNT 1

This conviction was overturned by the Court of Appeal on 16th November 2017 on the grounds that it was unsafe.

# ABOUT THE AUTHOR

William Merritt is a Specialist Investigator who was born in England and raised in New Zealand, where he developed a passion for rugby, boxing, and surf lifesaving.

In 1972 William joined the New Zealand police. He was stationed as a uniformed officer at West Auckland before being selected to join the Criminal Investigation Branch. During his time as a Detective Constable he was instrumental in solving many serious crimes and received recognition from senior officers for his work on a major homicide.

William resigned from the New Zealand police to follow a career as a Specialist Investigator after identifying a gap in the market for the investigation of insurance claims that were suspected of being fraudulent. After proving his worth to several insurance companies, he went on to pioneer insurance claims investigation in New Zealand.

In 2000 William moved to the UK to further his experience. This move enabled him to accept assignments in London, Europe, the USA and the Caribbean.

It was in October 2013 that William's expertise in criminal and civil investigation was first called upon to assist Defence Counsel in historic sex offence cases.

The Rolf Harris case is one of many that William has worked on. His success in establishing the truth has been acknowledged by some of London's leading criminal defence barristers.